The
Underwater Dig
Introduction to Marine Archaeology

SECOND EDITION

9 781559 920315   52395

The
Underwater Dig.
Introduction to Marine Archaeology

SECOND EDITION

Robert F. Marx

Pisces Books
A Division of Gulf Publishing Company
Houston, Texas

for Hilary Toby Marx

Library of Congress Cataloging-in-Publication Data
Marx, Robert F., 1933–
    The underwater dig: an introduction to marine archaeology/
Robert F. Marx.—2nd ed.
        p.   cm.
    Includes bibliographical references.
ISBN 1-55992-031-9
    1. Underwater archaeology.   I. Title.
CC77.U5M37   1990
930.1'028'04—dc20   89-70973
                                                                   CIP

Contents

Preface

The most challenging problem confronting all archaeology is the accelerating pace at which sites are being destroyed. As bulldozers scar millions of acres each year and whole valleys are inundated for reservoirs and recreational lakes, irreplaceable opportunities to unravel and illuminate the past are lost. Man is indeed earth's most destructive force, but until recently most of his depredations were confined to the land. Today, however, he dredges and fills, floods, pollutes, and plunders. Although many underwater sites of archaeological significance are looted and destroyed by scuba divers, a much greater number are actually obliterated by dredging and landfill operations. In fact, hundreds of shipwrecks are lost every year and yet no outcry has been uttered either by archaeologists or the public. Because most underwater archaeologists are employed by governments and it is the governments that permit this deplorable destruction to continue, they tend to regard keeping their jobs more important than protecting these sites from destruction. Years ago in Florida, prior to any dredging or landfill projects commencing, a cultural impact study had to be undertaken. This is no longer being done in Florida or any other state for that matter. Due to extensive beach erosion in Florida in recent years, it is estimated that more than 200 miles of dredging and beach replenishment will be done in the next five years and absolutely nothing is being done to protect the hundreds of shipwrecks that lay in these areas.

An eloquent example of site destruction is found at Cadiz on the south coast of Spain. Cadiz is an important seaport that has been in continuous use since 800 B.C. Beneath its waters lie several thousand shipwrecks of many types, nationalities, and historical periods. The earliest known shipwrecks were Phoenician, which were then followed by those of the Greek and Roman merchantmen and warships. Countless ships of many European and northern African nations were also lost there. Even the Vikings came to grief at Cadiz. In A.D. 957 after months of sacking various ports of the Mediterranean, a fleet of 70 Viking ships went to the bottom in a storm in Cadiz Bay. In the sixteenth century alone more than 600 ships were lost, most of which were ships engaged in New World navigations.

There are many seaports in Europe, the Mediterranean, and other parts of the world where vast numbers of ships were lost spanning long periods of history. However, Cadiz is one of the most important underwater archaeological sites because of its unique anaerobic bottom sediments. In most areas very little wooden remains have survived over the centuries, but such is not the case at Cadiz. Even intact Phoenician hulls are known to lay under this harbor's protective mud.

Many of the shipwrecks lay in less than 50 feet of water and some have been subjected to damage and destruction by the forces of nature, such as huge seas caused during storms. Nothing can be done to prevent this from occurring in the future, other than actual salvaging of the shipwrecks to prevent their further destruction.

On the other hand, much greater destruction has occurred to the shipwrecks around Cadiz in the last three decades than has occurred to them through the forces of nature over thousands of years. Under the auspices of the Archaeological Museum of Cadiz, a visual survey was conducted during 1960–62. Within a three-kilometer radius of the modern port, 54 classical period shipwrecks and 97 of later dates were located. During a recent survey of the same area, it was discovered that more than two-thirds of these shipwrecks had been totally obliterated by dredging operations, which are still going on today. Most of the dredged material has been used as landfill and is now covered over by newly constructed buildings. Just a few years ago a container-ship port was constructed in which the landfill completely covered over the remains of a Phoenician sunken city.

Fishing boats also account for a greater amount of destruction to shipwrecks. Not only are archaeological objects caught in their fishing nets, but the cables pulling these nets cut across the seafloor, and sometimes beneath as well, destroying everything in their path.

In neighboring Portugal the situation is equally grave. During the recent construction of a deep-water port at Sines, a port first used by the Carthaginians and later by the Romans, dredging operations completely destroyed at least four Punic shipwrecks and many others of later periods. Further down the coast at Portimão, recent dredging operations destroyed three classical period shipwrecks and, no doubt, many other shipwrecks were also lost forever in this port as more than a third of the port has been covered over with fill to form the base for a large ship wharf.

In the area of Lisbon, where at least 500 ships are known to have sunk since the late fifteenth century, the devastation is even worse. In a recent interview, the captain of a dredge boat reported that "rarely a day passes in which some vestiges of an old shipwreck are not seen spewing out of the discharge end of the dredge pipes."

On the other side of the Atlantic the problem is equally acute. Dredging and landfill operations at Cartagena, Colombia, one of the most important seaports during the Spanish colonial period, have resulted in the destruction of more than 50 percent of Cartagena's known shipwreck sites. At Veracruz, Mexico, another major colonial port, the devastation is deplorable. Probably less than 10 percent of the area's colonial shipwrecks remain. At Rio de Janiero, Brazil, landfill used in constructing an airport completely covered the anchorage area used during the colonial period.

Shipwreck sites are not only being erased in protected harbors, but offshore as well. Dredging operations are conducted in the process of laying offshore petroleum pipelines, building breakwaters, gathering landfill and beach replenishment materials, opening new entrances to ports and rivers, and for other reasons. Several years ago during the dredging of a new channel at Padre Island, Texas, one of the Spanish shipwrecks from the 1553 fleet that lay offshore was sucked up in the hungry jaws of the dredge pipe and spat out on a nearby beach.

For years I have been leading a one-man delegation trying to educate many governments of the great historical and archaeological resources that they have in their waters and advising them to prevent further destruction of these sites by dredging and other types of destruction. In every single instance my pleas have been received by hostile reactions from the government bureaucrats with whom I met. Their usual answer is that the economics of the country are at stake and supersede the importance of protecting shipwrecks. In some instances I was told that they have so many objects in their museums that those in the sea are of no importance or interest. I have also taken my battle to UNESCO and other than being paid lip service, I accomplished nothing.

In the United States I have faced the same reaction from both bureaucrats and scholars. Nobody seems to want to step on Big Brother's toes and stick their necks out and criticize the shameful destruction of our underwater sites, which our government is permitting to occur. Yet these same people think nothing of trying to stop sport divers and treasure hunters from exploring shipwrecks, claiming that their plundering is destroying shipwrecks at an alarming rate. The fact is that shipwreck plundering accounts for less than five percent of the destruction that man is waging on our underwater heritage!

Another major problem confronting underwater archaeology is the ownership of shipwrecks and other underwater cultural sites. Throughout the world, all but 11 nations have specific laws concerning shipwrecks. In the United States 27 states have passed widely divergent laws laying claim to sunken historical sites. These laws were challenged in the Supreme Court in 1981 and the states lost the rights to shipwrecks. Federal laws give the federal government control over natural resources within the 200-mile limit except for state ownership of resources lying within the coastal three-mile area; however, these laws do not cover shipwrecks or other man made objects. Unlike archaeological sites buried on land, the right of states to manage the sites on their submerged lands was not explicitly stated in U.S. law. Until recently, in absence of such a law recognizing the special nature of ancient shipwrecks, these shipwrecks were covered by the "finders-keepers" principle that applied to modern wrecked and abandoned commercial vessels. It meant that Federal Admiralty Law took precedence over state laws.

During the last seven years, Congress has labored over the passage of a new law granting states the right to jurisdiction over all shipwrecks within three miles of the coast. Numerous hearings were held in Congress by the House Merchant Marine and Fisheries Subcommittee, and sport divers, treasure hunters, and archaeologists all contributed their points of view on the management of shipwrecks. In April 1987, the Reagan administration endorsed a new bill entitled the "Abandoned Shipwreck Act of 1987." The new bill was approved by the Senate on December 19, 1987 by a vote of 340 to 64 and the House of Representatives did likewise by an overwhelming majority on April 14, 1988. On April 28th the President signed the bill and it is now known as Pubic Law 100-298.

The new law would cover five to ten percent of the estimated 50,000 shipwrecks in the three-mile range. Other shipwrecks within three miles or beyond this area would continue to be covered by Federal Admiralty Law. The shipwrecks affected by the law are (a) those defined as historic abandoned shipwrecks that are "substantially" buried in submerged state lands, (b) those held in coal formations, and (c) wrecks that are listed in the National Register of Historic Places—of which fewer than 100 are currently designated. The states will decide how to divide the artifacts and treasures recovered and set up guidelines on the methods that must be used in locating and salvaging shipwrecks.

I hope this new law will eliminate the serious problems that have been prevalent for the past ten years. What we need now is another new law to protect shipwrecks from man made destruction.

Robert F. Marx
Indialantic, Florida

Introduction

More than 70 percent of the earth's surface, 197 million square miles, is covered by water. Only recently has man begun to plumb the depths of his watery planet, where, at the bottom of seas, lakes, rivers and springs, countless traces of the past await the underwater explorer. Like the artifacts scientists painstakingly unearth from land sites, these submerged relics furnish clues to help archaeologists and historians reconstruct the past.

Underwater archaeology is a new discipline, one to which the nonprofessional with high motivation and a fair level of competence can contribute significantly. There are far too few professional marine archaeologists for the great deal of work to be done. In many areas there is particular urgency to excavate underwater sites threatened with destruction by man and nature. Archaeology is a science to which committed amateurs have made valuable contributions. Now, more than ever, it is imperative an effort be made to train more lay underwater archaeologists to carry out excavation of the many sites threatened by dredging, filling or looting.

The vast, unfathomed storehouse of sunken ships and cities offers a unique opportunity to the diver-archaeologist. Underwater sites are generally far less disturbed than those on land. With the exception of a few sites such as Pompeii, Herculaneum and Thera, entombed in a fiery flood of lava, land sites typically present stratum after stratum of occupation. One site often spans thousands of years and frequently artifacts from one period become mixed in with those of another when the site is disturbed, making it difficult for the archaeologist to assign precise dates to his findings.

A sunken ship, however, is often an encapsulated unit. At the moment when disaster struck, time stood still: The vessel sank to the bottom and lies there, representing a single unpolluted moment of a bygone era. There are exceptions: Ships which sunk in port areas where other craft subsequently sank on top of them, wrecks littered by trash from ships anchored above them, and shipwrecks on which salvors have left traces of a later time.

From a sunken city or a sunken ship the underwater archaeologist can recover virtually every artifact that might be found on a land site of the same era. And sometimes he finds objects never seen before. Everything from the smallest coin to marble columns weighing several tons has been found, even such seemingly perishable items as foodstuffs, cloth and paper. A shipwreck can be a time capsule from which the archaeologist gains important information about construction, rigging and armament. Like artifacts found in a sunken settlement, the cargo and personal effects of the crew and passengers yield valuable data about the time.

Underwater archaeology ranges from the excavation of shipwrecks to excavation of submerged cities, towns, ports and ceremonial wells or cenotes and includes sites once occupied by prehistoric man. Along coastlines throughout the world hundreds of former settlements and seaports lie underwater. And lakes, rivers and springs conceal sites once inhabited by man. At some underwater locations, such as the sacred cenotes of Central America, man deliberately threw in objects; at others small craft overturned, spilling their contents accidentally. Any site bearing traces of man's history, whether a shallow pond or the ocean depths, is of potential significance, and any diver coming upon such a site is either a potential archaeologist or a potential destroyer. The choice may depend on the training and knowledge available to him as a potential archaeologist.

Underwater archaeology is still an infant science, its development closely linked in the past few decades to the introduction of scuba and the sport of skin diving. Before World War II, in the days of helmet diving, there were few discoveries of note, and most scholars were skeptical of any potential for underwater archaeology. Unfortunately a number of land archaeologists continue to consider anyone who works an underwater site a romantic treasure hunter. The skepticism, however, is declining in the face of the contributions to marine archaeology by professionals and disciplined amateurs. Some divers

Underwater archaeologist holding a ceramic Bellarmine jug, recovered from a Dutch shipwreck off Australia. (Credit: Western Australian Museum.)

have been interested only in recovering salable treasure, but many others would have been eager and able to do good work had they only known some basic archaeological principles and techniques. The future of undcrwater archaeology hinges in part on encouraging the motivated layman to acquire the basic tools necessary for archaeological research and excavation. Because funds to train professionals are severely limited, the vacuum must be filled by the competent amateur for whom underwater archaeology is an avocation.

There are now fewer than 100 underwater archaeologists in the world, most of them self-taught. There are few incentives to lure young people into the field full time. Until a few years ago it was impossible anywhere to earn a college degree in underwater archaeology. During the spring of 1974, the University of California at San Diego became the first school to offer undergraduate courses in this field. At that time, the University of Pennsylvania was the only school for post-graduate studies in underwater archaeology. Currently, there are six other universities in the world with graduate programs in underwater archaeology. Texas A&M is the best known and by far has the best program available. Other institutions include East Carolina University in Greenville, North Carolina; the University of Haifa in Israel; the University of Western Australia at Fremantle; St. Andrews College in Fife, Scotland; and the University College of North Wales at Bangor.

Most school-affiliated underwater archaeologists find themselves limited to a relatively few months of field work a year because of their academic responsibilities. After more than ten years of chafing under such limitations, Drs. George Bass and Michael Katzev gave up well-paid teaching posts to work full time doing actual marine archaeological projects. They founded the American Institute of Nautical Archaeology based on Cyprus. Their endeavors are concentrated in the eastern Mediterranean, where Bass believes more than ten thousand ships of historical interest lie sunken along the nine hundred miles of Turkey's coastline. During 1973, their first year of work, they explored the sites of some twenty ancient shipwrecks first discovered by sponge divers, one of which turned out to be the oldest shipwreck ever discovered at the time.

Few land archaeologists have shown interest in learning to dive, and yet it is some of these professionals who categorically state that underwater excavations, when they should be undertaken at all, should only be attempted by professionals. There are two schools of thought. Although most land archaeologists subscribe to the above, those who have worked on marine sites generally feel important work can be accomplished by anyone who is intelligent, a competent diver, and interested enough to learn the basics. The techniques are relatively uncomplicated and can be mastered with practice. Expertise in archaeology is not essential in the preliminary phases of searching and locating sites, although preparatory reading and research and some familiarity with excavation on land sites is certainly useful.

As proof of the contribution of nonprofessionals one has only to realize that every important underwater site excavated was discovered by amateurs. Furthermore, they have designed and built most of the equipment used in underwater excavations.

Public interest in archaeology has grown, so that the gap between the trained, paid archaeologist and the serious, disciplined amateur is narrowing. The media report the latest techniques and finds, encouraging more amateurs to become involved. More than three-quarters of the members of local, state and regional archaeological societies are amateurs, so-called because they hold no degree in archaeology. They undertake more field work, laboratory research, and publish more reports of findings than do the limited number of professionals. Many nonacademics contribute special qualities—diving, use of special equipment, surveying, drafting or photography—which they acquired in the pursuit of their avocation.

There are close to 5 million scuba-divers in the United States and about a million in Europe. During the past 35 years some have done more damage than the combined forces of nature during the past three thousand years. The first culprits were commercial salvage divers. During World War II, when there was a great demand for scrap metal, they combed lakes, rivers and oceans, and recovered, along with the modern scrap, thousands of old anchors, cannon, and metal ballast from sunken ships. They were probably unaware they were often making it impossible to find again a historical wreck site after they had removed the only clues that could be detected by special equipment or, indeed, the only clues available in the case of ships with ballast of iron or lead ingots rather than stones.

The havoc wreaked by souvenir collectors and treasure hunters is similar. The weekend diver who simply picks up a cannon ball or a bronze spike from a wreck and carries it home to decorate his living room perhaps doesn't realize he may be removing a valuable clue to the location and identity of a site. Professional treasure hunters often inflict damage on a far greater scale since they are not content with simply removing an artifact from the surface but dig down and destroy objects buried in coral, sand or mud. Dynamite and huge dredging devices, their standard excavation tools, can rapidly demolish a site including valuable glass and ceramic artifacts. It is hoped the souvenir collector and the treasure hunter will change their approach if given the opportunity to participate in the kind of archaeological excavation which yields not only treasure and artifacts but enhances their value by establishing their place in the context of history.

Several years ago amateur divers stumbled on a famous Revolutionary War wreck, the *New Hampshire*, near Boston. Their discovery precipitated a stampede. Divers descended on the wreck in droves and ripped it to pieces. Their main quarry was brass spikes and nails fashioned by Paul Revere which they sold for a dollar each. Such looting is by no means confined to the United States. In 1971, newspaper headlines proclaimed: "Underwater Pirates Loot Wreck of Charles II's 1675 Yacht." The royal yacht *Mary* was considered the most important historic shipwreck ever found in British waters. Yet, as soon as word of her discovery leaked out, she was stripped of everything visible, including a number of beautiful bronze cannon. Fortunately none of the pirates had access to equipment for digging into the sand which covered much of the wreck. When this was accomplished by members of a diving club working under the direction of an archaeologist, many important artifacts were recovered to be displayed in museums where such treasures belong. Along the French Mediterranean coast, sport divers are reputed to have plundered every old wreck lying above a depth of 150 feet. It has been difficult to convince divers, who can sell amphorae for $150 each, of the real threat they pose to archaeology.

Most disturbing is that for lack of knowledge of scientific preservation methods most items divers loot from sites are allowed to deteriorate or disintegrate. It is a sad sight to see a once splendid iron cannon rapidly turning to dust in front of a restaurant or shop.

The governments of countries where indiscriminate destruction of underwater sites has been allowed must share the blame. Until recently there was little official concern regarding archaeological sites in general and virtually no laws protecting underwater sites. Most European countries have now introduced legislation designed to protect such areas. However, putting a law on the books does not always ensure it will be followed. Several persons who plundered shipwrecks have been prosecuted, but most offenders have gone free because of the difficulty of catching the culprits in the act.

It is virtually impossible to patrol efficiently coastlines hundreds, even thousands, of miles long. Most nations of the Western Hemi-

A mound of Rhodian amphoras, indicating the presence of a shipwreck beneath them, off Cyprus in the Mediterranean Sea. (Credit: Michael L. Katzev.)

sphere have statutes stipulating that the country is entitled to a share of what a diver finds, but few of them have laws protecting the sites. Mexico was the first country in the Western Hemisphere to prohibit the excavation of underwater sites except under official supervision and by accepted methods. In 1958, the Mexican Underwater Archaeological Society founded CEDAM, and this semiofficial organization is in charge of directing all underwater projects in the country. Canada and Jamaica followed soon after with stringent legislation protecting their marine sites. Steps should be taken immediately on an international level to halt the further destruction of such sites.

It is imperative that governments be alerted to the importance of not only protecting such areas from looters but also of actively supporting qualified projects. Unfortunately, governments often hinder or prohibit any work at all. Thus far, governmental assistance appears to be generally reserved for excavations involving national prestige, such as the raising and preservation of the seventeenth-century Swedish warship *Vasa* in Stockholm Harbor. Nationalistic pride in some countries has kept qualified foreign archaeologists from undertaking any excavations. Certain countries have insisted such work be carried out only by their own nationals, which would be fine if they had qualified archaeologists. Such policy has meant no work at all has been done. Such a place is Greece, potentially one of the world's richest areas for underwater archaeology. The bias against non-Greeks can be traced back to the early nineteenth century when Greece was under Turkish rule. In 1803, Lord Elgin secured permission from the Turks to survey and later remove to England a great collection of Greek marble sculptures, chiefly from the Parthenon at Athens. That flagrant abuse of the Greek patrimony has rankled ever since. Peter Throckmorton, one of the pioneers of underwater archaeology, has collected information on nearly a thousand old wrecks in Greek waters, most of them pinpointed by sponge divers and fishermen. Throckmorton reports most of these are gradually but steadily being stripped, the loot smuggled out for sale in Europe and the United States.

The Swedish warship Vasa, *which sank in 1628 in Stockholm Harbor, on a special barge after it was raised. (Credit:* Vasa *Museum.)*

The accessibility of many sites in shallow water makes them vulnerable to greedy divers. If sport divers could be enlisted to participate in underwater excavation projects, many would gain far more reward than from random removal of artifacts. Until recently historians and archaeologists have failed to communicate to the general public the significance of underwater sites. Most divers are unaware of how much damage they can do with so little disturbance. Most would probably rather make a contribution, even a small one, to archaeology than pick up an anchor or cannonball for display out of context. How much more exciting to research the name, history and exact fate of a wreck. A few professional archaeologists who have collaborated with amateurs have been pleased with the results, but even closer cooperation on a larger scale is needed.

The British were the first to take the logical step of coordinating the activities of divers and vocational archaeologists, who for so long had been in conflict with each other. In 1963, in London the Committee for Nautical Archaeology was formed by representatives from such institutions as the British Museum, the Science Museum, the National Maritime Museum, the Institute of Archaeology and the National Institute of Oceanography. Since the establishment of this organization great progress has been made. Archaeologists have begun to value the contribution devoted amateurs can make and have worked with them on a number of projects. In 1969 the Committee founded the School for Nautical Archaeology at Plymouth to teach divers techniques employed on marine sites.

In Britain such incidents as the plundering of the royal yacht have decreased dramatically since the Committee came into being, even though the ranks of amateur divers are swelling rapidly. In almost every instance in which an old wreck is located there is a report to the Committee, which in turn provides both technical and financial assistance for the excavation. Unfortunately, there is no comparable body in any other country. There is a critical need for an organization such as England's on a national level.

In the United States the Council of Underwater Archaeology was founded in 1959, but it is little more than a name. As one of the original founders and a member of its Board of Advisors since its inception to the present time, I feel I have a right to criticize this body. The Council started off on the right track but has been dominated by governmental bureaucrats who seem to think their main function is to prevent everyone else from exploring and salvaging shipwrecks. The statement by one of the members: "You shouldn't be on a shipwreck unless you have a Ph.D." seems to be how most of them think. The basic function of the Council was to serve as a clearinghouse for information. Another important function of the Council was to keep data on all underwater archaeological sites that were discovered throughout the world, as well as information on new techniques. The average diver stumbling across a shipwreck or finding vestiges of a submerged place of occupation has no idea of where to turn for aid in determining exactly what he has found or what to do about it. The Council has not only failed to fulfill the reasons for which it was originally founded, but has actually made it a practice to keep as much distance as possible between its members and the rest of the diving world. In fact, until recently it was the practice to prevent even archaeologists, or anybody for that matter, who worked with treasure hunters or sports divers from presenting archaeological papers at its annual conferences. Thus far, its only important contribution has been to organize annual conferences at which professional underwater archaeologists present papers—a number of which deal with laws preventing the amateurs and treasure hunters from working on shipwrecks. Trying to convince them that working with these people would be beneficial to all mankind is not difficult.

The aim of this book is not to turn a competent diver interested in history and archaeology into an instant professional. For those interested in making underwater archaeology a career, I urge study leading to a college degree. However, it is my hope this book will contribute to the much needed education of enthusiastic amateurs in the basic methods of working an underwater site. The amateur who is motivated to learn and disciplines himself can achieve results every bit as interesting as can the professional, although he may leave analysis of his finds to the professional archaeologist.

There is water almost everywhere, and almost everywhere there is the possibility of finding and excavating underwater some part of man's past. This pursuit is pleasurable in itself and beneficial to all mankind.

1

Historical Background

The Mediterranean is known as the cradle of civilization because along or near its shores grew up the world's first great cities. Since prehistoric times, the men who inhabited these cities put to sea in various types of craft in search of exotic products they could not find at home. Although the early history of water craft is a matter of speculation, scholars believe Stone Age man probably used inflated animal skins, wooden rafts and dugouts for crossing rivers and lakes and possibly for short sea voyages along familiar coasts. Archaeological evidence discovered on mainland Greece reveals man had some type of vessel capable of making open sea voyages in the Aegean more than nine thousand years ago. Those early mariners traveled to the island of Melos to obtain obsidian, a hard volcanic stone used to make sharp-edged knives, scrapers and other tools. Unfortunately, there is no record of the vessels ancient men used.

A clay model of the oldest known sailing ship, dating around 3500 B.C., was found in a grave at Eridu in southern Mesopotamia. Similar vessels, rigged with large square sails, appear in prehistoric Egyptian art, scratched or painted on pottery. The Gerzeans, who migrated from Asia to Egypt during this same period, provide us with the earliest known representation of boats

11

made from planks. These vessels, depicted on pieces of pottery, had twin cabins and were propelled by oars and sails. As early as 3000 B.C. the Babylonians had established regular sea intercourse with India and may have ventured even farther on the high seas. The Egyptians began sea trading about 3000 B.C. and by 2500 B.C. were constructing wooden merchant ships well over 100 feet long and propelled by big square sails. These vessels traveled by way of the Red Sea as far south as the Somali coast of Africa for incense, ivory and gold.

a. Model of a Phoenician warship (a bireme), eighth century B.C.

b. Model of an Egyptian merchant ship, c. 1300 B.C.

c. Model of a Phoenician war galley, c. 500 B.C.

d. Model of a Sidonian merchant ship, c. A.D. 200. (Credit: Maritime Museum, Haifa.)

Diverse cultures dominated the Mediterranean during different periods. Between 3000 and 2000 B.C. the Egyptians controlled most of the sea trade in the western Mediterranean. Then the Mycenaeans in Greece and the Minoans on Crete appeared, soon gaining control of commercial sea traffic. Industrious merchants, they did a great deal to advance the fledgling science of navigation.

However, the Phoenicians outshone all others as the greatest maritime people in history. Their skill, knowledge of navigation, ability in commerce and willingness to venture where others dared not sail gave them for more than a thousand years an undisputed monopoly over the sea routes and maritime trade throughout the whole of the Mediterranean and in other areas of the known world. During much of their heyday few ships of other nations were able to put to sea without great risk of being sunk, captured or having their crews sold as slaves. As early as 1500 B.C. the Phoenicians made frequent voyages to the British Isles, the Azores and other outlying Atlantic islands. They may well have been the first to reach the New World from the Old. They also sailed to many lands in the Indian Ocean and were the first to circumnavigate Africa, a three-year voyage. They sailed wherever a profit was to be made, for they were not only unsurpassed seamen but consummate traders and merchants. Their homeland, an area of limited natural resources, was a narrow strip of land on the Syrio-Palestinian coast with Byblos, Tyre, Sidon, Arvad and Tripoli their chief centers and ports. They were a practical people, adopting the scientific and navigational knowledge of other cultures and then improving them. One of the advantages which enabled the Phoenicians, or Canaanites as the Bible referred to them, to become such a powerful nation was the abundance of the famous cedars of Lebanon. These were essential not only in shipbuilding but as major items of trade as well, in great demand by nations, like Egypt, where good timber was not to be found. Their more powerful and militaristic neighbors depended on them not only for the transport of their merchandise but also on many occasions to fight their naval battles. Phoenician vessels were used to maintain supply lines and to transport the legions of such great ancient military leaders as Sennacherib, Necho, Xerxes and Alexander the Great.

The Etruscans and Greeks gained in power in the eighth century B.C. and soon eclipsed the Phoenicians in maritime power. From the sixth century B.C. on, they were using merchant ships as large as five hundred tons and able to carry as many as six hundred passengers on long voyages.

Rome started its rise to power in 510 B.C., and by the time of the birth of Christ its fleets dominated the Mediterranean. Roman ships rarely ventured beyond the Straits of Gibraltar, known to the ancients as the Pillars of Hercules, but they did sometimes voyage to the British Isles. They were never superb sailors like the Phoenicians, using their ships chiefly to transport their legions to conquer other lands. Although Roman merchant ships were impressive in size, they were clumsy and sailed badly. From the number of Roman ship-wrecks found along the ancient sea routes, it appears their ship casualties must have been enormous. Following the decline of the Roman Empire in the third century A.D., the Byzantine Empire ruled the seas for three centuries.

The invaders from the north, who conquered most of the lands bordering the northern Mediterranean shores, had never lived near the sea. They disliked and distrusted this alien environment and during the so-called Dark Ages which followed they turned their backs on the sea, so that seamanship and navigation became lost arts for almost a thousand years.

Sailing vessels were not used until the seventh century A.D. in northern waters. The Viking Age began about A.D. 800 when the fearless Norsemen started pirate raids on settlements along all the coasts of Europe. Around A.D. 1000 they were making open ocean

The original tenth-century Viking ship (Gotstad) in Oslo museum.

voyages, apparently reaching Newfoundland and other points on the North American continent.

Europeans were not the only great seafarers of the Ancient World. From time immemorial even such relatively unsophisticated people as the Polynesians were sailing in outrigger canoes thousands of miles across open water. They traveled the South Pacific region as far north as Hawaii and as far south as New Zealand—when their culture was still Neolithic. The Japanese were most likely the first to make extended voyages in sailing vessels on the Pacific Ocean. A great deal of indisputable evidence shows that the Japanese reached the coast of Ecuador in South America as early as 3200 B.C. From historical documents, we know that in 219 B.C., a period when the Chinese were greatly concerned with discovering new medicinal drugs, a man named Huš Fu received permission and an enormous subsidy from the emperor of China to search for drugs in the eastern ocean. He assembled a fleet of ships and set sail with three thousand persons. At a site in Ecuador archaeologists have discovered evidence of a Chinese settlement dating from this same period, so it would appear that Huš Fu and his followers settled in the New World.

The Chinese were still crossing as late as the middle of the sixteenth century. Spaniards on an exploratory voyage to the Gulf of California in 1544 reported finding several large Chinese junks at anchor. The Chinese told them they had been coming to those regions for many centuries to trade with Indian tribes. A wealth of other archaeological evidence indicates Asians reached the New World long before Columbus laid claim. It is hoped remains of an ancient Asian vessel will one day be found in American waters.

During the Renaissance, European man threw off the cloak of fear and superstition covering the sea. The shining Age of Exploration began. Shipbuilding was revived, the art of navigation relearned, and old trade routes re-established and new ones sought out. The Portuguese made the first great leap forward in discovering hitherto unknown lands. The Spaniards followed soon after.

Until the discovery of the New World by Columbus, the European nations were stagnating because of a severe lack of precious metals, the main ingredients in expanding mercantile trade. One of the principal motives which stimulated discovery of the New World was the conviction that by sailing westward from Europe or Africa, Marco

Polo's Golden Land of Zipango (Japan) might be reached and great quantities of gold and silver could be brought back to satisfy Europe's needs. However, as it happened, treasure poured forth not from Zipango but from the mines of Mexico and South America. The treasure returning from the New World was important to all the European nations because it provided nearly 95 percent of the precious metals upon which their, monetary systems were based. It is popularly believed that only Spain benefited from these riches. The truth is that Spain benefited less than most of the European powers including England, France, Holland and Italy. Throughout the sixteenth, seventeenth and eighteenth centuries, when ships, some nearly keeling over from their loads, were bearing immense amounts of treasure home, there was virtually no industry in Spain. She was dependent on other European nations for manufactured goods of all kinds, both for export to the New World and for domestic consumption. As a result, nearly all the gold and silver brought to Spain flowed out of the country and into the coffers of foreign nations. It has been computed that between 1492 and 1803, more than 4 billion pesos (a peso was not a coin but a monetary unit equal in value to one and one-eighth ounces of pure silver) in gold and silver reached Spain from the New World. This does not take into account

Spanish galleon wrecking on a beach.

the staggering amounts of unregistered treasure smuggled back to Spain to avoid payment of the excessive taxes collected by the king's agents. Some experts believe the contraband treasure exceeded twice the amount of registered treasure which reached Spain.

The trade between Spain and her New World colonies, initiated soon after Columbus's discovery of America, had grown by the middle of the sixteenth century to involve more than 150 vessels a year, organized into annual convoys called flotas. This lasted until the 1820s, when almost all the colonies had gained independence. On the outbound voyage from Spain these vessels were laden with every conceivable kind of manufactured item from almost every nation of Europe: tools and weapons, cooking utensils, glassware and ceramics, cutlery, cloth and trimmings, hats, shoes, religious objects, furniture, window glass and even dressed stones and bricks for buildings. On the return voyage, in addition to gold and silver bullion and specie, which was the main cargo in value, they carried chests of pearls, emeralds and other gemstones; silks, spices, Chinese porcelain and other luxury items brought from the Far East to Mexico; agricultural products such as sugar, tobacco and dyestuffs.

The most dangerous route navigated by the Spaniards during these three centuries was that between Manila in the Philippines, a Spanish possession, and Acapulco in Mexico. Nearly every year between 1565 and 1815, large ships called "Manila Galleons" made the perilous voyage, sometimes lasting as long as eight months. The mortality rate for both ships and passengers was appallingly high.

To date, not a single Manila Galleon has been located despite the fact that four of these were lost on the coast of California and another on the coast of Oregon. One of them, the *St. Agustin*, lost in 1595 with a very important cargo, is known to lie in Drake's Bay near San Francisco. During storms, porcelain shards have been thrown up on the beaches of Drake's Bay and the exact location of the shipwreck is known within several hundred yards.

Recently, I applied for permission to locate and excavate the *St. Agustin* and ended up in a legal battle with the National Park Service. The Park Service has repeatedly stated that it does not have the funds to locate or excavate this shipwreck, and yet it refuses to have anyone else do it, which would be for the benefit of the general public and scholarship. The state of California now

Carpenters' tools found at the sunken city of Port Royal, Jamaica, lost in 1692 during an earthquake.

maintains that it has legal ownership of this shipwreck and has offered to give me permission to work the site, despite the protests of the National Park Service.

Although the famed Spanish treasure galleons were the richest ships to ply the Caribbean, they were certainly not the only ones. Hundreds of smaller vessels—coastal traders, advice-boats (for dispatches and intelligence), salvage vessels and fishing craft—also operated out of the many ports of the Spanish colonies. The wealth of these colonies soon attracted to the Caribbean the Portuguese, French, Dutch and English who sought a share of the shining wealth either through contraband trade or plunder. The volume of non-Spanish shipping increased after the establishment of permanent bases for privateering and smuggling. Some, like Jamaica, became important colonies in their own right. Shipping expanded dramatically after English settlements were founded in North America and on many of the West Indian islands. By the beginning of the eighteenth century an estimated 600 non-Spanish ships were visiting the ports of the Caribbean each year. By 1785, the number had grown to more than 1,300, and by 1800 more than 2,500. Some of these were warships but most were merchantmen and slave ships.

The voyage to and from the New World was hazardous. Thousands of ships were lost at sea, mostly in storms. Others were lost through incompetent navigation, fire and battle. Even today, the Caribbean, dotted with treacherous reefs and shallows and swept by tropical storms, as sudden as they are violent, claims more than its share of ships. In the days of dead-reckoning navigation and inaccurate or nonexistent charts, when sail-driven wooden vessels deteriorated swiftly in the tropical climate, and the sea teredo (shipworm) ravaged their hulls, the toll was even greater, and thousands of wrecks litter the sea bottom.

We don't know who first had the courage to penetrate the depths of the sea, nor can we be sure of what impelled them to enter such an inhospitable environment, although it was probably for fish, mollusks and crustaceans. It has been established that men were diving as early as 4500 B.C.; archaeological excavations in Mesopotamia have unearthed shells that could only have been recovered from the sea floor by divers. Then there is a gap in diving history of more than a thousand years, until the Theban Sixth Dynasty in Egypt around 3200 B.C. Numbers of carved mother-of-pearl ornaments from this epoch have been found by archaeologists indicating that diving was widespread. Greek free divers were active as early as 2000 B.C., bringing up sponges and the highly prized red coral from the Mediterranean floor. Since pearl diving was done in China at this same time, we know that diving was widespread in the ancient world.

Our admiration for the ancient free diver is great when we consider he performed without any eye protection. Anyone who has ever opened his eyes in salt water knows how uncomfortable it is and how difficult it is to see clearly. He must have been very skillful, for red coral is seldom found in water shallower than 100 feet and diving to such a depth without the aid of any breathing apparatus or fins is no mean feat. Gulping air into his lungs, he jumped in the sea with a stone weight grasped in his arms to carry him down and guide ropes from a boat tied to his waist to bring him up again. Once on the bottom, he jettisoned the weight and pursued his objective. When he ran out of air, he either tugged at the rope and was pulled back to the surface or ascended hand-over-hand by himself. His work was not limited to plucking valuables indigenous to the sea. He dove for other reasons too: for construction work in rivers and harbors, for military purposes and for salvage.

The earliest account of divers in quest of sunken treasure is found in Herodotus, the Greek historian who wrote about the middle of the fifth century B.C. About fifty years earlier a Greek diver named Scyllias and his daughter, Cyane, had been employed by Xerxes, the king of Persia, to recover a fabulous treasure from several Persian galleys sunk during a battle with a Greek fleet. After they had brought up the treasure, Xerxes refused to give them the promised reward and held them aboard his galley, probably for other diving jobs. Seething at this treachery, Scyllias and Cyane jumped overboard in the midst of a storm and gained revenge by cutting the anchor cables of the Persian ships, causing many collisions. They escaped in the confusion.

By the third century B.C., diving for sunken treasure was so common among the Greeks that special laws regarding the division of finds were passed. Treasure recovered in two cubits of water or less (a cubit was equal to a foot and a half) entitled the salvor to a tenth of the value; treasure recovered from water between two and eight cubits deep entitled the diver to a third of the value, and treasure recovered in depths over eight cubits entitled the diver to half the value. The part of the treasure not given to the diver was the property of the original owner or, in the event of his death, the property of the ruler from whose waters it was recovered.

Nearly as famous as the brilliant exploits of the early free divers of the Old World were those of the Indian and Negro pearl divers of the Caribbean who remained free divers long after the advent of diving equipment. Even before the Europeans arrived in the New World, diving was practiced by many of the aborigines. Like Old World divers, they found on the sea floor an abundant supply of food. Although diving for pearls did not become a major occupation until the coming of the white man, it was done on a small scale in the Caribbean by the Lucayan, Carib and Arawak tribes. In 1498, during Columbus' third voyage of exploration, his fleet anchored one day at the island of Cubagua, near the coast of Venezuela, where his men noticed the local Indians wearing pearls found in the surrounding waters. On his return to Spain, Columbus reported his find to the king, who ordered that a

pearl fishery be immediately established on Cubagua. Other large
oyster beds were found in nearby areas, including one off Margarita
Island, which eventually became the center of a pearl industry that still
flourishes today. The Spaniards so overworked the Indian divers that
by the mid-sixteenth century few were left. The Spanish then began
employing slaves brought from Africa to dive. Over the centuries these
Caribbean pearl divers brought up vast fortunes in pearls which were
sold all over the world.

The Spanish also used slave divers for salvage work. In major
colonial ports, such as Havana, Veracruz, Cartagena and Panama,
teams of divers were kept aboard salvage vessels ready to leave at a

Early helmet divers at work on the British warship Royal George, *which sank off
Spitshead, England, in 1782. The drawing was made in 1844 while the divers were
salvaging her. (Credit: National Maritime Museum, Greenwich, England.)*

moment's notice to recover valuable sunken cargo. From the sixteenth century to the end of the eighteenth more than 100 million ducats were salvaged from Spanish wrecks by these divers, who more than once saved the monarchs of Spain from bankruptcy. Ironically, when other European nations began colonizing the West Indies, runaway divers were instrumental in depleting the Spanish exchequer: their new employers used their talents to salvage Spanish treasure wrecks, but the profits went into English, French and Dutch treasuries.

In 332 B.C., when Alexander launched his conquest of the world, the Phoenician island stronghold of Tyre offered such a long and fierce resistance that both attackers and defenders had frequent recourse to divers. There is a legend that Alexander himself descended into the sea in some sort of a chamber to watch divers destroy the harbor's boom defenses, lines of spars designed to obstruct invading vessels. Scanty as the details are, Alexander's descent is a milestone in man's struggle to make a place for himself in the sea. However, it was not the first such technical advance in diving. Three decades earlier, in 360 B.C., Aristotle's *Problematum* mentions divers using diving bells—inverted containers, with air trapped inside.

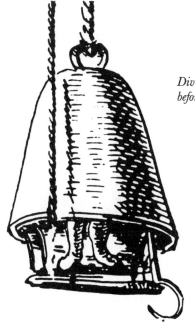

Diving bells were in use several centuries before the birth of Christ.

Almost two millennia passed before there is another account of a diving bell. In 1538, two Greeks designed and built a diving bell and demonstrated it in Toledo, Spain, before the Emperor Charles V. More than ten thousand spectators observed the two men in a bell large enough to hold them both. They sat inside with a burning candle as the bell was lowered into the water. To the crowd's amazement the flame still burned brightly when they surfaced. News of the Toledo bell spread throughout Europe, stimulating the construction of many like it. Practical application varied. Some divers worked inside the bell. Others, hindered by the confinement, used it as an air bank, swimming outside to work and returning at intervals to gulp air into their lungs. Over the years many improvements were made and the diving bell remained in use as the chief diving tool until replaced in the eighteenth century by such innovations as the diving suit, in which the diver had breathing air pumped down from the surface through a hose. In the Caribbean the diving bell was little used because virtually all of the wrecks salvaged were in relatively shallow water.

One of the most notable uses of a diving bell occurred in 1677 when an enormous bell—13 feet high and 9 feet across—was built in Spain and used to salvage two shipwrecks off the port of Cadaqués. Two Moorish divers were employed and stayed down for an hour at a time. They claimed they could have stayed even longer were it not for the terrific heat created in the bell by their breathing. They worked without leaving the chamber and the venture was highly successful. Several million pieces of eight and a quarter of a ton of gold bullion was recovered. The divers were paid in a novel manner: each time they surfaced with treasure they were permitted to keep as much of it as they could hold in their mouths and hands.

The greatest single treasure ever recovered in the New World was the work of William Phips, an American, in 1683. In 1641 a Spanish treasure galleon was wrecked on a reef (Silver Shoals) some ninety miles north of the coast of Hispaniola. This was one of the richest ships ever lost and the Spaniards searched for years without finding it. In his childhood, Phips had listened raptly to the tales sailors on the wharves of his native Boston told of this wreck and others. Bitten by the treasure bug, he took the savings he had earned as a young shipwright and in 1681 made his first Caribbean treasure hunt. Although he did not recover the vast treasure of his dreams, he did locate several wrecks and more than met his expenses, a promising beginning.

He then went to London to enlist the aid of King Charles II for an expedition to search for the lost galleon on Silver Shoals. It was eighteen months before he was finally granted a royal audience; but Phips was determined and persuasive. The king agreed to back the venture in return for a large share of the profits.

After getting together about twenty Negro pearl divers, refugees from the pearl fisheries of Margarita Island, at Port Royal on Jamaica, Phips set off for the wreck area in late 1683. After reaching the reef he drove himself and the men almost to the breaking point, the divers forced to scour the miles of reef from dawn to dusk. Perseverance was at last rewarded. A diver, sighting a large sea fan, dove down to retrieve it as a souvenir and upon surfacing discovered silver coins attached to its base. Phips burst into tears of exultation. The next month was a daily struggle to bring up the treasure while fighting the weather and pirates who had heard of the windfall. More than thirty-two tons of silver, a vast amount of gold, chests of pearls and precious stones were recovered before bad weather and exhaustion of provisions ended the salvage operation. The total value of his haul in today's currency was over $20 million. Phips received one-sixth, enough to make him the richest man in the colonies. He was knighted by the king and named governor of Massachusetts Colony.

Several years ago, a treasure hunting firm working under an agreement with the National Museum of Santo Domingo relocated this shipwreck and recovered a large amount of treasure and artifacts. An excellent documentary movie was made of this recovery and numerous books and articles also published, which brought the history of this shipwreck to the public's enjoyment. A traveling display of the find also toured across the United States over a period of several years.

Man has always been curious about his past. Thousands of years ago the Babylonians and Egyptians not only kept records of contemporary history but tried to delve into earlier times. Herodotus traveled thousands of miles eagerly investigating the histories and oral traditions of many peoples. The kings of the last Babylonian dynasty were antiquities collectors, and the Romans were avid antiquarians, collecting art treasures from all over the known world to adore their palaces and villas. Interest in ancient art dimmed along with scientific curiosity in the Dark Ages because of a religious orthodoxy which frowned on rational inquiry about man's past. Many priceless Greek art objects which had endured centuries were burned for lime or melted down for their mineral content during that long epoch. Fortunately for mankind, not all the Greek art shipped to Italy and other Roman domains reached its destination. Many of these plundered masterpieces were saved for a more appreciative posterity by being lost at sea.

During the Renaissance the liberated spirit of man focused great interest on ancient art, thought and life, and a cult of antiquity grew up. Treasure seekers and antiquity hunters were busy digging up objects to sell to the rich for private collections and museums. Even the Spaniards in the New World found grave robbing a lucrative business: Aztec, Olmec, Mayan and Incan artifacts have been found in recent years on dozens of Spanish wrecks. Unfortunately, most of the handwrought artifacts of precious metals or gems were destroyed by the Spaniards for their intrinsic value.

The first so-called archaeologists were nothing more than grave robbers who cloaked themselves in official titles, looted countless sites and shipped the treasures back to their own countries for great profits. Egypt, Greece and Mesopotamia were plundered so ruthlessly that many museums in other European countries have more extensive collections of antiquities than their own.

Archaeology ceased to be looked upon solely as a treasure hunt with the discovery in 1748 of the sites of Pompeii and Herculaneum which had been entombed beneath volcanic ash and lava when Mount Vesuvius erupted in A.D. 79. Archaeologists found that a great deal of knowledge about the way the people of these two towns had lived could be derived by disciplined, scientific excavation instead of stripping the sites of artifacts. Many deplorable errors were made in the early days but it was a start in the right direction. However, archaeology didn't emerge as a full-fledged scientific discipline until early in the present century. Even as late as the beginning of World War I, the teaching of archaeology in many universities meant art history, and many excavations were still conducted by people more interested in finding valuable artifacts than in gaining knowledge of the past or perfecting scientific techniques such as the establishment of a reliable system of comparative dating.

Two Englishmen deserve most of the credit for developing archaeology as a science. From 1880 onward, Flinders Petrie and A. H. Pitt-Rivers developed painstaking methods for proper excavation and recording. They emphasized the importance of stratification, the

Bronze statue of Poseidon, ancient Greek god of the sea, recovered by sponge divers about fifty years ago off the coast of Greece. (Credit: Greek National Museum.)

significance of associated finds, and the need for accurate and detailed recording. Their meticulous approach to all phases of field work remains the basis for sound excavation work today.

In 1928, a leading Hellenist, Salomon Reinarch, wrote: ''The richest museum of antiquities in the world is still inaccessible to us. It lies at the bottom of the eastern Mediterranean. We are able to explore the land and air without much difficulty, but we are very far from rivaling the fish in their element, who in the words of St. Augustus, 'have their being in the secret ways of the Abyss.' Those ways remain closed to us.'' Reinarch's remarks came before great steps were taken to enable man to discover the treasures of the undersea museum.

The first people to show interest in underwater archaeology were a group of English antiquarians who in 1775 sponsored an expedition to recover historical artifacts from the Tiber River near Rome. Greek divers, using a diving bell, worked for three years with little success because they had no way of removing the centuries' accumulation of river mud covering a number of wrecks containing a wealth of artifacts. After that there was little interest in underwater archaeology until early in this century when objects brought up by Greek and Turkish fishermen and sponge divers aroused the enthusiasm of archaeologists. When it was seen how beautiful and valuable many of these items were, archaeologists hired divers specifically to hunt for more. Most of the magnificent bronzes now displayed in the National Museum in Athens were recovered by sponge divers and fishermen.

Fishermen have no doubt been finding unique, handcrafted antiquities for centuries, but many ended up in the melting pot for their scrap metal value. As early as the beginning of the eighteenth century fishermen near Livorno, Italy, recovered bronze statues of Homer and Sophocles. Several years later fishermen in the Gulf of Corinth off Greece snagged a bronze statue representing the "Zeus of Livadhostro." Near Piombino off the coast of Tuscany, close to the site of the ancient city of Populonium, fishermen in 1832 hauled up in their nets a bronze statue of Apollo. This exquisite work is one of the Louvre's major exhibits. Until 1966, when a dredging operation at Piraeus near Athens uncovered a large group of spectacular bronze statues, the Apollo bronze was the only extant bronze original from the Greek Archaic Period (before 480 B.C.).

In 1900, sponge divers reported finding a large cache of statuary at a depth of thirty fathoms off the island of Antikythera. The Greek Ministry of Education and the Greek Navy sponsored a salvage operation there. Because of the depth, the sponge divers working on the project had only five minutes or so of bottom time. One who exceeded this died from the bends. It was not a proper archaeological excavation since the uneducated divers had no idea what was worth saving and what was not. A number of huge marble statues, which the divers mistook for boulders covering the site, were mistakenly picked up by cranes and thrown into deeper water. The site was never worked systematically, so that when the exhausted divers stopped many more valuable objects remained on the bottom. The wreck proved to be a Roman argosy laden with a cargo of works of art looted from the sanctuaries and temples of ancient Greece. Amphoras and other ceramics found on the wreck place the date of the wreck at about 75 B.C. In addition to a number of priceless bronze statues, including the well-known Antikythera Youth, thirty-six marble statues and a bronze bed decorated with animal heads were raised. Smaller objects, including a gold earring in the form of Eros playing a lyre, a number of exquisite glass vessels and the gears of a unique astronomical computer, were brought to light. This fantastic discovery provided magnificent examples of original works by master sculptors of the Argive and Athenian schools. The site was briefly revisited in 1953 by a team of French divers who claim the wreck is buried deep in the sand and that many more works of art await recovery.

Another Roman argosy dating from the first century B.C. was found by Greek sponge divers in 1907 three miles off the Tunisian coast near Mahdia. The bulk of the ship's cargo consisted of stone bases, capitals and sixty columns weighing over 200 tons. Between 1908 and 1913 sponge divers worked on the site in 150 feet of water. Under the direction of the Tunisian Department of Antiquities, divers recovered a large part of her cargo. Among the most interesting finds were well-preserved bronze busts, dancing dwarfs, a heron and a large statue of Agon. In 1948 a team of French divers led by Captain Jacques Cousteau, using scuba equipment for the first time on an underwater archaeological site, employed waterjets to remove a great overburden of mud covering the wreck and raised more of the ship's cargo to the surface. The site was again worked on in 1954 and 1955 by amateur divers from the Tunisian Club of Underwater Studies, but more remains to be done on this wreck.

Another accidental discovery was made by sponge divers in 1928 off Cape Artemision in Greece. They found a Roman shipwreck from about the time of Christ. The Greek Navy, using helmet divers, conducted a brief salvage effort which ended prematurely when a diver died of the bends. The famous statue of Zeus, or Poseidon, the god of the sea, a bronze jockey and parts of a galloping horse of the Hellenistic period were among the objects found. Although this wreck is buried in sand in only 130 feet of water, nothing has been done to excavate it properly in recent years.

The first disciplined archaeological work on an underwater site occurred in Lake Nemi near Rome in 1928. Legends had grown up about two Roman ships which sank there during the first century A.D. Both ships were enormous and sumptuous: each over 230 feet long with decks paved in mosaics and colored marble, heated baths, marble columns and other decorative features and luxurious appointments. They were probably pleasure craft used by the Roman rulers and nobility. Feeble attempts with primitive equipment had been made to salvage the wrecks as early as 1446 and again in 1535. Twice in the nineteenth century divers recovered artifacts from the site. The last operation was halted by the Italian government in 1895 when divers were found removing a great quantity of wooden planking from the wrecks.

Then, in 1928, Mussolini decided the government should salvage both ships. During a four-year period the whole lake was drained. After the ships were exposed, archaeologists had a unique opportunity to study two well-preserved hulls of the Roman period before they were disassembled and carted off to a Rome warehouse. Fortunately the archaeologists made good detailed plans of the hulls, because they were later burned in 1944 by German troops. Only scale models remain for study.

In the Western Hemisphere the first major excavation of an underwater site was led by Edward Thompson, the American consul in Mérida, Yucatán, in Mexico in the early part of the twentieth century. Thompson had a passionate interest in archaeology and purchased an area of land that contained the ruins of Chichén Itzá, the most important city of the Mayan civilization. Under the auspices of the American Antiquarian Society and Harvard University's Peabody Museum, he began a systematic exploration of the many ruins on the site. Near one of the temples he discovered a large cenote—a hole formed in the limestone terrain by the collapse of the roof of a subterranean cave and filled with collected rain water. Thompson's cenote was 190 feet in diameter, the water within was 65 feet deep, and the walls surrounding it rose 60 feet above the water's surface. The local Indians informed him that the cenote was called the Well of Sacrifice and according to legend contained immense treasure. Thompson's research corroborated the Indians' story. For centuries before the Spanish conquest, the Mayans had worshiped Yum Chac, a rain god believed to inhabit the cenote. Dependent on maize for food, the Mayans made offerings to appease Yum Chac in times of drought, offerings which included gold and jade and sometimes young maidens as wives for the god.

After returning from the United States, where he raised money from the Peabody Museum and learned to dive in a helmet suit, Thompson began work on the project in 1909. A derrick was erected for lowering and raising him and for holding a suction dredge to remove the mud at the cenote bottom. His first dives revealed that mud lay ten feet deep over much of the bottom and the inkiness of the water made vision impossible. For months Thompson had to rely completely on the suction dredge, manipulating it from the surface. Tons and tons of mud were pumped up but the ooze failed to yield even one artifact. At last, just as he was ready to concede that perhaps the rain god had made his home elsewhere, the dredge brought up the first artifact: a round ball of resinous incense. Then, after Thompson put a steel-jawed grab bucket into use, scarcely a day passed without relics coming to light. Thompson dove in the gloomy depths and working by touch found more incense balls, ceramic incense burners, vases, bowls, plates, axes, lance points, arrowheads, copper chisels, discs of beaten copper and even human bones. Among the valuable artifacts were some $800,000 worth of gold bells, figures and discs and pendants, beads and earrings of jade. Thompson, unlike so many of the earlier archaeologists, was a dedicated amateur, not interested in making money from his work. The priceless collection was shipped to the Peabody Museum, where it was on display until 1960 when it was given to the Mexican government.

During the American War of Independence a number of British warships were sunk in 1781 in the York River off Yorktown, Virginia. In 1934, oystermen discovered the hulks of several of them and the Colonial National Historical Park Service and the Mariner's Museum of Newport News joined forces to salvage them. Navy divers used water jets to blow the mud off two of them and reported that they were too poorly preserved to be raised. Consequently, a grab bucket operated off a barge recovered a good, representative collection of late-eighteenth-century armament and equipment: cannon, anchors, weapons, ship's fittings, tools, bottles, crockery and pewterware.

The state of Virginia recently decided on having one of these shipwrecks excavated in a proper archaeological manner. A cofferdam has been constructed around one of the hulks, which still contains wooden structure in a good state of preservation. Within the cofferdam the dirty water is chemically filtered and clarified. A team led by underwater archaeologist John Broadwater is currently working this site.

The grab bucket employed by Thompson was still in use as late as 1950. The techniques and standards of underwater archaeology had progressed little in forty years when Nino Lamboglia, director of the Institute of Ligurian Studies, in 1950 undertook a project which pointed up the destructive capabilities of the grab bucket. In 1925 in 140 feet of water off Albenga in northwest Italy fishermen had snagged amphorae from what proved to be a first-century B.C. Roman shipwreck. Lamboglia was unable to procure government funds for a salvage project nor could he arouse interest among amateur divers. Offered the assistance of a commercial salvage firm, he accepted. Helmet divers under his direction removed a few of the amphorae by hand. Then he used a large grab bucket, directed by an observer in a diving chamber who had telephone communication to those on the surface. Giant steel claws smashed into the wreck, wrenching up amphorae, wood and other objects. This drastic method lasted ten days during which 1,200 amphorae were raised, all but 110 broken. This haphazard destruction of an archaeological site was to stimulate the development of scientifically acceptable techniques for future underwater archaeological projects. Lamboglia was the first to admit that he had made a grave error in his methods, which made no provision for making plans or drawings of the site.

The next major excavation of an ancient wreck was undertaken in 1952. Divers working on the construction of the great Marseilles sewer outlet came upon the remains of a second-century B.C. Roman ship in 150 feet of water off the little island of Grand Conglo018. The excavation of this wreck was the proving ground for many of the tools and techniques in use today, including the airlift, high-pressure water jets, photography and underwater surveying and mapping.

Captain Jacques Cousteau joined forces on the project with Fernand Beinoit, a land archaeologist. A thick mud layer and sand covered most of the site and Cousteau employed an airlift—sort of an underwater vacuum cleaner—to suction it off. Airlifts had been used in the 1930s in the Florida Keys by treasure hunters but never before on an archaeological dig. Benoit and other non-diving archaeologists watched the operation over closed-circuit television, but were frustrated because they couldn't communicate with the divers to control their actions.

The divers were limited by the water's depth to three dives a day for a total of forty-five minutes of bottom time. Although a total of several thousand dives were logged during the project, only one serious accident occurred, in which a diver lost his life.

Many unusual and priceless artifacts were recovered but, in spite of this, the excavation was not considered an unqualified archaeological success by many scholars because of failure to gather pertinent data while the artifacts were in situ. No plan of the site was ever made, and both Cousteau and Benoit failed to provide information on how they had arrived at various conclusions concerning the wreck site. No matter how fragmentary excavation material may be, it is the obligation of the archaeologist to record it and publish his findings, because what seems inconsequential at the time may prove highly significant in the future to another archaeologist. Like Heinrich Schliemann, excavator of Troy and Mycenae, these men were pioneering a new frontier and their mistakes should be judged accordingly.

The first complete and successful excavation of an ancient shipwreck directed by a professional archaeologist working underwater took place at Cape Gelidonya on the Turkish coast. The project was initiated by an enthusiastic American, Peter Throckmorton, an erstwhile student of archaeology, a diver, and in the throes of a wanderlust that brought him to Turkey after roaming all over the globe. In 1959, after sharing countless bottles of raki with a number of garrulous Turkish sponge divers, Throckmorton learned the location of many areas with "old pots in the sea," or amphorae. Almost every sponge diver in the Mediterranean knows of a wreck site or two. During the course of a year Throckmorton managed to check out about thirty-five of these locations and most proved to be the sites of ancient vessels spanning a period of more than two thousand years.

One of those wrecks, located in ninety feet of water off Cape Gelidonya, turned out to be the oldest shipwreck ever found: a Bronze Age wreck dating from 1300 B.C. During an exploratory dive on it, Throckmorton quickly realized its great importance. He was able to convince several sponge divers, who had planned to dynamite the site and raise the cargo of copper and bronze to sell for scrap, to leave it untouched. He then reported his find to the University of Pennsylvania's Department of Archaeology. Dr. Rodney Young, the director of the university's Institute of Classical Archaeology, offered to find the funds and personnel to mount a major expedition to the site.

The following summer a team of twenty specialists in different aspects of underwater archaeology, including Frédéric Dumas, who had previous experience in underwater projects off the French Riviera, and George Bass, a young graduate student in archaeology at the university, arrived to join Throckmorton at Cape Gelidonya.

Because of the depth of the wreck, every diver was limited to only 68 minutes a day of working time underwater, but since each man's task was carefully planned the group was able to make the most of the short bottom time. After the area had been thoroughly cleared of seaweed, the team made drawings and plans of all visible traces of the cargo. They then filmed a photographic mosaic of the site. On the bottom, the site looked like a conventional land site with meter poles staked about and numbered plastic tags marking all visible objects. Every item was drawn, photographed, triangulated and plotted before being raised to the surface.

A thick lime deposit, as hard as concrete, covered most of the cargo and only an occasional piece protruded through the hard seafloor. To attempt to extract individual pieces underwater was both too time-consuming and too dangerous because of the fragility of many of the artifacts. Working with hammers and chisels, the divers broke off large clumps of conglomerate, some weighing as much as four hundred pounds, and sent them to the surface in lifting baskets where they were broken apart. Some of the larger masses were so difficult to separate from the bottom material that the divers had to use automotive jacks. Until each day's recoveries could be treated, they were stored in a freshwater pond on the beach. When the clumps were broken apart a vast array of artifacts from the ship's cargo came to light: bronze chisels, axes, picks, hoes, adzes, plowshares, knives, spades, a spit and a large number of copper ingots. An airlift used in the few sand pockets on the site yielded other artifacts including four Egyptian scarabs, oil lamps, polished stone mace-heads, apothecary weights, pieces of crystal, mirrors, awls, a cooking spit, whetstones, olive pits and animal, fish and fowl bones.

Very little of the hull was preserved but the distribution of the cargo suggests that the ship was approximately twelve meters long. Brushwood dunnage, as described in the *Odyssey*, was still lying over fragmentary planks. The cargo and personal possessions found indicated the ship was a Syrian merchant vessel which had picked up its cargo of metal on Cyprus. This wreck shed new light on seafaring during the Bronze Age and furnished a wealth of information on early metallurgy and trade.

The expedition was a clear-cut success and opened the door for future underwater archaeological projects in the Mediterranean. Bass, convinced of the importance of this fledgling science, decided to make it his life's work. Before he had first gone to Turkey he had consulted many land archaeologists and found that the majority felt

Divers on the Bronze Age Cape Gelidonya wreck raising lumps of concreted cargo with plastic salvage balloons. The "Hookah" equipped diver, drawing his air from a surface compressor, fills a balloon. Note that nothing is visible that seems like a shipwreck. (Credit: Peter Throckmorton.)

that underwater archaeology was impossible and could never become an exact science. They stated such reasons as: "Nothing could be preserved underwater," or "It is impossible to make proper plans underwater." Some said it was too dangerous and far too expensive for the amount of information that could be gained.

During the excavation of the Bronze Age wreck Bass and the others had been able to prove all these predictions unfounded. They discovered a remarkable portion of the cargo was in an excellent state of preservation despite having lain underwater for nearly 3,300 years. They had made accurate plans and drawings underwater, more professional than many produced on land excavations. Although most of the expedition members had had little previous diving experience, no diving accidents occurred. To the surprise of the skeptics the whole project, including the air passage of all involved, cost under $25,000, a modest sum and considerably less than that spent on many land excavations of the same duration. The only disappointment felt by Bass and Throckmorton, in this and some of their subsequent excavations as well, was the scarcity of preserved wood from the original ship. This hindered them in determining important aspects about the methods used in the ship's construction.

In 1982, sponge divers accidentally located a still-older Bronze Age shipwreck off Ulu Burum in Turkish waters dating back to 1400 B.C. Bass and his team are still excavating this fantastic discovery. Laying in 150 feet of water on a rocky shelf, the fifty-foot-long trading ship carried a cargo representing seven civilizations of the Late Bronze Age. Thousands of artifacts have been recovered, providing an astonishing portrait of an era symbolized by the fall of Troy and the reign of Egypt's Tutankhamen. Enough ship's timbers have survived to extend our knowledge of ship technology back a thousand years.

Less than a year after Bass began his excavation of the Bronze Age shipwreck off Cape Gelidonya, the most important and challenging underwater archaeological project ever undertaken in Europe was finally completed after five years of hard work. On April 24, 1961, the 64-gun Swedish warship *Vasa*—which sank with more than fifty passengers and crew in Stockholm Harbor in 1628 in full view of the king and thousands of spectators shortly after being launched— was raised to the surface. All early salvage efforts had failed. The deepest part of the wreck lay in a hundred feet of water, too deep for early divers working out of bells to accomplish much. The wreck lay for more than three hundred years in a silent tomb of harbor mud. Generally, salvage of a wooden vessel is impossible after fifty years because the wood is eaten away by shipworms. However, Stockholm Harbor is one of the few places in the world where there are no shipworms and the *Vasa* remained intact.

In 1956, a Swedish petroleum engineer, Anders Franzen, became interested in the *Vasa*. After several years of research he narrowed down her location and used a core sampler (a device with which geologists obtain samples of sediment on the sea floor) operated from a small boat to find the wreck. Swedish Navy divers were sent down to identify and investigate its condition. As Franzen expected, they found it intact. With the aid of the government and funds from private sources, a team of helmet divers under Franzen's supervision began the tedious job of raising the ship. It was far from simple: the *Vasa* was large for her day, with a displacement of 1,400 tons (four times the size of the *Mayflower*) and was deeply buried in the harbor mud. The divers had first to remove all of the loose objects aboard. Then they had to blast tunnels under the wreck with a water jet—a perilous undertaking because the ship could easily have slipped deeper into the mud and crushed them—so that steel lifting cables could be inserted under the hull. The construction of the tunnels alone took three years. While this was going on, other divers were employed removing the masts, spars and rigging. Finally, the cables were strung through the tunnels and pontoons were used to lift the ship.

The *Vasa* was then towed into dry dock and placed on a specially built concrete barge equipped with a sprinkler system to keep her

The Vasa *shortly after is was raised, being hosed down to keep the timbers wet to prevent them from cracking. (Credit:* Vasa *Museum).*

wet until she could be preserved. (This is discussed in greater detail in Chapter 7.) Franzen was incredibly busy the moment the ship broke the surface. With scores of archaeologists and historians he entered every accessible part of the vessel and found himself in a fantastic time capsule. Everything lay as it had fallen three and a half centuries before: sea chests, leather boots, weapons, carpenter tools, beer steins, cooking implements, money and powder kegs. More than ten thousand artifacts were found. Franzen even discovered lying among the cannon carriages the remains of some victims of the disaster. And twelve partially clad skeletons were dug out of the mud inside the ship. One of the seamen had his sheath knife and a leather money pouch with twenty coins still attached to a belt around his waist. The ship was an underwater Pompeii where mud and cold water instead of volcanic lava and ash preserved a moment in history.

Although the discovery and recovery of a section of the Tudor warship of Henry VIII, the *Mary Rose*, has received much publicity in recent years, only the starboard half of the ship's hull was recovered. It had the consistency of wet cardboard when brought to the surface on October 11, 1982. Preservation is still underway in a specially-built museum in Portsmouth, England, and eventually its wooden remains will be stabilized and preserved for posterity. When lost during a battle with the French in 1545, this 700-ton ship with 91 cannon and a crew of 700 was one of the most formidable ships afloat. The more than 17,000 priceless artifacts that the site yielded have revealed many unknown factors about life during Tudor times.

In recent years the Western Hemisphere has also produced a number of well preserved ship hulls to rival those of the *Vasa* and *Mary Rose*. Two American gunboats, the *Hamilton* and *Scourge*, two-masted schooners fighting in the War of 1812, were discovered in 1973 in Lake Ontario near Niagara Falls in 275 feet of water. The expedition was sponsored by The Royal Ontario Museum and led by amateur archaeologist Donald A. Nelson, who is a dentist by profession. Several years ago a National Geographic Society sponsored expedition using ROVs (remote operated vehicles) equipped with video and still cameras discovered that both ships were in a remarkable state of preservation, appearing as if they had just sunk months before. Under a slight coating of silt both vessels looked like models in a Walt Disney production. Plans have been discussed for many years now by both the United States and Canadian governments, but nothing conclusive has developed in relation to raising these intact time-capsules of the past.

Although not intact and more on the order of the remains of the *Mary Rose*, three lower hull sections of mid-sixteenth century Basque whaling ships were discovered in Red Bay, Labrador in 1977. Archaeological work under the direction of Robert Grenier and James A. Tuck commenced in 1977 and continued each summer until 1985, when the program came to a halt due to lack of funds. Even though considered one of the major underwater archaeological discoveries in this hemisphere, to the great chagrin of many scholars, the Canadian government did not provide the necessary funding to raise these precious hulls, as was the case in England of the *Mary Rose*.

Still another major Canadian discovery that met a similar fate was the *HMS Breadalbane*. The ship was lost in August 1853 near Queen Elizabeth Island in the Arctic, searching for the 128-man crew of the ship of Sir John Franklin, who was seeking a Northwest Passage connecting the Atlantic and Pacific Oceans. A team headed by Canadian physician Dr. Joseph B. MacInnis, who specializes in diving under the ice and has led seven Arctic expeditions, used side-scan sonar and ROVs to locate the shipwreck under the thick ice. Except for photographing the site, no other funds were available for future salvage. Researchers believe that the low water temperature has kept all of the artifacts and ship's hull well preserved.

2

What Is Underwater Archaeology?

Before defining underwater archaeology we should try to understand what archaeology is all about. According to more than one dictionary, archaeology is the "scientific study of antiquities," but this is inadequate. Some people think of archaeology almost in terms of art history of ancient civilizations, which is also a totally inadequate interpretation. One dictionary says archaeology is the understanding of ancient civilizations in their totality through the discovery of objects belonging to ancient peoples. Sir Leonard Wooley, the great archaeologist who discovered Ur, the city of Abraham, wrote that "The purpose of archaeology is to illustrate and to discover the course of human civilization through the excavation of ancient places of habitation." Many people still think of archaeology as the search for man-made objects, when, in fact, it is the search for knowledge of man's past derived from the interpretation of the things found rather than the things themselves. To quote Wooley again: "The archaeologist, being after all human, does enjoy finding rare and beautiful objects, but wants to know all about them, and in any case prefers

40

the acquisition of knowledge to that of things; for him digging consists very largely in observation, recording and interpretation.''

Thus the function of the archaeologist is not simply to identify an object and determine its application. It is equally important to record the situation in which the object was found, its association with other objects, and its similarity or dissimilarity to objects found on other sites. The only way we can learn about man's early history is through archaeology, since man has no written records going back more than five thousand years. Moreover, the earliest records of literate man are scarce. Until recently all archaeological investigation of material remains of past human activities was confined to dry land, man's natural habitat. Increasingly, however, in the past several years awareness has grown of the potential of rich archaeological evidence lying beneath the waters that cover two-thirds of the earth's surface.

There is something about the term ''underwater archaeology,'' or its variants, ''submarine archaeology'' and ''marine archaeology,'' which provokes uneasiness in the minds of certain land archaeologists. Actually there is little difference between land and underwater archaeology; each is archaeology but practiced in different environments. Whether a person is excavating an ancient ruin under a scorching desert sun or working on a shipwreck beneath the freezing waters of the North Sea, he is engaged in archaeology, provided he is following accepted techniques and procedures.

Another term sometimes confused with underwater archaeology is ''naval archaeology.'' However, they are not synonymous. Naval archaeology has been practiced for several centuries and is the study and reconstruction of ancient ships from literary and iconographic evidence.

There is often a lack of distinction between underwater archaeology and underwater salvage. Underwater salvage is the simple recovery of objects found on a shipwreck or other underwater site without particular regard for the site itself. Underwater archaeology implies working on a site for the chief purpose of obtaining archaeological data. The recovery of artifacts is secondary. Salvage archaeology is a ''quickie'' form of excavation done both on land and in the water before a site is destroyed to build a road, or an irrigation project, or to dredge a harbor. However, this does not imply such an excavation is carried out with no regard for the cannons of archaeological procedure. Rather, the scope of the excavation is limited. And the primary objective is still to gather pertinent data and not only to save artifacts from destruction.

Ancient cultures were located between seas, and the greater portion of ancient trade was conducted across water. From underwater sites a great deal can be gleaned about man which is not revealed from land excavations of dwellings, sanctuaries, public buildings, burials, etc. Ships have sunk every year since ancient man first lashed two logs together. Before long, wrecks from almost every generation of antiquity will have been found and excavated. From them archaeologists will fill in the sketchy outlines of cargo these ships carried, where they sailed, and how they were constructed. Ships found in association with coins or other materials which can be ascribed to a precise date or period are of great help to land archaeologists dealing with the same period or roughly the same period and can aid them in dating different strata on land. The principle of stratification asserts that the latest dated objects are on the top, the oldest at the bottom.

Underwater archaeology has brought to light many artifacts never found on land. Although tens of thousands of silver and gold bars were shipped to Europe from the New World, until a number were recovered from shipwrecks in the Caribbean in recent years, not one existed anywhere. According to modern texts on metallurgy, platinum was not in use until the mid-nineteenth century because until then, it was thought, man could not produce the intense high temperatures required to refine and work the precious metal. In light of the recent discovery of a platinum bar dated 1521 found on a shipwreck off Grand Cayman Island, the texts must be rewritten.

Contrary to popular belief, many objects survive better underwater than on land. Rarely does a land archaeologist find ceramic artifacts intact. Usually he unearths small shards which must be painstakingly reassembled. On the other hand, the average shipwreck may yield hundreds, sometimes thousands, of intact ceramic items; not just the bulky terra cotta amphorae found on ancient shipwrecks in the Mediterranean and the Spanish olive jars found in the Caribbean, but even small, fragile cups and saucers of delicate Chinese porcelain. Clay smoking pipes are almost never found intact on land sites, but more than six thousand unbroken pipes were brought up from the sunken Jamaican city of Port Royal. Glass bottles are another item

Silver- and pewterware recovered from the sunken city of Port Royal, which sank in 1692 in Kingston Harbor, Jamaica.

rarely found unbroken on land; at Port Royal more than twelve thousand intact bottles were recovered from the muddy bottom.

Some seemingly ephemeral objects have lasted better underwater than underground—such as the complete human skull, containing an intact brain from ten thousand years ago, which was found in Warm Mineral Springs, Florida. Another nearby sinkhole, Fig Springs, was excavated by the late Professor John Goggin, one of the pioneers in underwater archaeology in North America. He found Indian artifacts such as corncobs, peach pits, gourds, woven cane matting, worked wood and animal hides, none of which would normally be preserved on a land site. At Port Royal such delicate items as tobacco leaves, human hair wigs and fragments of cotton and woolen clothing survived. In 1941, a page of a printed Bible published prior to 1695 was recovered from a wreck and in 1961 a complete book of sailing directions in Dutch was found in a wreck from circa 1590 off Cape Canaveral, Florida.

Depending on a number of important factors, some underwater sites should be treated in the same way as a land site. Not all of the archaeological techniques developed for use on land are applicable or relevant underwater, however. A point of disagreement George Bass has had with other archaeologists has been his dogmatic belief that every underwater site can be surveyed and excavated stratigraphically by the same or similar methods employed on land sites. Proving this point is one of the main reasons he gives for becoming interested in underwater archaeology. In the relatively deeper water where he has done his work, he has been able to prove his point because the sites were undisturbed over the centuries by storms, wave action, currents and men. The opposite is true of sites in shallow water—which include most in the Western Hemisphere— where they have been badly battered by nature and man and are scattered over extensive areas of the sea floor. Also, in spite of the limitations involved in diving on the deeper Mediterranean wrecks, once on the bottom the diver is able to work comfortably, with good underwater visibility. On most wrecks in shallower water the diver works in rough seas and is hampered by poor visibility, which makes it impossible to utilize the same type of surveying, photographic and excavation methods used on the deeper wrecks.

As on land, the excavation of an underwater site results in its obliteration, so every means possible should be employed to record accurately by measurement, drawing and photography the excavation and the objects uncovered. Detailed reports should be published. This is an obligation the archaeologist must fulfill lest the information gained be lost like the site itself.

To date, the sunken city of Port Royal, which went down in an earthquake in 1692, is one of the few sites in the Western Hemisphere on which any attempt has been made to excavate completely and thoroughly under the accepted standards of the "old school" archaeologists. Here, the excavation methods were akin to those used on land sites and by Bass and Throckmorton on the Bronze Age wreck. The site was marked off on a grid, a thorough survey was made, and the position and stratigraphy of all artifacts and sunken buildings uncovered were recorded and photographs and drawings made of everything recovered. All artifacts were properly preserved and a number of reports dealing in detail with all aspects of the excavation were published. However, as in the case of the Mediterranean wrecks Bass and Throckmorton have excavated, Port Royal was unique in a number of ways in comparison with the majority of underwater sites in the Western Hemisphere. The wrecks and the city sank quickly; the wrecks in deep water beyond the reach of disruptive forces, and the city, beneath harbor sediment. Thus, most of the artifacts and buildings remained undisturbed and unjumbled. Port Royal, located in a protected harbor, has not been greatly molested by the natural forces which have ravaged most shipwrecks in shallow-water areas.

During my three-year excavation of Port Royal between 1965 and 1968, more than one million artifacts were recovered, yielding a vast amount of archaeological data. More than two dozen archaeological monographs and two books were published and permanent displays of the finds set up in three of the island's museums. Traveling displays were also shown all over the United States and Europe, and replicas of many of the finds have been manufactured and sold by the Jamaican government for the past twenty years. Each summer since 1981, there has been a two-month summer field school directed by Dr. D. L. Hamilton and sponsored by Texas A&M University and the Jamaican National Trust, and over 100 students have been trained in underwater archaeological techniques at this important site.

Of the more than ten thousand vessels that were lost in the Western Hemisphere prior to 1870, more than 95 percent were lost in shallow water of less than fifty feet. Since very few of these shallow-water sites fit into the same category as Port Royal or the deeper Mediterranean wrecks, just how much archaeological data can they relinquish? Some archaeologists feel that so little information of value can be obtained from them that it is fruitless to undertake any serious excavation. In some cases this may be so, but not always. Documentary sources can provide a great deal of information about the colonial ships, their cargoes and the men who sailed them. However, there are no corresponding literary sources documenting the ancient ships found in the Mediterranean. There are many things that historians have been unable to find out about the ships that plied the seas of the Western Hemisphere over the past five hundred years. In many instances underwater archaeology can provide answers to such intriguing questions as how various ships were constructed, what their rigging was, what anchors and armament they carried, and what their cargoes were.

Normally, in the case of shallow-water wrecks, only the type of cargo, armament and anchors can be determined. This is not the fault of the archaeologist but of nature. Consider what happens to most ships wrecked in shallow water. Either immediately upon running aground or soon after, the vessel begins to break up, even in good weather. The superstructure of an old ship was the first to go. Since it was buoyant, it was generally washed up on a beach or carried some distance from the main hull, spilling cannon and other objects along the way. Waves or currents eventually dispersed the ship's timbers and the sea teredo or other marine borers eventually devoured it. Consequently, virtually nothing remains to furnish clues to how the ship was constructed or how and where she carried her stores, cargo and armaments. In some cases ships' cargoes have been scattered over areas of several square miles, are intermingled with cargoes and vestiges of other wrecks—some older, some more recent—making it almost impossible to determine what belongs where. Such wrecks are less important than those in deeper waters where the wrecks are sealed containers for their contents.

Although stratigraphy—the origin, composition, distribution and succession of strata—is of prime importance on land sites, most of which span long periods of time, it is not always relevant or even possible to establish on many underwater sites, especially those in shallow water. On deeper wrecks, particularly when more than one wreck lies on the same spot, stratigraphy determines what each ship carried. It is also of prime importance on deep wrecks when any portion of the hull remains to determine the manner in which it was constructed. On some of the deeper sites when a ship settled upright and intact, even though most of the wooden hull may have disappeared, the cargo may still lie in situ as it was stored on the ship. Stratigraphy in this case might aid in determining the sequence in which the ship stopped at different ports by establishing how the various cargo items were stored. However, this only holds if the newer cargo was stowed on top of cargo loaded earlier. Heavier items would naturally be stowed under lighter cargo, which would confuse the situation.

A number of archaeologists overestimate the importance of precisely recording the exact location, or establishing the horizontal relationship between every single object discovered on a marine site. In regard to shallow wrecks scattered over large areas, this practice is a waste of time. Plotting the position of some of the major finds will help in establishing how the ship broke apart and where the various components ended up. This can help in deciding which areas are to get priority in excavating. It is more important to make detailed records of the deeper wrecks, providing the ship sank more or less intact. In such a case it may be possible to establish where various items were stowed aboard ship and to reconstruct the ship's form from fragmentary pieces.

One of the major problems is determining in the early stages if an underwater site is of archaeological merit. To be safe, each site should

Underwater archaeologists at work on a Roman wreck, located off the coast of Israel. (Credit: Elisha Linder.)

be treated as if it were of great value until it proves not to be. A site that turns out to be where a ship anchored and trash was thrown overboard is not in the same category as one of Columbus's shipwrecks, but it may take days or even weeks of work to determine what it is one has found. Thus, the amateur underwater archaeologist should seek help from experts to ascertain the importance of a find in establishing the methods by which it is to be worked. What Flinders Petrie wrote more than sixty years ago is still valid:

> *To suppose that excavation—one of the affairs which needs the widest knowledge—can be taken up by persons who are ignorant of most or all the technical requirements is a fatuity which has led, and still leads, to the most miserable catastrophes. Far better to let things lie a few centuries longer*

underground, if they can be let alone, than repeat the vandalism of past ages
without the excuse of being a barbarian.

No two archaeologists will agree on how old a site or object must
be before it can be considered of archaeological importance. A
number of classical archaeologists working in the Mediterranean feel
a site has to be more than five hundred years old before it is important.
While working in Israel several years ago, I was astonished to hear
several archaeologists say that a Crusader shipwreck, dating circa
A.D. 1200, had recently been found but that it would not be worked
on because it was too recent to interest them. If we took this attitude
in the Western Hemisphere, we would, of course, have virtually no
underwater sites of archaeological interest. If we accept the dictionary
definition of archaeology as "the study of antiquities" at face value,
we have a problem because "antiquities" refers to objects from
ancient times or those made before the Middle Ages.

For the purposes of this book let us say that any find that sheds
light on man's past—how he lived, worked, traveled and interacted
with others; what he constructed and how—will have archaeological
significance, regardless of age. For practical purposes let us consider
of potential historical interest any artifact over one hundred years
old. This takes us back to an important time in shipping, for it was
the period of transition from sail to steam and from wooden hull to
steel. More important, it was the time when the art of shipbuilding
evolved into the science of shipbuilding. Ships began to be built from
plans, most of which are still in existence, rather than by traditional
craftsman techniques handed down from father to son. As each year
passes, modern technology makes yesterday's miracles obsolete, and
thus objects, not necessarily very old, become things of the past and
disappear. Consequently, even the recovery of machinery manufactured during the Industrial Revolution, which began around 1800
in the United States, has archaeological merit, even though drawings
for them may exist.

Isolated finds of a single artifact can sometimes be of conse-
quence, as in the case of a recently discovered glass bottle dating
from the mid-seventeenth century. This bottle, found underwater,
bore the date 1654, but prior to its discovery, experts identifying
similar bottles by their style of manufacture had placed manufacture between 1670 and 1680.

A gold pocket watch recovered from an eighteenth-century Spanish shipwreck in the Caribbean.

The recovery of a pocket watch, evidently dropped overboard by a man being rowed across a river in England during the early 1600s, has yielded a great deal of information on early watchmaking which wasn't known before. A person coming upon a solitary anchor, seemingly unassociated with a shipwreck, might think it inconsequential. However, what if experts identified it as from the fifteenth century or even earlier? This would be of enormous help in establishing that others had reached the New World before Columbus.

Man left traces of his presence not only on land across continents but also in rivers, lakes and springs as well as along the shallow coastal fringes. Due to navigational limitations, early mariners tried to stay within sight of land whenever they could, steering courses from headland to headland. Sailing close to shore assured the seaman of finding a safe haven for the night. Most of the ships which came to grief and sank in the Old World before the Renaissance were fairly close to shore. Even after the Age of Discovery, when long, open voyages were commonplace, most ship disasters occurred close to coastlines. Thus, most of the world's underwater archaeological sites are in waters shallow enough to be explored by scuba divers.

Basically there are four different types of sites, different in number and the amount of archaeological data potentially available. Shipwrecks in seas, lakes and rivers far outnumber all other types of sites, and because of their time-capsule nature provide the most important archaeological information. The other types—submerged or inundated settlements, religious sites and refuse areas—are comparable to land sites because they generally span long periods of time and yield less relevant information than do wreck sites.

SHIPWRECKS: Until recently all information about the history and evolution of ancient shipping had been gleaned from the interpretation of ancient literary references and iconography (mosaics, frescos, decorations of ceramic objects, medallions, seals and coins). However, these sources furnished meager information about a vessel's appearance, construction, means of propulsion and performance. Most ancient authors were not well versed in seafaring matters, and artists sacrificed many details for decorative reasons. Thus, the only way to fill this gap in our knowledge of ancient shipping is by locating and excavating shipwrecks. The trireme, for example, was the common warship for more than five hundred years, yet virtually nothing is known about it. During the great Athenian expedition to Sicily in the summer of 413 B.C., more than 350 triremes were sunk off Syracuse in naval battles. The discovery of even one of these wrecks could provide a staggering amount of information.

The ultimate goal of the underwater archaeologist is to find a completely intact and well-preserved shipwreck such as the seventeenth-century warship *Vasa*. Unfortunately, the ravages of the seas in most areas make this an impossible dream, at least in the depths which can be penetrated with present diving equipment. There are some exceptions at the bottom of freshwater lakes and rivers and in a few saltwater zones.

In recent years three *bateaux* (small gunboats) from the mid-eighteenth century were raised intact and remarkably well preserved from Lake George, New York. Except for some Indian canoes, they are the earliest existing examples of American-built vessels. The gondola *Philadelphia*, lost in a battle with the British in 1776 on Lake Champlain, was also found well preserved. When she was raised, her cannon were still mounted and there were more than five hundred pieces of military equipment aboard. The *Philadelphia* is now on permanent exhibit in the Smithsonian Institute in Washington.

An excellent example of ship preservation was seen in the recent recovery of a large section of Henry VIII's warship *Mary Rose* from the muddy bottom of Portsmouth Harbor, England. The discovery, excavation, and raising of which could not have been accomplished

Land archaeologists excavating one of the Viking ships found in Denmark, after a cofferdam was erected around them and the water was pumped out. (Credit: Danish National Museum.)

without the painstaking work provided by more than 250 dedicated amateur sports divers, under the direction of Dr. Margaret Rule. The British, with their traditional appreciation of the amateur who engages in cultural or scientific activity for pleasure rather than gain, lead the way in using trained amateurs.

The Baltic and North seas are unique because they contain thousands of extraordinarily well preserved shipwrecks. Although the water is salt, the saline content where ships lie, all within diving depths, is less than in other seas. Consequently there are no coral-forming organisms and the waters do not sustain the sea teredo or other marine borers. This means that wood and other organic materials are in no way affected, even when unprotected by sedimentary deposits. Although divers have located dozens of old ships standing as if they had sunk just the day before, diving in these areas and working on these wrecks is difficult because the cold water restricts the length of time a diver can spend on the bottom, and underwater visibility is seldom more than three feet.

During the past three decades more than 150 old ships, some dating as early as the twelfth century, have been found in the land-reclamation project draining the Zuider Zee in Holland. Most of these wrecks are as well preserved as the *Vasa*. In 1957 five Viking ships were discovered buried in mud under the shallow waters of Roskilde Fjord in Denmark. All five had been deliberately scuttled to protect the entrance to a settlement in the tenth century. Because of the difficulty of diving in those northern waters, a cofferdam was erected around the wrecks, the water was pumped out, and they were excavated by land archaeologists. They have been removed from the site, reassembled and placed on display for all to see and enjoy. To the disappointment of archaeologists the ships had been stripped before they were scuttled so little was learned about the rigging used by the Vikings.

Since the second millennium before Christ, men have been sailing the Black Sea where the saline content is only about half that of the Mediterranean. Although nothing has been done to verify the fact, it is believed old ships found in the Black Sea will be in a state of preservation similar to those found in northern waters.

In some instances much can be learned from documentary sources about the construction of ships lost in the Western Hemisphere. Around the year 1650 the British Admiralty passed a regulation stipulating that all ships had to be constructed from plans, a copy of which had to be preserved in the Admiralty archives. Not only are thousands of these ships' plans extant but also plans of British-built merchant ships and even of many foreign ships which were captured or bought. There is a long period—from the time of Columbus until this period—about which we still know very little of ships' construction. Archives in Spain, France, Holland and other European countries house countless plans and even ship models, but most date after 1700. Another considerable gap in information concerns early American-built ships. Most extant plans and sketches of ships built in America date after 1800. Prior to that most American vessels were made by "rack of the eye," by craftsmen without plans or sketches. To fill in these hazy areas, a modest amount of information can be derived from the excavation of shipwrecks in shallow water, and far more will come from wrecks which may be discovered in fresh water or in areas such as the Baltic and the North seas.

The Mediterranean has become the acknowledged focus for most of the professional excavations of shipwrecks. This is natural since the Mediterranean is virtually the sole repository for ancient shipping as well as the resting place for all classes of shipping from medieval through modern times. During a span of 5,500 years thousands of ships were lost. Many of them, types not to be found anywhere else, contained cargoes and other materials not found on land sites. In some cases, such as the Bronze Age wreck found off Turkey, articles have been recovered for which no comparative material has ever been found on land.

The well-preserved remains of a Roman ship-wreck, located in the Mediterranean. Note the grid over the hull and the diver recording data. (Credit: Elisha Linder.)

Two Roman amphoras recovered by the author off the coast of Lebanon.

Although hundreds of ancient wrecks have been discovered in the Mediterranean in the past twenty years, virtually nothing has been learned about the ships themselves because of the paucity of wood on the sites. On the other hand, a great deal of information has been gathered concerning trade routes and the cargoes and other items carried on the ships. As more wrecks are found and identified, trading routes of the ancient mariners are better understood. Already we know their range was wider than previously thought.

The cargoes of most Mediterranean wrecks excavated have been amphorae used in the wine trade. These "five-gallon jerry cans of antiquity" were also used to transport other liquids and such products as brined fish, olives, dried fruits and pitch. A small number of wrecks carrying cargo varying from plundered works of art to architectural components and sarcophagi have also been found and studied. It is too bad that most of the wrecks found in Mediterranean waters have been stripped by sport divers, and only about ten properly excavated by archaeologists who gathered, interpreted and published the results of their work.

Although the wreck of a seventeenth-century Spanish galleon is likely to arouse less academic interest than the remains of an ancient Greek or Phoenician merchantman, it is nevertheless certain that New World shipwrecks will eventually receive their due share of attention when more trained people are available to work on them. Certainly to an American historian one of Columbus's wrecks is as important as a Roman argosy. Perhaps more so.

In the early days of scuba diving most of the work on New World shipwrecks was undertaken by treasure hunters. The academic world displayed little interest and so ships were ripped to pieces, artifacts wrested from the sea floor, carried off and lost to archaeology forever. Fortunately the situation in the United States has changed in recent years. Many sites are still worked by treasure hunters and amateur divers, but increasing numbers are protected and excavated under the supervision of state archaeologists hired by treasure hunting firms such as Treasure Salvors of *Atocha* fame. In the state of North Carolina more than a dozen Civil War shipwrecks have been discovered by amateur divers interested in marine archaeology and have been salvaged under the watchful eye of the state's underwater archaeologist. Through these excavations much was learned about these ships, their cargoes and armaments. In South Carolina most of the effort has been concentrated on three Confederate blockade runners sunk off Charleston. They were located and excavated by a young amateur underwater archaeologist, Edward Lee Spence, who heads a group called the Sea Research Society. Initially local scholars took a dim view of his activities, but as they became aware of the significance of his work they not only changed their views but offered him assistance and support. Dr. Robert L. Stephenson, South Carolina's state archaeologist, said of Spence's work: "The artifacts recovered off these wrecks are clearly a datable series of items which can be used as comparative materials, particularly when digging on land sites." Unfortunately, archaeologists in many states do not express interest in helping with underwater projects, and most divers working on wrecks are left to their own devices.

Most of the shipwreck salvage in the United States has to date been confined to the sea, particularly off the Florida coast. However, there are countless ships at the bottom of the Great Lakes, in many North American rivers, and in many other areas in this hemisphere. The chief deterrent to locating and salvaging them is that which hinders work in the Baltic and North seas: cold, dirty water. In spite of this, an increasing number of people willing to meet the challenge have made interesting finds.

Most of the ship losses on American rivers and in the Great Lakes are of recent vintage. Although by the latter part of the seventeenth century a small number of vessels were plying the Great Lakes, supplying the needs of the early settlers and transporting the products of forest and field, commerce really didn't open up until the beginning of the nineteenth century. Lake traffic was stimulated by the discovery of iron ore in Minnesota, and locks were built connecting the lakes to one another and to the St. Lawrence Seaway in 1855. Around this time the rapid expansion westward made Chicago the stepping-off point by train for the settlers headed to the frontier. For a time there were no connecting rail lines from the east, so settlers were transported on the Great Lakes to Chicago, as were locomotives and rolling stock. At least five thousand vessels are sunk in the Great Lakes and await examination by underwater archaeologists.

A large number of British, French and American warships were also lost in these lakes. The first warship built for use on the Great Lakes was the snow (a small vessel resembling a brig) *Halifax*, launched by the British in 1756. Lost on Lake Ontario several years later, it was located not too long ago and salvaged. During the War of 1812 both British and Americans lost many vessels on the Great Lakes in inclement weather and battles, such as the *Hamilton* and the *Scourge*. They were located by a magnetometer and identified through an underwater television camera lowered down to them.

More than five hundred vessels from the era of the wooden-hull sailing ship were lost in rivers along the United States eastern seaboard. Most were seventeenth- and eighteenth-century merchantmen sunk in storms on rivers or near settlements of early colonists. The remainder were warships such as the British ones lost at Yorktown in 1781. Some have undoubtedly been destroyed by dredges, but many still under the mud should be relatively easy to locate.

A great number of paddle wheel steamers were lost on America's major rivers, including the Mississippi, Missouri, Ohio and Hudson. The cover of the October 1972 issue of *Archaeology* magazine depicted a map showing the locations of fifty-eight steamboat wrecks lost between 1842 and 1862 along just two hundred miles of the Missouri River. On the smaller Tennessee River upwards of two hundred paddle wheelers were lost.

During the Civil War a number of blockade runners and gunboats sunk in rivers. The *Cairo*, one of the first ironclads ever built and the only gunboat which exists from the war, was sunk in 1862 on the Yazoo River near Vicksburg, Mississippi. It had the distinction of being the first ship ever sunk by an electrically detonated mine. The site of this wreck was discovered in 1956 and the 176-foot-long ship was cut into three sections, carefully raised, reassembled and placed on display in a museum at Vicksburg. This is a good example of how amateur divers overcame almost total lack of visibility. They worked entirely by feel. Using water jets to remove the mud covering the *Cairo* and slinging cables under her hull to assist in raising her, the divers found a large number of weapons, crockery, tools and other artifacts—all without being able to see an inch.

In addition to larger vessels, many smaller craft such as ferry boats, fishing boats and even canoes sank in rivers. In many cases these small craft were buoyant, so that when they capsized in strong currents or rapids the items aboard, but not the craft themselves, were lost. An example of this type of accident was the loss of many birchbark canoes by the French voyageurs. Many lives as well as merchandise were lost along the water route of lakes and rivers which form the present boundary between Minnesota and Ontario. The lucrative fur trade began early in the seventeenth century. Trade goods were brought to Grand Portage on Lake Superior from the East and then transported by the voyageurs over long distances to trade for furs with the Indians. The many dangerous rapids along their route bear testimony to the hazards they faced, because the river bottoms near these rapids are strewn with remnants of the canoe cargoes. Since 1962, with the help of amateur divers, the Minnesota Historical Society has investigated many of these sites and recovered a wealth of material including kettles, tools, axes, lead musket balls, gunflints, whetstones, knives, beads, buttons and thimbles. When any items from an overturned voyageur's canoe can be dated and compared with similar articles found on land Indian sites, the chronological framework for many North American Indian sites is strengthened.

Although anchors are not in the same category as shipwrecks, they are so closely associated with ships that they fit for all practical purposes into the shipwreck classification of a site. Tens of thousands of anchors were lost in ports and harbors over the centuries. Sometimes an anchor became fouled in something on the bottom and couldn't be raised. Anchors were sometimes deliberately lost when a ship had to make a sudden departure and there wasn't time to do anything but cut the anchor cable. Anchors were lost along coasts when ships stopped to await a change in wind direction or for another ship to catch up or even when ships anchored for the night along hazardous shores. The discovery of old anchors provides invaluable information about early sea routes. When identified and dated they furnish excellent clues about exactly what areas various seagoers reached. In some cases the discovery of an anchor leads to the finding of a shipwreck, since any ship swept onto a lee shore during a storm would try to drop anchor in attempting to stay offshore in safer water. In most such instances the cables parted and the anchors were lost. Over a period of years I have located dozens of ships after first finding an anchor in an unlikely area, such as near a shallow reef, and then searching closer to shore for the ship itself.

SUBMERGED OR INUNDATED SITES OF HUMAN HABITATION: At the end of the last Ice Age melting ice caused the sea level to rise from three to six feet a century between 18,000 and 3000 B.C. Scientists disagree on this point, but even nine thousand years ago

Divers inspecting and filming a submerged wall off Bimini, Bahamas, believed to have been constructed by some pre-Columbian civilization. (Credit: Dimitri Rebikoff.)

when men were laying the foundations of Jericho, the world's oldest city, the oceans were between one hundred and three hundred feet below their present levels. The shorelines of all the continents stretched far beyond their present boundaries; most of the North Sea was dry land, and England was connected to continental Europe by a land bridge. Land bridges also existed in other areas of the world such as the Bering Strait. Since early man lived along the shores of the continents, many of their places of habitation are now covered by the sea.

Some seven thousand years ago the coast of southern California, particularly the area near San Diego, was inhabited by a primitive people more technologically advanced than most other groups then living in North America. The sea level then was about one hundred feet lower and the coastline extended nearly two thousand feet farther offshore than it does today. In 1954 a sport diver discovered off La Jolla, California, the first of many sites of these Indians. Since then quite a number of sites have been found along with thousands of artifacts including mortars, food grinders, weights, scrapers and projectile points. Due to the movement of the sea floor in the shallow water, stratigraphic sequences do not exist and all perishable material such as bone, wood and fiber has long since disintegrated. The dating of the material recovered from these sites is done by comparison with similar objects found on land sites where stratigraphic and geologic dating is possible.

Off Gibraltar in the Mediterranean archaeologists have discovered submerged caves at a depth of 117 feet containing evidence of occupation by prehistoric man sixty thousand years ago—a time when Europe and North Africa were connected by land across what is now the Strait of Gibraltar.

The melting of glaciers elevated the water level of lakes, rivers and other bodies of water on land. In many areas pooling of melting ice formed new lakes and flooded sites of settlement. Since time immemorial the shores of lakes and rivers have attracted settlers with the promise of food and drink.

During the nineteenth century a number of fields of wooden pilings, like fence posts, were discovered in several Swiss and German lakes together with a number of prehistoric artifacts. Archaeologists assumed these were palafittes, i.e. villages built over the water by Neolithic and Early Bronze Age peoples referred to as "Lake Dwellers." Scuba divers, beginning in 1951, excavated a number of these sites on lakes Zurich and Neuchfâtel. Analysis of pollen samples they recovered from the muddy bottom led to a startling discovery: Vegetation grew in the soil at the same time the pilings and artifacts were made. This meant, of course, that the dwellings were not built over the water but on marshy land at the edge of the lakes and were eventually covered by rising water. Excavation has continued and a great deal of material recovered, much of it surprisingly well preserved. Even such normally perishable items as wickerwork, fabric and wood have been brought up. Because sites of this type are not subject to the destructive forces of marine wave action and currents, stratigraphic dating has been possible, enabling archaeologists to establish a sequence pattern of the various cultures which lived on the same sites between 3300, and 1800 B.C.

More than a third of the freshwater lakes in the United States are man-made, and their number is expected to double in the next ten years. In California the growing demand for new reservoirs has meant that hundreds of Indian middens (refuse heaps) have been drowned. The Indians of California were so culturally and linguistically diversified that the inundation of a single valley could eliminate traces of an entire culture which had lived there for thousands of years. This is the kind of situation in which underwater archaeology can be most helpful. A handful of dedicated amateur underwater archaeologists have located and excavated a number of these sites. Where the water is still they have been able to spot many sites from the air. They are visible because for some unknown reason dark clouds of suspended matter hang over the sites.

Prior to recent discoveries made in a number of fresh-water springs (sinkholes or cenotes in Mexico) it was commonly accepted that early man did not reach Florida until 3,500 years ago. We now know that Stone Age men were living in caves in Florida 12,000 years ago, eking out a miserable subsistence in a climate similar to that of Minnesota. They lived in competition with a fearsome array of mammoths, mastodons, giant ground sloths and saber-toothed tigers. Amateur divers have been finding the bones of these creatures in Florida rivers and springs since scuba diving became a sport. During the summer of 1973, a group of students from Northern Arizona University, directed by Dr. Charles Hoffman, conducted an expedition on the Silver River in central Florida. Beneath eight feet of sediment under the river bottom they discovered the bones of a mammoth, dating back approximately eleven thousand years. With it they found a rock-point spearhead probably used to kill the beast.

This find ignited a great deal of excitement among scholars since it signified that early man was in Florida eight thousand years earlier than previously thought. However, if the scholars had accepted discoveries made by an amateur diver in Warm Mineral Springs, they would have known this startling fact much sooner. Bill Royal, a retired Air Force colonel, began diving in Warm Mineral Springs, near Sarasota, in 1958. On the very first of the thousands of dives he was to make, Royal discovered a large number of prehistoric animal bones in submerged caves and noted that stalactites hung down from the roofs of the caves in the spring which reaches a depth of 230 feet. The caves began on ledges at a depth of 45 feet and were found at varying depths all the way to the bottom. Royal realized that many of the animal bones he was finding were of species extinct since the last Ice Age and he knew the stalactites could only have been formed when the caves were out of water, so he was justifiably sure he was on to a major discovery. During the next few months he also discovered the remains of seven human skeletons, a number of projectile points, two bone needles and several bone tools. Excited by what he had come up with, Royal wrote to dozens of experts, but none replied. Finally an anthropologist from the University of Florida visited him and after no more than a cursory visual inspection of the bones stated they couldn't be more than five hundred years old. Royal was subsequently referred to in academic circles as "that crazy diver."

Undeterred, he pressed on with his explorations. In the summer of 1959, while diving with Dr. Engenie Clark, a noted marine biologist, he discovered a complete human skull containing an intact brain. The high hydrogen sulfide content of the 87-degree water is devoid of oxygen below twelve feet, creating an anaerobic condition responsible for the remarkable preservation of the brain tissues and other organic materials found in the spring. Radio carbon- 14 dating established the brain was more than ten thousand years old. Although this find was heralded throughout the world, the academic establishment accused Royal of perpetrating a hoax and publicity stunt. One expert went so far as to claim Royal had found the skull in Europe and planted it in Warm Mineral Springs.

Anyone else might have given up, but Bill Royal pressed on, although he would have to wait years before having the pleasure of hearing the experts corroborate his finds. Over the years he spent more than five thousand hours underwater, discovering many more bones and artifacts. These, he always left in situ for the day when he would finally be able to show it all to an interested archaeologist. Finally, in 1972, Dr. Wilburn Cockrell, Florida's state underwater archaeologist, somewhat reluctantly agreed to investigate the validity of Royal's finds. Near the entrance to the cave where the skull and brain had been found, Cockrell found a pile of stalactites lying in a pattern which could only have been arranged by man. Digging around the perimeter of the pile he found a number of human bones and realized it was a burial site. Months later, with the assistance of other archaeologists, he began meticulously to excavate the site, after first removing more than seven tons of rock and stalactites covering the site. Pollen samples were analyzed, helping to determine the climatic conditions and date of the burial. They recovered a complete skull and a number of bones which proved to be those of a man buried some twelve thousand years ago. These are the oldest human remains found in North America. Months afterward Cockrell discovered an atlatl, or spear-thrower hook, in the same area. Used to throw a spear a long distance with great force, it is the oldest artifact ever found in association with human remains in North America. Thanks to funding from the Florida state government, Cockrell and Royal are presently working and will continue for several more years exploring Warm Mineral Springs. They have also extended their activities to investigate a few other of the more than five thousand other springs scattered throughout Florida. Royal's perseverance paid off and his fantastic discovery has changed historical record.

Submerged towns and harbors have long captured public imagination. Fishermen's tales about church bells tolling beneath the waves have always had eager listeners. Storytellers have written book after book about divers walking into submerged buildings and finding immense riches still guarded by complete skeletons swaying in the currents. Countless movies have fed children's fantasies with visions of pirate captains still at the helm of sunken sailing ships and trunks lying on the sea floor, guarded by a giant octopus, waiting for the intrepid adventurer who will discover piles of gleaming gold and brilliant gems. Many land archaeologists, although admitting that examination of such sites contributes to a better understanding of the past, feel that excavation of them is not merited since there are so many similar ones waiting to be dug on land where it is less difficult and less expensive to work. However, many underwater sites, although certainly not fulfilling a Hollywood fantasy, and far from easy to work on, are well worth excavation. Many are located in harbors and bays; some have already been destroyed by dredging and others are likely to be obliterated soon.

In 1965, a large portion of the sunken city of Port Royal, Jamaica, which sank in 1692 with a loss of two thousand buildings, was almost destroyed by dredging planned in the construction of a deep-water port. Fortunately UNESCO and other organizations intervened and won a reprieve. During the spring of 1974 dredging and the construction of a large deep-water pier were begun at the island of St. Eustatius in the Caribbean. In the course of work a large portion of the sunken city of Orangestad, drowned in an earthquake in 1687, was destroyed. With similar sites fast disappearing throughout the world, it is imperative that as many as possible be excavated as soon as possible.

The walls of a submerged building located off Italy, probably dating about A.D. 200. (Credit: Gerhard Kapitän.)

In the Mediterranean there is much work to be done on at least 280 such historic sites. Some will never be located since the areas have been filled in and modern settlements built over them. Many of these sites sunk as a result of catastrophes such as earthquakes and volcanic action. Like Port Royal and Orangestad, they are of the time-capsule variety, similar to Pompeii or a ship sunk in deep water. Few land sites can compare with them. However, a number of submerged sites are in many ways similar to land sites. These sank because of isostatic movements of the earth's crust. The water level didn't rise, but rather the land sank slowly over a long period. A small number of sites of human habitation were inundated by a gradual rise in sea level, of several inches per century, known as a eustatic change. Usually where sites were slowly covered over by water, most of the buildings were destroyed, the material reduced to indecipherable rubble. This is especially true in areas where the sites were exposed to the open sea and heavy wave action.

Enthusiasm for work on underwater settlements appears to be limited for a number of reasons. First is the lack of people qualified to undertake proper excavation, and then there is the reluctance of many land archaeologists to employ divers to work under their direction. Time and expense are also cited. Many of these sites encompass vast areas and are covered by centuries of sedimentation, especially those located near river mouths. Whereas a shipwreck may only take a season to excavate, one of these sites could take many years. At Port Royal, for example, the site was covered by as much as twenty feet of sediment in some zones and although my team and I spent three years excavating, we covered only about 5 percent of the site.

Except for the work at Port Royal, virtually no submerged cities and ports have been excavated. A few test holes have been dug on a number of sites in the Mediterranean but none approaches the scope of an excavation. Most of the work on those sites has been restricted to surveying and mapping the remains protruding through the sea floor from under tons of concealing sediment.

The most important surveys conducted to date were done by a French Jesuit, Père André Poidebard, who pioneered the exploration of harbor sites. He was the first to use aerial search and photography on an underwater archaeological site. After locating the sites of two ancient harbors and a number of other breakwaters and stone installations off Tyre, the best-known Phoenician port on the coast of Lebanon, he spent three seasons between 1934 and 1936 surveying and mapping. He accomplished a good deal by using local helmeted sponge divers to investigate structures he spotted from the air. The divers used various hand tools to remove marine growth from the structures and obtained accurate measurements. Père Poidebard directed the operation, peering through a glass-bottom bucket. He took photographs through the bucket and sketched plans of all the structures. In 1946, he also made a similar survey of Sidon, another important Phoenician port, before much of this site was destroyed by dredging. An English archaeologist, Honor Frost, who followed in Poidebard's footsteps and surveyed the same two sites in recent years, found the French priest had made a few major errors in identifying a number of natural rocky reefs as man-made structures. If the Jesuit had been able to dive himself, these mistakes might well have been avoided.

Since 1958 another English archaeologist, Nicholas Flemming, has spent every summer investigating more than one hundred submerged towns and harbors. His first survey was undertaken at Apollonia, once a great Greek city on the north coast of Africa. Like the others he has surveyed over the years, it was investigated on a limited budget and with just a few assistants. Unable even to afford the luxury of an airplane for searching and photographing, Flemming usually first employs snorkeling equipment to locate structures. They are then buoyed, measured, plotted and photographed. To obtain aerial photographs of a site, a small helium-filled balloon equipped with a special camera is sent aloft to shoot a series of still pictures. With these Flemming can produce a complete photographic mosaic of a site and complement other information gathered underwater. His main aim is to establish patterns in which ancient harbors and towns were laid out and the extent of their areas. To confirm relative dates when these settlements sunk or were abandoned, Flemming relies on collecting small amounts of pottery and other sampling materials which can be approximately dated.

In 1960 Edwin Link, the inventor and underwater explorer, briefly surveyed the submerged seaport of Caesarea on the coast of Israel. The city, built under Herod the Great, was later occupied by the Romans, the Saracens, the Crusaders and finally the Arabs in the thirteenth century. In its days of grandeur, it was one of the most important seaports on the Mediterranean. After the city was abandoned many years ago, the majority of the massive stone port structures gradually sank into the sea because of isostatic movements of the earth's crust. From the air, Link located and mapped jetties built to protect the port. Then, with the assistance of Israeli archaeologists and divers led by Dr. Elisha Linder, a number of test holes in the inner harbor were dug with airlifts. The weather was abominable while Link was there and excavation was possible only on a few days. However, they did recover an important collection of artifacts which included Hebrew and Roman pottery and amphorae, bronze ship nails and other fittings, large numbers of coins, hairpins of sculpted ivory, a bronze seal bearing the likeness of the god Horus and an unusual shelf-shaped oil lamp.

Happy over his success at Caesarea, Link headed for Greece, a move he was later to regret. He got permission from the Greek Department of Antiquities to explore, but not to excavate, the sunken city of Helice on the Bay of Corinth. He also asked for and thought he had received oral permission to stop at Perachora, another sunken city along the way to Helice. Shortly after anchoring at Perachora, Link's vessel was boarded by police. The police, who had been harassing and shadowing the expedition since it entered Greek waters, arrested Link, claiming his permit did not include the site over which he was anchored. Link left Greece after paying a $740 fine. And thus ended his interest in sunken cities.

Since 1976, the Israeli government has undertaken a major underwater archaeological exploration of Caesarea and tens of thousands of man-hours have been spent exploring, mapping, and excavating the site, which has resulted in numerous important discoveries. The site is used every summer for training students of archaeology from many nations.

RELIGIOUS SITES: In many areas of the world are lakes and springs that cultures of the past endowed with sacred properties. Such sites are often the repository of ceremonial artifacts cast into the waters as offerings to the deities. High in the mountains of Colombia the Indians of the Chibcha tribe believed that Lake Guatavita was the home of their gods. For hundreds of years, until the Spanish

Author and wife with a human skull and ceramic figurine recovered from a sacrificial Mayan well, or cenote, in Yucatán.

conquest, they threw such valuable offerings into the lakes as gold and emerald necklaces, nose rings, earrings, beaten-gold breast plates and helmets, and gold figurines. Since the arrival of the Spaniards a number of attempts have been made to recover these treasures, with only token success. Lake Titicaca on the Peru-Bolivia border and Lake Chapala in Mexico were also sacred sites.

Lake Amatitlan in the volcanic highlands of Guatemala was the center of the Mayan civilization during its Classical Period. To placate the fierce gods who ruled over the nearby volcano, Pacaya, which towers over the lake, the Indians made many offerings over two thousand years. Accidental discovery of a pottery vessel in 1955 by an amateur diver led to the salvage of many remarkable artifacts. After the first find, several scuba divers joined the search and recovered more than six hundred ceramic vessels, incense burners and stone sculptures lying exposed on the lake bottom. After news of this reached the United States, the late Dr. Stephen F. Borhegyi, then curator of the Milwaukee Public Museum, joined forces with the amateur divers. Over the next several years, in water varying from 10 to 130 feet deep, they recovered more than five thousand artifacts dating between 1000 B.C. and A.D. 1000. There is still a great deal of work to be done in Lake Amatitlan and other lakes in the vicinity, because all the artifacts recovered were found on the surface of the lake bed and no attempt has been made to excavate the many items that must have sunk into the sediment.

The Yucatán peninsula is dotted with more than two thousand deep natural wells carved out of friable limestone. Many of these cenotes, located near Mayan ruins, are believed to have been revered by the Indians and to contain ceremonial offerings such as Thompson found at the sacred cenote at Chichén-Itzá.

Although Thompson accomplished an amazing amount, it was suspected he missed a lot because of the salvage methods available so many years ago. In 1959, the National Institute of Anthropology and History of Mexico, with the assistance of members of CEDAM under the direction of Pablo Bush Romero and an American team led by Norman Scott, started further excavation in the cenote. This time, instead of a grab bucket, scuba divers used airlifts, recovering more than four thousand artifacts. However, the project was cut short because land archaeologists felt that better excavation methods could be devised which would not damage fragile items as the airlift did. In 1967, the same people resumed work on the site. After failing to drain the cenote, they used sophisticated and expensive equipment to purify the water and render it crystal clear. Excavation was then resumed with a modified airlift which did not damage artifacts. In two and a half months they recovered a fantastic collection of objects, including two beautifully carved wooden stools, many sculpted stone items, hundreds of ceramic vessels, various types of gold and jade jewelry, obsidian knives, flint projectile points and human bones. When the expedition was called to a halt still more work was left to be done.

During the spring of 1957, at the request of Dr. E. W. Andrews of Tulane University, I made a number of exploratory dives in a cenote at Dzibilchaltún. He was excavating the Mayan land site, about a hundred miles from Chichén-Itzá. On the first dive I found two unique and perfectly preserved Mayan vases dating circa A.D. 500. Since I was not free to spend time on a full-scale project in the

Diver recovering artifacts from the cenote at Dzibilchaltún, Yucatán, once a religious site of the ancient Mayan Civilization. (Credit: National Geographic Magazine.)

cenote, Dr. Andrews sought and received assistance from the National Geographic Society, which recruited two outstanding divers, Luis Marden and Bates Littlehales. Shortly before, Marden had distinguished himself by locating and salvaging artifacts from the wreck of the H.M.S. *Bounty* off Pitcairn Island, where it had been sunk by mutineers in 1790.

Marden and Littlehales, without excavation equipment, explored every inch of the 140-foot-deep cenote and recovered a staggering amount of artifacts. Among the more than thirty thousand items they brought up were many intact ceramic vessels and figurines, stone statues, human bones, a clay flute, bone nose plugs, obsidian knives and a bone awl inscribed with hieroglyphs. As in the case of Lake Amatitlan, use of an airlift and other types of excavation equipment should yield many more priceless artifacts.

REFUSE SITES: Throughout the world, wherever man lived near water, underwater accumulations of refuse can be found. In some cases refuse was thrown into the water to dispose of it, and in others, kitchen middens, once on dry land, were covered by water. What the peoples of the past considered trash the archaeologist considers important clues in piecing together a picture of extinct cultures. In most cases, freshwater kitchen middens are by far the most rewarding refuse sites because objects are found much better preserved than those in saltwater or even many of those found on land. Freshwater refuse sites are generally also easier to locate and explore than those in the sea.

Underwater kitchen middens reveal the dietary habits of early men, and the relative amounts of various types of animal and fish bones, shells and seeds offer evidence of climate and climatic changes at different times. Such interesting artifacts as projectile points, the stone they were shaped from, bone tools, shell implements, charcoal and ceramic shards are also found in kitchen middens of early peoples.

In 1955, the late Dr. Goggin began taking his anthropology students from the University of Florida on field trips to find and explore refuse sites in many of the state's rivers. They accomplished a lot, recovering much material not only from where Indians had lived along rivers but also from where early Spanish mission settlements had been. In 1958 they made their most significant find, recovering from the Suwanee River the largest collection of

Seminole pottery extant, plus clay pipes, glass beads, spurs, scissors and flintlock muskets.

The term refuse site would seem to indicate that only unwanted debris is present, but this is not always so. Beneath many rivers, streams and lakes in the southeastern United States lie large amounts of war materiel from the War Between the States. As the Confederate armies retreated toward the end of the war, they threw great quantities of weapons and equipment into various bodies of water to keep them out of enemy hands. Divers have recovered pieces of artillery, projectiles, small arms and even crates of ponchos. Such discarded items as bottles and broken crockery have often been found in water near where military forts stood or troops encamped.

Places where ferry boats crossed rivers or bridges spanned them have proved rewarding to both amateur and professional underwater archaeologists. Old maps and sometimes commemorative plaques reveal the location of such sites. The English seem to be doing most of this kind of underwater work, and innumerable finds dating back to the Roman and Viking periods have been made in recent years. Several years ago near the village of Farnham, a diver searching in the Tilford River discovered the handle of an elaborate presentation sword. It was fashioned from seven and a half ounces of gold and encrusted with 635 diamonds. Months of research proved it was part of the sword presented to Lord Nelson by the king of England after winning the Battle of the Nile in 1798.

Harbors and ports or wherever ships have dropped anchor are choice refuse sites. The bottoms of these areas are littered with a vast accumulation of debris either thrown overboard or lost. In some areas such as Cadiz in southwest Spain, continually used as a port for almost five thousand years, the sea floor contains a wealth of material that boggles the imagination. The Guadalquiver River, which runs through the middle of the Spanish city of Seville, is perhaps the most lucrative refuse site in the world. All the ships sailing to and returning from the New World anchored there, and in the course of loading and unloading, small craft bearing merchandise and treasure frequently spilled their cargo either because they were overloaded or collided with other vessels. During three hundred years it is estimated that more than 10 million pesos' worth of merchandise and treasure was lost in an area covering only about a quarter square mile. And the vast majority of it has never been recovered.

The refuse site is a good choice for an excavation project by an amateur underwater archaeology enthusiast. Relatively little research is necessary to locate a promising site, and permission is rarely required from authorities to explore such an area. The diver can usually work from shore instead of a boat. Providing excavation equipment is not used, the only expenditure is for diving equipment. These sites seldom have stratigraphical importance, and survey work such as measuring, mapping and photographing objects in situ is not essential. In many ways excavation of a refuse site is similar to a treasure hunt, but one that does no damage to an important archaeological site—provided everything found is shown to an expert capable of determining whether any of it has any archaeological significance. The only problem is that in discovering objects on the bottom it is not always easy to determine quickly if one is working on a refuse site, on a shipwreck site or on a sunken settlement. This is especially true in harbor areas, and the search and excavation techniques covered in the following chapters will help distinguish between one type of site and another.

3

～～／／／／／／／～～

Research

The key to success in any underwater archaeological project is thorough research, with primary source material used when available. Failure to prepare scrupulously the groundwork generally results in a great waste of time, effort and money. Rarely can the specific site one seeks be found without painstaking research. During the past twenty years, millions of dollars have been spent by those who either did no or insufficient research, depending on unreliable sources such as popular books or magazine articles.

Some years ago, a professional underwater archaeologist, who ought to have known better, attempted to locate the city of Charlestown, which sank in 1687 off the island of Nevis in the Caribbean. He failed to find the site because his research had been inadequate; he was searching three miles from the actual sunken settlement. Had he researched more thoroughly he would have found the documents which give the precise location.

Many mistakenly believe only a limited amount of research is necessary to locate underwater sites. They think that with today's sophisticated electronic location equipment, any site can be found if even the general location is known. Recently an international mining company entered the field of treasure hunting. Equipped with a submersible vehicle and the latest in electronic detection gear, it

72

boasted it was about to make the biggest treasure recovery in history. Hearing of their plans, I contacted the director of the operation and offered to supply them with original documentation I had concerning their quarry. The shipwreck they were after had been the flagship of a Spanish treasure fleet carrying over 22 million pesos in treasure when it was sunk off the coast of Colombia during a naval battle between the Spaniards and the English. The ship, the richest galleon ever lost in the New World, was blown up in the battle and sank in six hundred feet of water. The director declined my offer. He was sure that with only a general location, obtained from secondary source material, the wreck site could easily be located. Three months later, after an expenditure of more than a quarter of a million dollars, the director contacted me, imploring my help. However, I had decided in the interim to eventually find the wreck myself and no longer wanted to share the information I had.

After an expenditure of more than $20 million, last winter an international group of treasure hunters announced that they finally located the above-mentioned Spanish galleon *San Jose*. Thus far they have been unable to come to terms with the Colombian government over the division of what they hope to recover from this shipwreck, so there are no immediate plans for her recovery.

Like many of my friends in the field of underwater archaeology, I started my career as a treasure hunter and learned the hard way the importance of research in primary source material. When I first became interested in old shipwrecks in 1950, I read countless books that fired my imagination with tales of galleons lying intact beneath the waves, their holds crammed with treasure, skeletons gently swaying in the currents. I found any number of "authentic treasure charts" as well, pinpointing the locations of many wrecks "containing millions in treasure." In 1959, after three years spent finding and excavating several exciting old wrecks (without the "help" of any of those books and charts) which yielded myriad artifacts and even some treasure, I was eager to move on to other wrecks in the Caribbean. I reasoned, "Why spend weeks and months snorkeling over coral reefs and combing the sea floor for wreck sites when all I had to do was make use of the information I had already accumulated from those books and charts I had read?" So, from the lists I had compiled, I chose 100 wrecks scattered all over the Caribbean and set off to track them down.

Fifteen months later, after exploring from the Gulf of Honduras to the San Blas Islands off Panama and from Trinidad to the Bahamas—diving off almost every island and on every reef and rock in between—I had found only 2 of the 100 wrecks and neither of those had yielded anything of interest. As I learned later, while doing years of research in European and American archives and libraries, this was not surprising.

Out of the 100 "authentic wrecks," 74 never existed but were the creation of highly imaginative writers. Of those that did exist, 18 had in fact sunk with treasure on board; however, they sank in very deep water on the high seas far from the shallow coastal waters where the writers had conveniently placed them and where there was almost no chance of recovery. Four others had indeed sunk in shallow waters but hundreds of miles from the locations given in the books and charts; the remaining 4 existed and I found 2 of them.

Professional treasure hunters and underwater archaeologists have long since realized that most of the information in such books is fictional. They label those wrecks "ghost wrecks," and have a hearty laugh when they hear of a newly organized expedition setting out after one of them. Even the assistance of so-called experts on maritime history cannot always be relied upon. An example of this is what happened to the late Kip Wagner, considered one of the most successful treasure hunters in the world. In the early days, before he realized the only place to get reliable information was from original documentation in archives, he sought assistance from an expert at the Smithsonian Institute and was told that the eleven ships of a Spanish treasure fleet lost in 1715 were all wrecked in the Florida Keys. If Wagner had researched no further, he would never have recovered the more than 10 million dollars' worth of treasure and artifacts from these shipwrecks which he located, not in the Florida Keys at all, but more than two hundred miles away.

However, quite a few important underwater discoveries were made by men who never did a bit of archival research and paid no attention to information of the "ghost wreck" variety. One, Teddy Tucker of Bermuda, has worked closely with underwater archaeologists from the Smithsonian Institute on many shipwrecks in Bermuda waters over the past twenty years. Tucker started off by searching the reefs surrounding Bermuda using a glass-bottomed bucket. When he sighted something that did not appear to be a natural formation he dived to check it. This led to significant discoveries, but he is one of the few who have been successful with this method. For everyone who has found a good shipwreck, there are hundreds who have not. Most professionals would agree it is best to have the odds in one's favor, which involves scrupulous research before setting out after a wreck.

There are two approaches to research. One is to explore areas of probable sites, as Tucker does, and then concentrate research on a particular site after it has been located so one can identify and learn everything possible about it. The other is to select a particular promising site or sites as objectives and do in-depth research on them before any attempt is made to locate and excavate. The latter method has proved the more successful for me and many others in the field. Following are two examples of how research bore fruit in my work.

In 1503, during Columbus's fourth and last voyage of exploration, he was forced—to keep two of his badly leaking ships from sinking— to run them aground in St. Anne's Bay on the north coast of Jamaica. After he and his men were rescued by another vessel, these two ships settled beneath the bay's muddy bottom and were soon forgotten. From historical documents I unearthed in the Spanish archives, I

Artifacts recovered by the author—ceramic shard, fragment of glass, piece of striking flint, and coral-encrusted tack—from one of two shipwrecks lost by Columbus on his fourth voyage, in St. Anne's Bay, Jamaica.

found sufficient clues to enable me to locate the wrecks without difficulty. In his diary Columbus mentioned he had run both ships aground "about a bow shot distance from the shore [usually about one hundred yards] and close to two freshwater streams and an Indian village," from which he had received supplies of victuals to feed his hungry men before they were rescued. Although the streams no longer exist, old maps of the area showed their courses. It was easy to find traces of the Indian village near the shore. With this information I was able to narrow the probable location of the wreck site to an area about the size of a football field. With the assistance of Dr. Harold Edgerton of M.I.T., using a sub-bottom profiling sonar, we located both wrecks in a matter of minutes after laying out a grid-search-pattern system with buoys.

In 1656, the Spanish galleon, *Nuestra Señora de la Maravilla* carrying a prodigious treasure, was lost on the Little Bahama Bank. Contemporary salvors were able to recover only a small portion of her wealth before the wreck was covered over by shifting sands. For centuries repeated attempts have been made to locate this wreck, but all failed. In recent years it intrigued many treasure hunters who spent more than a million dollars searching for her. A book on sunken ship locations came out in 1960 giving the *Maravilla*'s location in the Florida Keys. A stampede, reminiscent of the Gold Rush, ensued and almost everyone in the treasure-hunting business searched for her—but in the wrong area.

I, too, became fascinated with the *Maravilla*, the second richest ship to sink in the Western Hemisphere. I concentrated a great deal of research effort on her in the Archivo General de las Indias and in other manuscript collections in Spain. After culling more than twelve thousand pages of documents dealing with this ship, including a copy of her original manifest listing and describing every item she carried when lost, I came upon a 144-page book published in Madrid in 1657 by one of the few survivors of the wreck, Doctor Don Diego Portichuelo de Ribadenyra. He wrote an exciting and vivid account of everything he had observed from the time he boarded the ship in Porto Bello, Panama, until he was rescued. The book included an excellent narrative of the ship's loss. I was unusually fortunate in locating three different contemporary charts showing the precise location of the *Maravilla*. Armed with all this research, I was able to find this shipwreck in the summer of 1972 and recover a substantial amount of treasure and artifacts from her. The three charts had placed her location in 27 degrees and 15 minutes of latitude, and I found her only a half mile south of this spot.

Another underwater archaeologist who learned the importance of research the hard way, and has since found a number of fantastic shipwrecks through research, is the Belgian, Robert Stenuit. When he started in the field he wasted several years locating and salvaging a number of shipwrecks which were part of a Spanish treasure fleet sunk by an Anglo-Dutch fleet in 1702 in Vigo Bay, Spain—only to discover that the Spaniards had taken off all their treasures before the ships sunk. Later, after he had spent several years researching hundreds of shipwrecks, Stenuit decided to go after a galleass named *Girona*, one of the many ships lost after the ill-fated invasion attempt by the Spanish Armada in 1588. When the *Girona* was dashed to pieces on rocks off northern Ireland, she was carrying the survivors and treasure from four other Spanish ships, so that to find her would be equivalent to finding five ships. Many had tried to locate the wreck, but until Stenuit, no one had succeeded. He spent 650 hours just in pinpointing her location and the tedious work paid off when he found her in less than an hour of searching and eventually recovered enough artifacts to fill a museum.

In 1975, Stenuit again showed his skill as a professional researcher with his discovery of the Dutch East Indianman, *Slot Ter Hooge*, lost enroute between Holland and the Far East with a cargo of three tons of silver ingots and three large chests of coinage. Soon after this ship met its fate in 1724, off a small island named Porto Santo, close to Maderia Island, the famous British diver John Lethbridge, using a wooden barrel full of air in his endeavors, recovered a large portion of the treasure. Historical documents only gave a vague location, but Stenuit was able to locate a silver tankard once owned by Lethbridge, which had an engraving on it showing the precise location of the shipwreck. Like on the *Girona*, Stenuit made some startling discoveries on this site.

At the conclusion of my wild goose chase after ''ghost wrecks'' in the Caribbean I realized so little was known about actual shipwrecks and other types of underwater sites that I would have to undertake a thorough and intense program of original research myself. Since that time I have devoted years to researching in all the major archives, libraries and museums in Europe and throughout the Western

Hemisphere and have been privileged to have access to private collections of documents and manuscripts. I have worked in Spain, Portugal, France, England, Holland, Denmark, Norway, Sweden, Austria, Italy, Mexico, Colombia, Panama, Venezuela, Cuba, Santo Domingo, Puerto Rico and many of the smaller Caribbean islands. In Spanish depositories alone, I spent three full years reading old documents, and since 1962 I have had Spanish researchers continuing work for me. As by-products of this research, which has led to my discovery of numerous worthwhile sites, I learned to read five languages and wrote fifteen books on maritime history, underwater archaeology and related subjects.

I have amassed a file of data on more than thirty-five thousand shipwrecks throughout the world from the time of the Phoenicians until the end of the American Civil War, where my interest in shipwrecks ends. To write in any detail about these wrecks is not within the scope of this book. I suggest anyone interested in underwater archaeology in the Western Hemisphere may read my book, *Shipwrecks of the Western Hemisphere 1492–1825*, published in 1971. It contains a lot of pertinent information regarding thousands of the most significant shipwreck and other types of sites in this hemisphere. I selected approximately one-quarter of the sites I have researched for inclusion in the book. The locations of each wreck are given to the best of my ability, but it must be remembered that it generally takes hundreds of hours of sharply focused researching of each site to find all the relevant information one should have before initiating any search. To do this for each of the sites covered in the book would take many lifetimes. My aim was to provide a guide to aid in selection of a particular goal which would then require further research. The book is also a good source for identifying sites found by accident.

There are myriad printed sources available for researching ship losses after 1825, the cutoff date in my book. This is particularly true of ships wrecked in United States waters. The most reliable book is the *Encyclopedia of American Shipwrecks* by Bruce D. Berman, published in 1972. As a result of eight years of intensive research the author managed to collect data on more than fifty thousand wrecks in American waters. Of these, he selected over thirteen thousand to write of, excluding all vessels of less than fifty gross tons. A small number of these wrecks are pre-Revolutionary, and his list includes ships lost up to 1971. Included in the information about each wreck is the name and tonnage of the vessel, the year of construction, the date and cause of loss, and the location.

Another excellent reference work is *A Guide to Sunken Ships in American Waters* by Adrian L. Lonsdale and H. R. Kaplan, which lists 11,000 wrecks off the coasts of the United States as well as many in rivers and the Great Lakes. Although most of the wrecks mentioned in this book are also listed in Berman's, they are covered in somewhat greater detail here. Dozens of other books deal with shipwrecks in particular areas or with ships lost during specific eras. For the Great Lakes I recommend reading *Memories of the Lakes* and *Shipwrecks of the Lakes*, both by Dana Thomas Bowen. New England area wrecks are dealt with in *Wrecks Around Nantucket* by Arthur H. Gardner and *Shipwrecks of Cape Cod* by Isaac M. Small, both especially interesting. A good book on West Coast shipwrecks is *Shipwrecks of the Pacific Coast* by James A. Gibbs, Jr. The best book about river wrecks is *Steamboat Disasters and Railroad Accidents* by S. A. Howland. For information on almost every military and merchant ship lost during the Civil War there is the forty-two volume work entitled *Records of the Navies of the Civil War*, published by the U.S. Government Printing Office in Washington, D.C.

In addition to books a number of pamphlets published by various government agencies contain wreck information postdating 1825. The best source is the Treasury Section of the National Archives in Washington, D.C., which will furnish the following reports for a small fee: "Marine Disasters North of San Francisco, California, from January 1870 to August 1886"; "Marine Casualties on the Great Lakes from 1862 to 1873"; "Wreck Reports of the Great Lakes, 1886-1891"; and "List of Wrecks and Casualties—Coast of Rhode Island and Fisher's Island, 1752-1907." This last report gives the location of 600 vessels lost in the area.

Over the years the Public Information Division of the United States Coast Guard has also published (free of charge) lists of ship losses including "Principal Marine Disasters, 1831-1932" (with data on more than six hundred vessels lost on rivers, lakes and at sea); "Life Saving Annual Reports, 1878-1914"; and "United States Merchant Ship Losses: December 1941-August 1945." Other good sources for information are the U.S. Naval Hydrographic Office and the U.S. Maritime Commission, both located in Washington, D.C.

Divers and some of the cargo they recovered from the Spanish merchantship, Matanceros, *lost on the coast of Yucatán in 1739. (Credit: Walter Bennett.)*

The most comprehensive general book on shipwrecks throughout the world is *The Treasure Diver's Guide* by John S. Potter, Jr. Books have also been published in various countries dealing with their own ship losses. For Spanish ships there are two major works: *La Armada Española,* in nine volumes, and *Disquisiciones Nauticas,* in six volumes, both by Fernández Cesareo de Duro. From French ship losses one should consult *Histoire des Naufrages,* in three volumes, by Jean L. Desperthes. British ship losses are covered in dozens of books by various authors. The best work on British warships is *The Royal Navy*, in three volumes, by William L. Clowes.

Although books published in recent years can be quite helpful in selecting and locating a site, it is wise to go back to the primary source whenever possible. Every state in this country has many books about its history, and it is a good idea to read all of these, especially when doing research on a specific wreck, the oldest or those written soon after the time of a particular ship loss.

Books written before 1800 are generally difficult to find. However, they can be borrowed from large libraries or through interlibrary loans. As a guide in determining which older books might be helpful, I suggest consulting *Incunabula and Americana 1450–1800* by Margaret B. Stillwell. It lists over eleven thousand titles and gives the libraries which have them. Another source, international in scope, is the *Subject Index of Books Published Before 1800,* a four-volume work by Robert A. Peddie. It has an alphabetically arranged subject list of fifty thousand books written in various languages, and I have located hundreds of useful books through it.

Old newspaper accounts are also a valuable source of information on shipwrecks after the mid-seventeenth century. More than once I have been able to identify or learn more about a shipwreck or other type of site through newspapers. Some of the best descriptions of the 1692 earthquake which destroyed Port Royal, Jamaica I found in English and other countries' newspapers. In 1959, I found and salvaged a Spanish merchantship off the coast of Yucatán. In re-searching its identity I discovered a newspaper item which resolved all mystery. This wreck was located off a place called Matanzeros Point, and I thought this was probably the name of the sunken ship. I knew it sank between 1730 and 1740 from the artifacts I had salvaged, so I began searching through all newspapers and periodicals covering this period. I finally came across an item regarding the wreck in a February 1736 issue of *La Gaceta de México,* a daily newspaper published in Mexico City. My ship had been named *El Matanzero,* as I had thought, and from the paper and subsequent research in the Spanish archives I was able to learn her whole history.

Newspapers were first printed in the American colonies in 1690 and were the only medium for dissemination of news of all descriptions. In addition to listing the movements of all ships in and out of ports and their cargoes, the papers printed a great deal of information on shipwrecks, not only in America but throughout the world. To determine which newspapers were being published or were published nearest to the site of a wreck or site one is researching, it is helpful to consult the following excellent works: *History and Bibliography of American Newspapers, 1690–1820,* two volumes, by Clarence S. Brigham; and the *Dictionary of Newspapers and Periodicals* by N. W. Ayer and Sons, which covers the period until 1880. The *New York Times* was founded in 1851 and is a comprehensive source of information on later shipwrecks.

Original research undertaken in archives is by far the most rewarding, as well as the most challenging and time-consuming method of learning about underwater archaeological sites. However countless ships were lost and cities inundated for which no original documentation exists today and one must rely on secondary sources for information. In 1746 a Portuguese fleet of twenty ships heading from Brazil to Lisbon was struck by a storm and forced to run before it. The fleet was still intact when it entered the Caribbean and passed within sight of Barbados, but shortly afterward the storm matured into a full hurricane. The ships were widely dispersed and thirteen were lost without a trace. Consequently there is no documentation on these wrecks other than the fact they disappeared. During the third decade of the sixteenth century the town of Nueva Cadiz, on Margarita Island off the coast of Venezuela, sank during an earthquake, yet not a single document has survived to tell of this event and the only thing known about it is a brief paragraph in a book written in 1558.

Documents concerning various shipwrecks or other disasters were often lost when the ships carrying them back to the Old World sank themselves. Unfortunately we can never hope to know about many sites because thousands upon thousands of historical records have been destroyed by man and nature. Moreover, many thousands of manuscripts and documents dealing with ship losses are in various depositories in a number of countries, but until they are catalogued, which may take years, they are inaccessible to researchers.

All of the documents predating 1670 that were kept in Old Panama City were destroyed by fire when the pirate Henry Morgan and his men burned the city to the ground. In addition, many documents postdating 1670 have been destroyed by Panama's humid, corrosive climate. Complete archives in Cartagena and Bogota, Colombia, were destroyed during the War of Independence. Similarly, a great wealth of records was destroyed in Veracruz and Mexico City during the Mexican War of Independence. When Cuba revolted against Spain near the end of the last century, the colonial archives fortunately survived. After the war the Cubans turned over the archives to the Spanish, who took them to Seville. Eighty years later these thousands of bundles of priceless historical documents remain stacked and unopened as they were when they arrived, collecting dust and ravaged by mice and insects in an old building in Seville. The main archive in Lima, Peru, was twice destroyed by earthquake in the eighteenth century. Even in Spain, vast numbers of documents have been destroyed, particularly in 1551 when the House of Trade building burned to the ground, and recently, in 1962, when many documents were destroyed in a flood.

Spanish colonial history is not alone in suffering the destruction of records. Documents of other European nations have shared a similar fate. Portugal had the great misfortune of having its main depository of historical documents, the Casa da India, sink into the Tagus River in an earthquake in 1763. In World War II firestorms from bombing destroyed untold amounts of documents in London, Paris, Rotterdam and Amsterdam.

The greatest collection of Spanish colonial documents is stored in the Archivo de las Indias in Seville, which was the second House of Trade building. The original state archives of Spain was the Archivo de Simancas, near Valladolid in the north of Spain. It became so overcrowded that in 1784 the king ordered all documents dealing with the New World shipped to Seville, thus creating the Archivo de las Indias. However, in recent years it has been discovered that about seven hundred bundles of documents (called *legajos*) dealing exclusively with the New World still remain in the Simancas archives. There is a great deal of documentation on Spanish maritime history in other depositories in Spain, such as the Museo Naval, Museo Nacional, Biblioteca Nacional, Archive Histórico Nacional and the Academia Real de la Historia, all of which are in Madrid. Most of the documents dealing with ships lost off the Spanish coast are in these depositories.

Compared with the archives in Seville, the above have only a small portion of the overall documentation covering the Spanish colonial period in the New World. Of the more than two-hundred-fifty thousand *legajos* in the Archive de las Indias, the majority are not catalogued and about 20 percent of those shipped from Simancas in 1784 have never been opened. Anyone is permitted to undertake research in any of these depositories, provided he can read the archaic Spanish of the handwritten documents, which is quite different from modern Spanish. However, a number of professional researchers can be hired to do the research for those unable to read the documents or unable to spend the necessary time in Seville. Each year this archives receives hundreds of letters from those who desire information on shipwrecks, but unless one is willing to pay a research fee, the overworked staff is unable to help.

In many documents the precise location of shipwrecks is vague. In the early days, which would apply mainly to Spanish shipwrecks, there were few fixed place names on charts used by navigators. In Florida, for example, on most sixteenth-century charts only two places are named: Martires (spelled a number of ways) in the Florida Keys and Cabo de Canveral or Cape Canaveral. By the mid-seventeenth century a few more place names had been added to charts, including Las Tortugas (the Dry Tortugas), Vivoras and Matacumbe (two islands in the Florida Keys), Rio de Ais (Fort Pierce Inlet on the east coast) and La Florida (St. Augustine). By the beginning of the eighteenth century many other names were on charts, rendering them more accurate. One reason Spanish documents are often vague on shipwreck locations is because when writing to Spain to tell of a disaster little effort was made to pinpoint a wreck since officials in Seville were not interested except in what had been lost and in knowing how much had been recovered or could be recovered.

Another important factor to keep in mind when doing research in primary source material is that there was no standardized calendar system followed by all countries. In 1582 Pope Gregory XIII ordered that ten days of the year be omitted to bring the calendar and the sun once again into correspondence, thus creating the Gregorian calendar which we use today. All of the Protestant countries stuck to the old calendar, however, for many years. Until England adopted the Gregorian calender in 1752, her new year began March 25; so a date of February 11, 1733, to the English was February 21, 1734, to the other European nations.

Very few documents have survived in Holland concerning Dutch shipwrecks in the New World, although much information on Dutch shipping is found in Spanish and British depositories. References to Dutch ship losses elsewhere in the world can be found in the Netherlands Royal Archives in the Hague and the Netherlands Historical Ship Museum in Amsterdam.

Portugal had very little documentation concerning shipwrecks predating 1763 when the Casa da India was lost, but for information postdating that time there are three important depositories: the Museu da Marinha, the Arquivo Nacional da Torre, and the Arquivo Historico da Ultramar, all in Lisbon.

Although a great deal of documentation on French maritime history has survived the centuries, French depositories are so badly catalogued that it is almost impossible to accomplish much in them. The three main sources of information on French ship losses throughout the world are all in Paris: the Musée de la Marine, the Bibliothéque Nationale, and the Service Historique de la Marine. Other archives in the remaining nations of Europe are generally well catalogued but most of their shipwreck documentation deals with losses in areas other than the New World.

A researcher finds England the least taxing place to work, for the depositories are all well catalogued and the staffs helpful. The main places to research shipwrecks are the British Museum, the Public Records Office, the Admiralty Library, the National Maritime Museum and the Archives of Lloyds of London, all of which are in or near London. Because of the Great Fire of London in 1666, there are virtually no extant documents on British shipwrecks in the New World before the mid-seventeenth century; but then again, there was not much British shipping to the New World before then. Between 1666 and 1740, there is a limited amount of original documentation on British ship losses in New World waters. All of the ships built and used by the American colonies until the War of Independence were under British registry; and even after the war the vast majority were insured by Lloyd's of London, established in 1688. It is a great shame that a fire in 1838 wiped out Lloyd's archives, which contained all insurance records and reports of tens of thousands of shipwrecks throughout the world.

In 1740, a newspaper called *Lloyd's List* was founded and is still published. It has listed the movements of British shipping around the world, as well as brief accounts of ship losses and the movements of important foreign shipping such as the Spanish fleets or ships engaged in the East Indies trade. *Lloyd's List* has also published information regarding the salvaging of ships. Until recently it was necessary to go to England to consult these "lists," invaluable in gathering information on ships lost after 1740. Now, however, all the "lists" dating from 1740 to 1900 have been republished in a multivolume work which is found in a number of large United States libraries including the Library of Congress in Washington, D.C., and the New York Public Library.

Research in the Public Records Office, Britain's most important depository of shipwreck information, can begin in the United States by consulting the following reference works which deal with documents in the Public Records Office: the *Calendar of State Papers, Colonial Series, America and West Indies*, in forty-two volumes, and the *Journal of the Commissioners for Trade and Plantations from 1704 to 1872*, in fourteen volumes. These books contain brief extracts of tens of thousands of documents concerning the New World, many pertaining to ship losses. To get a copy of a complete document, one only has to write the Public Records Office requesting it and it will be sent for a small fee. In gathering information on British warships lost anywhere in the world, one first should consult *Lists of Admiralty Records Preserved in the Public Records Office*. If one knows the name of a ship, it is easy to find out through this index book what documents about it exist. Another good source for locating shipwreck documents in other British document collections is *A Guide to Manuscripts Relating to American History in British Depositories* by Grace Gardner Griffin.

Before doing any research in United States depositories, either on American or foreign ship losses, one should consult the *Guide to Archives and Manuscripts in the United States* by Philip M. Hamer to determine which archive or library would have relevant material. The National Archives in Washington, D.C., is the most important source of shipwreck data postdating the American Revolution, but there are many others with original documents, too. Each state has archives which should be looked into when you're interested in a wreck off the coast or in a river or lake of a particular state. In some cases many of the most important documents in state archives have been published, as have indexes of what the archives contain. If one is interested in ships wrecked off Virginia, for instance, the first step in researching them would be to consult the *Calendar of Virginia State*

Ten-foot long gold chain with reliquary pendant, found on a Spanish galleon lost in 1715 off the coast of Florida. These items were manufactured in the Far East and brought to Mexico for transshipment to Europe. ▲

Diver with 10th century Chinese ▲ *"dragon jar" on a site off Indonesia.*

View of two large prop-wash excavation devices used to remove overburden on a shipwreck site and reach the stratigraphic level of the artifacts. ▲

Pre-Columbian gold figurine of a cat-like animal found in a ceremonial lake in Panama. Such small objects were used as sacrifices to the gods. ▲

Divers sorting through the ballast rock and looking for artifacts, while a prop-wash excavation device is blowing away the sand in the hole. ▼

Dutch gin bottle with pewter top still on it found off Brazil on a Dutch warship that sank in 1648. ▲

Author with the tops of Spanish olive jars, the large storage jars used to transport all liquids and some solids on Spanish vessels. ▼

Archaeologist Bill Royal hand fanning away sedimentation on a human skull dating around 9,000 B.C., which he discovered in a deep sinkhole at Warm Mineral Springs, Florida. ▲

Diver inspecting a bronze cannon on a 16th century Spanish ship wreck in the Bahamas. Note that very little coral grows on bronze metal underwater. ▲

Intriguing ceramic head found in the sea off Dominica Island. Experts have identified it as Phoenician in origin. How did it get to the Caribbean? ▲

Diver locating a pile of coral encrusted iron artifacts from a Spanish merchantman lost in 1526 in the Caribbean. ▼

Small Chinese porcelain figurine from the late Ming dynasty found on a Portuguese East Indiaman off the coast of Brazil. ▼

One of the oldest seaports of antiquity, Byblos, dates from at least 6,000 B.C. Located on the coast of Lebanon, it was used by many different cultures over the centuries. ▲

Diver using a theodilite for mapping a shipwreck site. ▲

A large section of an oak keel of a 17th century French warship lost off Martinique Island ▲

◀

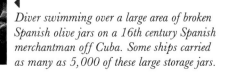

Diver swimming over a large area of broken Spanish olive jars on a 16th century Spanish merchantman off Cuba. Some ships carried as many as 5,000 of these large storage jars.

Archaeologist using a small airlift to remove sediment from a 6th century B.C. Phoenician shipwreck off the coast of Israel. ◀

Diver using an airlift to dig out an old anchor from a wreck site off Puerto Rico. ▼

▲ *View of a prop-wash in action blowing away a heavy concentration of sediment on a shipwreck site.*

Archaeologist recovering two clay jars and several Chinese porcelain plates on a 13th century Chinese junk off Indonesia. ▶

Four figurines of the Carthaginian goddess Tanit, found on a Phoenician shipwreck of the 6th century off Tyre, Lebanon. ▶

Section of a 12-foot long gold chain found on a Spanish ship wreck off Florida's coast. The chain was manufactured ◀ *in the Far East.*

Two small Spanish pieces of artillery called Falconetes, or Versos, used mainly as antipersonnel weapons. They shot a stone ball, instead of an iron one like larger weapons. ▶

Author with 16th century ceramic jars from a Manila Galleon lost off Guam in 1690. (Photo courtesy of A. Michael Jones.) ▼

Diver holding brass spikes next to a coral-encrusted iron cannon on a shallow reef. ▲

Markings on this Portuguese bronze cannon, found in Brazil, show a date of 1649 and also other valuable information that will help identify the shipwreck. ▶

Two earthenware Chinese figurines from a Chinese trading vessel lost in the 9th century off Malaysia. ▼

Archaeologist at work in the Red Sea on a 7th century Byzantine shipwreck. The grid is used in plotting the finds. ▲

Gold ring with coat-of-arms of the Ponce de Leon family, which helped identify this wreck as the Santiago, lost in 1522 off Grand Cayman Island. ▶

Diver cleaning a section of wooden hull of a 12th century Japanese ▼ *shipwreck lost off Taiwan.*

Here's one of the signposts in locating a shipwreck—one of an old ship's timbers protruding from the seafloor. ▼

Papers and other Manuscripts Preserved in the Capitol at Richmond, in eleven volumes, edited by Kraus Reprint Corp. of New York.

In addition to the state archives, many state and private universities have large manuscript collections. Some even contain a wealth of information from foreign archives. At the University of Florida there is a rich collection of documents on microfilm obtained from the Archivo de las Indias and other depositories abroad, dealing with early Florida history. Thus, when seeking primary source material about Spanish shipwrecks off the coast of Florida, one may first consult this source and quite possibly find there everything needed, so that a trip to Spain would be unnecessary. The Bancroft Library of the University of California at Berkeley has a good collection of documents and microfilm from many archives. These are relevant to ships lost not only off the California coast but throughout the Pacific.

A number of maritime museums also have original documents and microfilm. One of the most extensive collections is in the Mariner's Museum in Newport News, Virginia. The San Francisco Maritime Museum is the best source of information on West Coast shipwrecks, particularly for those lost after the Gold Rush. The indispensable reference work on microfilm collections is Richard W. Hale Jr.'s *Guide to Photocopied Historical Materials in the United States and Canada.*

All countries of the Western Hemisphere and many of the Caribbean islands have national archives worth consulting. The Archives of Jamaica not only has original documentation on the several thousand ships lost in her waters but on losses throughout the West Indies and even the East Coast of the United States. Unfortunately the best source for determining which archives and libraries might have pertinent information is Lino Gomez Canedo's *Los Archivos de la Historia de America,* which is in Spanish and has not been translated. This extremely helpful work describes what is in every depository in this hemisphere, and any others in the world which have documentation on New World history.

For Mediterranean shipwrecks and cities inundated before 1400 virtually no firsthand accounts by contemporary witnesses have survived. However, much can be learned by reading ancient histories and geographies, beginning with Ptolemy's *Geography,* Herodotus' *The Histories,* Pliny's *Natural History* and Thucydides' *History of the Peloponnesian War.*

During the Classical Period, sea battles accounted for the loss of some 5,000 oar-driven warships throughout the Mediterranean. Many of these battles are described in vivid detail by ancient authors. In the Battle of Salamis between the Greeks and the Persians in 480 B.C., more than one hundred vessels were lost between Salamis Island and the coast of Attica. When Anthony and Cleopatra fought Augustus in 31 B.C., off Actium in Greece, more than a quarter of the 450 ships involved were sunk. Many warships were lost because of bad weather and faulty navigation. During the Battle of Encomus in 225 B.C., only 16 of the 400 ships engaged were lost in the fighting; but shortly after, a storm sprung up and 250 ships were sunk. The Romans lost four warships to bad weather for every one lost in battle. Nothing has survived to indicate the numbers of merchant vessels lost during those same times, although it is known that 67 B.C. was a spectacular year for merchant ship losses. The Roman Senate was concerned because foreign merchants were giving Rome too much competition in sea trade. The Senate entrusted Pompey the Great to resolve this state of affairs and during a nine-month period, starting at Gibraltar, he swept through the Mediterranean destroying more than one thousand merchant and pirate vessels.

Thus far every ancient shipwreck discovered in the Mediterranean has been a merchant vessel, even though many careful searches have been conducted in zones where sea battles were fought and ships sunk in the Classical Period. A number of explanations have been offered for this disappointing situation. Honor Frost thinks that because warships were not completely decked over like merchant vessels, they would quickly fill with sediment and be covered over soon after sinking. Thus, no traces would be visible above the sea floor to indicate the presence of such a ship. Nicholas Flemming believes that, even after being destroyed in battle or storms, these ships, because of their light tonnage and lack of ballast, might not sink but would drift ashore where wave action would tear them apart. This seems a plausible explanation in light of the experience I had while sailing a replica of a tenth-century Viking ship in 1964. I found that although our vessel filled completely with water, right up to the gunwale, she did not sink.

Archives of the countries bordering the Mediterranean have a great deal of original documentation on ship losses after 1400. For example, I was researching one of history's greatest maritime battles, the Battle of Lepanto, in which a combined Christian fleet fought the Turks in the Gulf of Corinth in 1571. More than one hundred ships were lost in this battle, and I found documentation in more than two dozen archives and manuscript collections between Turkey and Spain because the ships and men in the Battle of Lepanto came from almost every country bordering the Mediterranean. An even greater disaster was the destruction of a Spanish invasion fleet of 150 warships carrying more than eight thousand men. The fleet was destroyed in 1541 during a storm just as it was about to attack Algiers, then held by the Ottoman Turks. I located more than ten thousand pages of documents about the calamity in the Simancas Archives in Spain and the Vatican Archives in Rome. The best source on ships lost in the Mediterranean after 1740 is *Lloyd's List*.

Old maps and charts are often valuable sources for locating underwater sites. In the course of doing research I have come upon hundreds of maps showing, with astonishing accuracy in some cases and equally astonishing inaccuracy in others, shipwreck locations. Three old maps by three cartographers show the exact

War galleys engaged in combat during the Battle of Lepanto, 1571. *(Credit: National Maritime Museum, Greenwich, England.)*

positions of all twenty-one ships of a Spanish fleet which sank in 1733 in the Florida Keys. On the other hand, a chart showing the locations of a number of galleons lost in 1622 in the same area was so badly drawn that it was useless. The most accurate maps or charts pinpointing shipwrecks were generally those drawn by contemporary salvors.

A number of important factors should be considered in referring to old maps and charts. Over the centuries, shorelines have receded in some places and extended farther into the sea in others. Those areas that have built out particularly affect the underwater archaeologist today, since many sites have been covered by land. Port Royal is a good example of this: of the original two thousand buildings which sank into the sea, approximately 60 percent are now covered by land. Near Port Royal, but on the other side of the harbor, the shoreline has been built out by sediment brought down the rivers. Recently three eighteenth-century shipwrecks were found buried on land in this area. This has also occurred in many other places. Many small islands or cays that existed years ago have disappeared. Others have built up and some have been made by man.

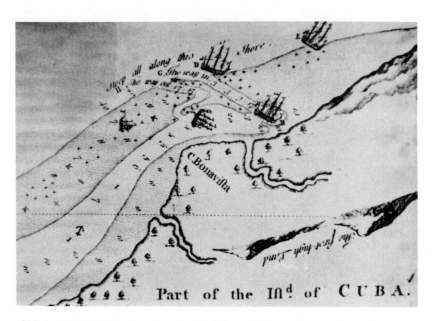

Old chart in 1720 showing where five English warships were lost on the northwest corner of Cuba.

Many old charts show north of Memory Rock on the Little Bahama Bank several small islands which no longer exist. However, I discovered they were by no means imaginary, for while searching for shipwrecks in that area and digging test holes in zones where a magnetometer indicated possible presence of wrecks, we located, attached to the limestone sea floor, the lower portions of large tree trunks where they had been rooted when those areas were islands. The mouths of rivers and streams have in some cases meandered considerable distances. Several inlets on Florida's Atlantic coast have closed up over the centuries and others have opened, some by natural forces and others by man. The present Fort Pierce Inlet is now two miles south of where it was about 1750.

Because positions of latitude taken from a rocking ship were often inaccurate, it was the practice, when possible, to establish the latitude of a shipwreck from the nearest *terra firma*. I have found that, on the whole, these reckonings, even those from the earliest days of New World exploration, are accurate to within a few miles. The distance, or measurement, of a mile and league was not universal in the old days. From the end of the fifteenth century and well into the nineteenth, the Spanish and Portuguese divided a degree of latitude into 70 miles of 5,000 feet each, or into 17½ half leagues of 4 miles each. The English and French divided it as we know it today: 60 nautical miles or 20 leagues of 3 miles each. The Dutch also divided it into 60 nautical miles, but used 15 leagues of 4 miles each. All nations used the fathom as the unit to measure the depth of the water, but its true length or depth was not uniform. The fathom varied between 5½ to 6½ feet, depending on the size of the seaman making the measurement, because a fathom was considered the distance between the outstretched arms of the man hauling in the sounding lead line. In areas where there is a considerable difference in tide levels, care must be exercised when relying on depths given in old documents and on old charts and maps, since they rarely mention what state the tide was in when water depth was reckoned.

Most depositories of primary source material have good collections of maps and charts. The most extensive, covering the entire world, is the Map Room of the British Museum. In the United States the two best sources are the New York Public Library and the Library of Congress. Several years ago the Library of Congress published a booklet entitled ''Treasure Maps in the Library of

Congress" by Hill and Ladd. Approximately half of the sixty-five maps listed deal with land treasures. The rest are of shipwreck locations, mostly of "ye olde sunken treasure" variety, pinpointing nonexistent "ghost wrecks." Many books of fine reproductions of old maps are available. An excellent guide to colonial maps and charts of Florida and several adjacent states is *The Southeast in Early Maps* by William Cummings. It lists where hundreds of old maps and charts covering these areas can be found.

A number of charts showing locations of ships lost during the last twenty years of the nineteenth century are available. In 1893 the U.S. Hydrographic Office produced a "Wreck Chart of the North Atlantic Coast of America," covering the area from Newfoundland down to the mouth of the Orinoco River in South America. It shows the locations and gives pertinent information of 965 vessels lost between 1887 and 1891. The U.S. Weather Bureau published two charts about the same time, the "Wreck Chart of the Great Lakes," which lists 147 ship losses between 1886 and 1891, and the "Wreck and Casualty Chart of the Great Lakes," listing all ships lost in 1894. In 1945 the U.S. Coast and Geodetic Survey published nine large "Wreck Charts" covering the area from Newfoundland to the Gulf of Mexico. Almost every wreck listed on these charts sank after 1900 and is of no archaeological interest at the present.

Modern navigation charts are sometimes useful in locating shipwreck sites. Many bear place names associated with wrecked ships. There is a Man of War Cay in the Bahamas and a Man of War Bay on the island of Tobago, both named after British warships lost in those areas. Rose Key near Nassau was christened after the H.M.S. *Rose* wrecked there in the eighteenth century. Spanish Cay in the northern Bahamas is so named because of three Spanish ships wrecked off it, the survivors coming ashore on the cay to await rescue. Golden Rock near Freeport on Grand Bahama Island got its name after two Dutch ships, carrying a fantastic amount of gold plundered from the Spaniards, were lost there in 1628. Throughout the world are many places named "Wreck Point" or "Wreck Bay" or other names indicative of past shipwrecks. In the Caribbean there are at least two dozen places with such evocative names as "Money Cay" or "Treasure Cay," implying ships sank with treasure or treasure was hidden ashore. On the southern coast of Spain between Cadiz and Gibraltar, there is a headland, Silver Point, which owes its name to a number of treasure-laden Spanish ships wrecked there in 1553. In the British Isles alone more than two hundred places are named from ships lost in those areas. On the northeast coast of Malta there is a St. Paul's Bay which has been called that for almost two thousand years to commemorate the apostle's shipwreck.

In a book of this length it is not possible to list every available research source. The following example, demonstrating how much material is available for one random area, should help show how one should approach shipwreck research. Assume you have either found a shipwreck off the North Carolina coast and want to identify it, or you want to research first before searching off the coast to determine what you might find. After thoroughly studying all relevant sources already mentioned in this chapter, you would turn to the following references:

There are two excellent books by David Stick listing hundreds of shipwrecks off North Carolina: *Graveyard of the Atlantic* and *The Outer Banks of North Carolina*. If the wreck appears from the evidence to have sunk after 1749, or if one is searching for a wreck postdating that year, when the first newspapers were printed in North Carolina, one would consult *North Carolina Newspapers on Microfilm* by Jones and Avant and their *Union List of North Carolina Newspapers 1751–1900*. Before researching any original documents one could refer to the *Index to the Colonial and State Records of North Carolina*, in four volumes, by Stephen Weeks; *The Colonial Records of North Carolina*, in ten volumes, by William Saunders; and the *Guide to the Manuscript Collections in the Duke University Library* by Tilley and Goodwin. The best source for old maps of the state, in addition to those already mentioned, is the Mariner's Museum in Newport News, Virginia, which has published a helpful guide: *Catalog of Maps, Ship's Papers and Logbooks*. Three years ago the Duke University Marine Laboratory published *An Oceanographic Atlas of the Carolina Continental Margin*, which contains a number of charts showing hundreds of shipwrecks in North Carolina waters, some dating back more than two hundred years.

Another approach to gathering information is to talk with anyone who may have accidentally found an underwater site. In the eastern Mediterranean the helmeted sponge divers, who walk the sea floor as a farmer does his fields, know where many wrecks lie and can be extremely helpful as Peter Throckmorton and others have found. If one is interested in a site in a port or harbor, commercial salvage divers and operators of dredging barges are good informants. Local sport divers who spend their time in pursuit of fish and lobster can sometimes furnish valuable clues to where shipwrecks or traces of them, such as ballast stones, lie.

In my experience I have found local fishermen or shrimpers to be excellent sources on shipwreck locations. They usually know the surrounding sea bottom as well as the palms of their hands, often snagging objects from wrecks or other sites in their nets. They know fish abound around wreck sites and many have their own "wreck charts," so they can either return to choice fishing grounds or avoid an area where they would lose valuable nets. During a ten-year period one shrimper working near Charleston, South Carolina, accidentally located more than thirty shipwrecks dating from 1650 to 1865. He gave their positions to the local historical society which hired amateur divers to explore them—an ideal example of cooperation in underwater archaeology. In August 1973, a shrimper snagged in its nets off the coast of Louisiana a wooden chest containing three hundred pounds of Spanish silver coins dated 1779 to 1783.

4

Search

In archaeology, underwater work generally costs more in time and money than similar work on land because a variety of factors determine how a project will be approached. They include weather conditions, water depth and temperature, clarity of water, nature of underwater topography and disposition of the site.

Weather conditions can severely restrict work on or under the water; an unseasonable blow can throw a schedule completely off. Once while working off Cape Hatteras, North Carolina, I had to wait in port a month before continuing work on a shipwreck I had been salvaging. Underwater work is extremely fatiguing and, depending on water depth and one's physical condition, less time can be spent working per day than on a land site. The depth of a site is the crucial limiting factor: at 80 feet a diver can make only two dives per day for a total of 70 minutes underwater; at 130 feet two dives totaling 35 minutes, and at 160 feet two dives totaling 20 minutes. Thus, when working a deep site, a project may take many years to complete unless there are many divers working. The French diving team that excavated the Roman wreck off Grand Congloué in the Mediterranean, slowly by the site's depth and rough seas caused by frequent storms, spent eight years on the project and even then had not completed it.

Fortunately, most Western Hemisphere sites are in relatively shallow waters where divers can accomplish far more in a given period of time than in deep water. At Port Royal, where the depth of the sunken city varied between 20 and 30 feet and the water temperature never went below 80 degrees, we were able to work on the bottom the whole day. Over three years each diver averaged 55 hours of bottom time per week. As long as one doesn't dive below 35 feet, no decompression is required and there is no danger of the bends. Physical stamina is the only limiting factor in shallow-water diving.

Although professional treasure-hunting firms can spend over $50,000 a month on a search project and twice that during a major excavation when more men are required, many underwater projects have been successfully accomplished on small budgets. Nicholas Flemming spends less than $1,000 a month to survey sunken cities by using unpaid volunteers, usually university students who are happy to have the experience and are hard workers. On many of my projects I have kept expenses to a bare minimum with the help of volunteer labor: members of local diving clubs, historical societies, tourists and friends. Local yachtsmen who enjoy involvement in underwater projects have often loaned me their boats.

Search and excavation equipment can be prohibitively expensive, but it isn't always necessary to use the elaborate and costly items. Teddy Tucker spent years locating shipwrecks with a glass-bottom bucket. To breathe underwater he used a small, homemade rig built from a paint-spraying compressor, a length of garden hose and a shallow-water helmet fashioned from a water-heater tank. A ping-pong paddle was the excavation tool to fan the sand away. With such inexpensive and rudimentary equipment he recovered over $300,000 worth of treasure and artifacts.

The two men who discovered the Civil War ironclad *Cairo* in the Yazoo River used a rowboat as a search vessel and a war-surplus compass as their only scientific instrument. Aware that a large mass of metal would affect the earth's magnetic field in the area of the wreck, they passed over the general area holding the compass. When they crossed over the wreck the compass needle swung around 180 degrees and remained in that position until they rowed away. They shoved a long metal rod into the muddy river bottom and knew they had located a wreck when the rod struck metal. Sophisticated equipment is not as important as thorough research before starting a search or excavation. The idea is to operate as efficiently as possible with the means available.

Almost all sport diving is done with scuba equipment, generally the best gear to use on deep sites such as those in 100 to 200 feet in the Mediterranean. However, it is not practical for most work on shallow sites, where bottom time is not limited. It hampers an operation for divers to come up each hour for a fresh tank of air and to provide someone to be responsible for continually refilling tanks. Back in the 1930s when treasure hunters began exploring shipwrecks in the Florida Keys and the Caribbean, the standard diving rig was the bulky shallow-water diving helmet, which required the diver to keep his head erect lest the air escape and water enter. After World War II this rig was superseded by the Desco diving mask, a full face mask connected to the surface air compressor by a rubber hose, like a shallow-water helmet. Around 1955, Hookah diving rigs came into use. They are basically like the Desco apparatus, except that the diver receives his air supply through a standard scuba regulator and wears a face mask covering only his eyes and nose. Today, both the Hookah and Desco rigs are standard equipment on most shallow-water sites, except where divers must work far from their air supply, as on a shallow reef where a boat might not be able to anchor or where a strong current drags on the air hose. In either of these situations, scuba gear would be more efficient. The Hookah and Desco rigs are far less expensive to use than scuba. An air compressor capable of pumping sufficient air for four men to breathe at the same time, plus the hoses and either Desco masks or Hookah regulator, would cost less than $750. To maintain scuba equipment sufficient to keep four men on the bottom all day and run the compressor to fill tanks would cost at least four times as much. The compressor used with Hookah or Desco can also be used for running excavating tools such as airlifts or pneumatic hammers. The high pressure compressor used for filling scuba tanks cannot be used this way.

In 1965, the Outboard Marine Corporation introduced a new SAS (Surface Air Supply) diving system which I found far superior to any other for work in water up to fifty feet deep. The same unit, differing only in exterior colors, was distributed by Johnson Motors as the Air Buoy and by Evinrude as the Aquanaut. The unit retailed for approximately $300 and weighed only forty pounds. It consisted of an engine-air compressor assembly encircled and floated on the surface by an inflatable tube. The 2-hp, 2-cycle engine delivered 2.5 cfm of clean air to each diver up to a depth of twenty-five feet, the length of the two hoses provided with each unit. This is actually twice the amount of air required at this depth. I found that by attaching additional lengths of hose I could safely and comfortably use these units as deep as fifty feet. It had several features I particularly liked. The air the unit delivers was the cleanest I have breathed underwater; the hoses did not kink or sink to the bottom and become entangled in obstructions; and the full face mask fit every face, child or adult. It had the great advantage of relatively low maintenance, a fact I'm sure of because my divers and I logged over thirteen thousand hours with these units during the three-year excavation at Port Royal. The chief drawback to the unit was its small fuel tank which ran an hour with each filling. As long as someone was topside to refill the tank, it ran continuously. The compact size and light weight were especially advantageous when working in a remote area. The unit eliminated the need for a boat if the site was close to shore. For work on most sunken settlements and refuse sites it was the ideal equipment.

Although the Air Buoy and Evinrude are no longer available, two firms in Florida presently market similar units ranging in price between $500 and $1200 depending on the size and the depth in which they can be used. Brownie's Third Lung in Fort Lauderdale has one model good for use up to 100 feet. Another, less expensive model for use only to depths up to fifty feet is sold by Innovative Designs, Inc. of Palm Harbor. However, an SAS, Hookah, or Desco should never be used when excavating with a prop wash, because of the danger of the air hose catching in the turning propeller where it could be cut or, even worse, pull the diver into it. When working under a prop wash, scuba is the only suitable gear.

Hollywood, with its fantasies of deep-sea divers fighting for their lives, grappling with giant sea creatures, has portrayed diving as one of the most hazardous occupations. Actually, the greatest dangers in the sea are those from man himself —his carelessness and lack of respect for an environment where he is an alien. Of course there is always the possibility of attack by shark or barracuda, but to my knowledge no one has ever been attacked while working on an underwater site. The noise of excavation tools tends to scare large marine life away. However, a number of trigger fish, moray eels and large crabs as well as many small fish have mistaken my fingers for worms as they darted around a site where tasty morsels were being uncovered as I dug into the bottom. Stinging corals and spiny sea urchins probably inflict the most common injuries when a site is near coral reefs. Caution and common sense prevent underwater accidents and there is no reason why underwater work should be particularly hazardous to a trained diver.

Weather, over which one has no control, causes many expeditions to fail. By gathering as much meteorological data as possible about an area while planning a search or salvage expedition, one can at least put the odds in his favor by selecting the season which should offer the best weather conditions and the calmest seas. Throughout the Western Hemisphere the summer months are generally the best, but there are exceptions. Off Padre Island, Texas, the winter months offer calmer water and better underwater visibility. The rainy season is not a good time to work, especially in rivers or estuaries where rain-washed sediment clouds the water. And, of course, in planning a project in the Southern Hemisphere remember that the seasons are reversed.

Hurricanes and other violent storms can help or harm the underwater explorer. Some may uncover sites buried for years. This happened in 1962 when a hurricane lashed coastal North Carolina. High winds whipped up surging waves which uncovered the remains of the *Modern Greece,* a British steamer wrecked in 1862 trying to run the Federal blockade into Wilmington with supplies for the Confederacy. The wreck's general location was common knowledge, but it had been covered by shifting sands and was inaccessible until the hurricane. Navy divers working with state archaeologists have excavated it. On the other hand, hurricanes have often deposited as much as fifteen feet of sand over known wreck sites or changed the bottom scenery of an area so that a site could not be relocated. Because of the huge seas associated with hurricanes, artifacts buried on an offshore site can be thrown up on adjacent beaches. In addition, when beaches are eroded by strong wave action, vestiges of an offshore wreck washed ashore and buried in a previous storm may be revealed. Finding a silver coin on a beach may be the first clue that a wreck lies nearby. If one is interested in an area, ask the local people whether any such items have ever been found. Most of the shipwrecks of the 1715 fleet were discovered by Kip Wagner, who first found coins and artifacts from them washed up on the beaches.

Photographic mosaic of the Spanish merchantman San Jose, *lost in the Florida Keys in 1733. Timbers and ballast of the ship seen here. (Credit: Dimitri Rebikoff.)*

A careful review of hydrographic and oceanographic data should precede any search attempt in a new area. Charts published by the U.S. Hydrographic Office and the U.S. Coast and Geodetic Survey provide information relevant to water depth, positions of reefs and other shallow or hazardous areas, the directions of prevailing winds and currents and other data useful in determining the most promising areas to search and the type of equipment most suited. Sailing directions and coastal pilot books furnish further information such as indications of areas where it might be difficult or impossible to work: areas restricted to military use, fishing grounds or areas such as shipping lanes with heavy traffic.

The charts are essential in defining the nature of the sea floor in the search area. The chances of locating a site depend a great deal on the topography of the bottom and local sediment conditions. About 95 percent of ships lost in shallow waters are found on sandy bottoms. The rest lie on or under mud, silt, coral or combinations of them.

The degree to which ships wrecked on sandy bottoms are preserved depends on two major factors: how quickly the weight of the wreck pushed the hull down into the sand and how rapidly ocean and tidal currents built up sand over a wreck. In areas where only a few inches of sand cover a limestone or coquina bottom, little of a ship's hull would be preserved. Sometimes wrecks were covered over so quickly that even contemporary salvors who knew their precise locations were unable to salvage them. The *Atocha*, lost in 1622 in the Keys, is a

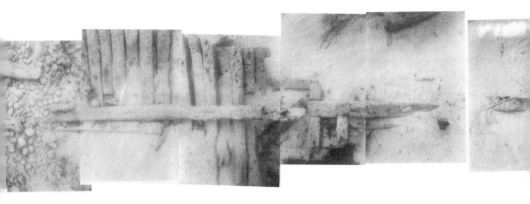

prime example. Since she sank on the edge of the Gulf Stream, where the currents run between 1 and 3 knots, the sand built up so fast over the wreck that within two months Spanish divers reported that only the masts protruded above the sea floor and an average two fathoms of sand lay over the ship's main deck. There is also much documented evidence that this happened to other wrecks which may be in a good state of preservation since the marine borers would not have had time to devour the wood.

The hull and cargo of most ships wrecked in a hurricane and sunk on a sandy bottom were scattered over a wide area, but there are exceptions. During the disaster which befell the 1715 fleet, ten of the ships were broken up and no traces of their wooden hulls remained. Yet the eleventh ship wrecked close to shore and its hull remained intact for a long time, enabling the Spanish to recover her complete cargo. Another exception occurred during a hurricane in 1733 when twenty-one Spanish ships were wrecked in the Florida Keys. Most remained almost intact until the Spanish salvaged them and then burned the parts sticking above the water. In 1968, I had an opportunity to excavate and learn something about how one of these ships, the *San Jose*, was lost. I plotted all the significant finds we had made and was able to trace her course. The ship had apparently been thrown clear of a shallow offshore reef in the high seas running at the time of the storm. She struck bottom about a quarter of a mile closer to shore on a sandy bottom approximately twenty feet deep, losing her rudder, five cannon (possibly carried on the stern) and a substantial amount of cargo that spilled out in this general area. Evidently, high seas then lifted the *San Jose* again and dropped her two hundred and fifty feet closer to shore, where she came to rest in thirty feet of water. Most of her cannon were discovered either on top of the ballast on the lower deck or relatively close to the main section of the hull, indicating she remained intact for a period after sinking and her cargo and remains were not scattered over a large area.

Usually when a ship strikes on a shallow reef it is so badly battered and broken up that no trace of its wooden hull remains. The wood either floats away or is devoured by borers. In some cases, parts of timbers might be washed into sandy areas and buried, but such fragmentary pieces are of no archaeological value. Coral growth varies considerably in areas of tropic and subtropic waters. Growth depends on water temperature, salinity and the amount of water action. In areas where growth is slow, most of the items on a sunken ship are carried away to areas at varying distances depending on their weight and shape. In some cases little or nothing at all can be found on the reef where the ship was wrecked. Along the Caribbean coastline of Yucatán, where the coral grows rapidly, the bulk of a wrecked ship's cargo would be buried in the living reef before it could be carried away by seas and currents. A good illustration of rapid coral growth is on Silver Shoals on the eastern end of the Bahama archipelago. When divers working for William Phips in the late 1600s located a treasure galleon forty-one years after it had been wrecked, they found the wreck completely buried in coral. In some places the growth was five feet thick and kept them from salvaging the entire wreck.

Ships lost in mud or silt are generally the best preserved. The weight of the ship quickly forces the lower hull and sometimes the entire vessel into the sediment where the wood is safe from attack by marine borers. In the harbor of Cartagena, Colombia, I dived on two large Spanish warships scuttled by the Spaniards in 1740 to prevent capture by the English. Several months before I arrived both wrecks had been uncovered during dredging operations to deepen the harbor. Because they had lain for so long in sediment they were remarkably well preserved.

The two ships of Columbus' which I discovered with Dr. Harold Edgerton on the north coast of Jamaica were also in an unusual state of preservation. Most sites in freshwater—rivers, lakes or springs— are buried in mud or silt whether they are shipwrecks, settlements, ceremonial or refuse. An annoying feature of this kind of bottom is that during excavation, unless there is a strong current, underwater visibility is nil because of roiled sediment.

Sites on rocky bottoms may offer better visibility but are the least rewarding if one hopes to find the remains of structures, ships or artifacts. A rocky bed is an underwater extension of the coastal relief above. No sedimentation has been deposited and, thus, anything settling on it remains exposed so that wood and other organic matter are devoured by borers and other organisms and objects are easily carried away by wave action and currents. Heavier objects such as cannon and anchors may remain and are eventually usually covered by biological concretions which merge them with their surroundings. Few sites in the Western Hemisphere are on this kind of bottom, while most Mediterranean underwater sites and most of those in the northern British Isles are rocky. In 1975, I spent some time exploring the waters of Ascension Island, a bleak dot lying in the South Atlantic about midway between Brazil and Africa. I found the site where the H.M.S. *Roebuck*, commanded by William Dampier, a successful pirate turned royal explorer, had wrecked on the rocky shore in 1701. Little trace of the wreck remained. Most of her heavier items like cannon had been dragged by wave action into deeper water and only small objects like spikes, nails and musket balls wedged in small rocky crevices remained.

On some sites, usually in harbors or near river mouths, the sea floor may present a combination of different materials. At Port Royal the surface of the bottom was fine silt, averaging from one to three feet deep, with coral growing in about 10 percent of this area. Below the silt was a four- to five-foot-deep deposit of about 50 percent hard-packed mud and 50 percent small gravel, stones and fragments of dead coral. Beneath this composition to a depth of more than twenty feet was material made of 70 percent coarse black sand and 30 percent gravel.

In areas where there appears to be only a small amount of sand or mud on the bottom, care must be exercised to ensure that what may look like bedrock is not a false bottom. Off Florida's east coast a limestone deposit called coquina, made up of broken sea shells and corals, grows fairly rapidly under favorable conditions. It can cover sandy or muddy areas, and shipwrecks have been found beneath the coquina, generally only one to three inches thick. Nature has other

Diver investigating a large seventeenth-century iron cannon after the coral growth had been removed by hand tools.

tricks of camouflage as well. In many zones in the Mediterranean and around the British Isles a species of sea plants and weeds grows thickly together, as high as six feet, hampering visual search efforts.

The scattering of the remains of a shipwreck over a wide area doesn't necessarily indicate the ship was ripped to pieces in a storm and her contents broadcast at the same time. Some ships wrecked in good weather and stayed together on a reef or shallows for years before either rotting or being ripped apart in a storm. At times when a ship struck on a reef which pierced her hull the captain would keep the sails up and try to run the vessel as close to shore as possible to lessen the loss of life and facilitate salvage operations. In such cases the ship would spill a great deal of her ballast and cargo between the point where she hit and where she eventually came to rest. I worked on a good illustration of this near Providencia Island off the Nicaragua coast. In 1641, a Portuguese ship, chased by several Spanish warships, struck on a shallow reef fairly close to shore. To elude pursuit the captain kept the ship sailing, staying on top of the dangerous reef, hoping either that the Spanish ships would wreck on the reef also or that they would cease pursuit to avoid danger. The ship traveled over two miles before it finally sank. In searching for the wreck by snorkeling, I discovered the area where she had first struck the reef and followed the path of the ballast stones until it brought me to the wreck itself. Mixed in with the ballast rocks were many artifacts which had fallen out through holes in the hull.

There are clues to where old shipwrecks lie. In the Western Hemisphere they are often cannon, anchors and ballast. In the Mediterranean an amphora or pile of amphorae may signal a wreck site, although finding any of these things does not mean they have to be in association with a wreck.

Often when a vessel was in danger of capsizing during a storm some or all of its cannon and even portions of the cargo were thrown overboard in an effort to stabilize the craft. When a ship ran aground on a reef or other shallows heavy objects were cast off in an effort to lighten and refloat her. In the vicinity of forts cannonballs and even cannon may be found which are not associated with a wrecked ship. During hurricanes or earthquakes they may have toppled into the water when sections of the fortifications collapsed, or they may have been thrown into the sea to keep them out of enemy hands. The enemy might have thrown them in after capturing the fort, or they were thrown in because they were too old and dangerous to use. In many cases cannonballs were lost in battles or training sessions, not only in proximity to forts but in areas where sea battles were fought.

Old, outmoded cannon were sometimes used as ballast on ships and occasionally jettisoned when not needed. An instance of this is found off the eastern end of Bonaire in the Caribbean. Diving there some years ago I found over two hundred cannon in a relatively small area. I was astonished and puzzled, especially since they ranged over a period of two hundred and fifty years. A local historian solved the mystery, explaining that ships coming from Holland anchored there to take on cargoes of salt from the island. The cannon, used as ballast, were jettisoned when the heavy cargoes of salt were loaded.

In most cases, when an isolated anchor is found without a nearby cannon or ballast pile, it is from a ship which lost it. However, sometimes a seemingly unassociated anchor can lead to a wreck. Anchors were lost, as I have mentioned, by ships being driven onto a dangerous reef or lee shore, and these can point the way to a lost ship. In 1964 near Taranto in southern Italy, divers located five enormous lead Roman anchors, each weighing about thirteen hundred pounds. They lay in a nearly straight line which began a

Raising an anchor off an eighteenth-century shipwreck in the Caribbean. (Credit: Walter Bennett.)

mile offshore. By following them toward shore, the remains of a first-century A.D. shipwreck which had been carrying a cargo of roof tiles and amphorae was discovered. Since most and, in some cases, all of a ship's anchors were carried high in the bow and stern of the ship, and since these sections of the ship were often broken off in a wreck and carried closer to shore than the main hull, anchors can also be found shoreward from a wreck site, providing a clue to the site's location. In either event, whether the anchor is seaward or shoreward of a wreck, knowing the wind and sea direction as well as the prevalent current directions in the area helps determine the approximate position of the wreck site.

Many ballast piles not associated with shipwrecks can be found in or near ports and harbors. Many sailing ships occasionally sailed without cargoes, carrying large amounts of ballast to stabilize them. Before or after entering a port, most and sometimes all of the ballast was tossed over the side. If the ship remained stationary while this happened, the ballast pile would resemble that on a wreck site. If the ship were swinging on its anchor, the ballast would be scattered as it is on a wreck site where the ship has been badly broken up and the ballast strewn about. Mariners in the old days were not especially concerned with sanitation aboard their ships. The Spanish were notorious for having the filthiest ships afloat. Many seamen and the poorer passengers lived below decks and tossed fish, meat and fowl bones into the hold along with the ballast. Other refuse such as crockery shards and broken glassware were also thrown into the hold and then thrown overboard along with the ballast rock so that items usually associated with artifacts from a wreck are found on a pile of ballast, confusing the underwater explorer into thinking he has found a shipwreck site.

Most old ships carried round ballast rocks ranging in size from several ounces to two hundred pounds. The larger rocks were normally placed over the lowest deck and smaller rocks used to fill in the spaces. On some of the early French and English ships, ballast rock was sometimes cemented together with mortar for use as permanent ballast which would not shift in rough seas.

The average ship took on ballast in a port or harbor, most of which had rivers or streams emptying into them providing the smooth, round pebble or river rock ballast most commonly used. Round rocks which had no sharp edges to puncture a wooden hull in rough weather were preferred. However, when these rocks were unavailable they turned to other types. A late-sixteenth-century wreck of either Spanish or French origin discovered in Bermuda contained flint rock for ballast. Documents dated 1570 tell of a Spanish merchantman sailing from Cuba for Spain with copper ore as ballast; of another Spanish ship sailing in 1638 from Venezuela to Spain with saltpeter as ballast, and still another in 1760 sailing from Cadiz to Venezuela with a ballast of gypsum.

As early as 1614 there is mention of Spanish ships carrying bars of iron from Spain to America as ballast, but this was done only when iron was shipped for sale in the New World colonies. From 1700 onward, English warships used large pigs of iron as ballast. The French followed this practice beginning in 1707. After about 1800, many merchantmen of all nationalities carried iron bar ballast.

Ballast is not always found on a shipwreck site. This is especially true of ancient ships in the Mediterranean. When ships transported heavy cargoes they avoided being dangerously overweight by not taking on ballast. Sometimes when ballast rocks were scarce sand was used which would not be recognizable later as ballast. On small vessels the limited space below decks made an alternate means of carrying ballast necessary. As the casks, barrels or amphorae containing liquids or solids were emptied of their contents they were filled with sea water. This method had the advantage of making it quick and easy to lighten the ship in a storm. The casks and barrels could either be emptied into the bilges and the salt water pumped overboard or they could be jettisoned faster than any other type of ballast.

One of the most important things to remember during a search is that nothing should be removed from the bottom where it has been found until the spot is marked in some way so that it can be found again. More than once a wreck has been found by location of an artifact or cannon on the bottom only to be lost again because the artifact was removed or the cannon covered over in the course of a windy night when sand shifted to bury it. If the broken neck of an amphora, for example, were lying on a sandy bottom in clear water, a diver might feel safe in rushing it to the surface to display to his excited comrades. Within minutes the surging sea could cause sand to fill in the depression where the amphora fragment had lain and the diver could not find the same spot again. The sea is vast and landmarks on the open sea don't really exist, so it isn't even safe just to leave a large object on the bottom. To make sure of finding a particular area again a buoy or other marker should be placed on it before the diver surfaces.

During a search operation three different kinds of buoys should be used. They should all be well built and self-unwinding. A diver can carry several small buoys which can be quickly dropped during a visual search when he sights something that seems interesting. They must be small enough to be attached to a weight belt without causing discomfort yet large enough to be spotted on the surface from at least one hundred yards. In my work I use a float cut from balsa wood. It is about six inches long, the thickness of a broom handle and painted an easily visible fluorescent orange. A length of strong fishing line is attached and wrapped around it and a four-ounce fishing weight is tied to the other end of the line. An elastic band holds it all together. When the buoy is dropped, the elastic band is first pulled off and the weight drops to the bottom as the line unwinds and the float races to the surface.

The largest buoys needed on a search operation are those for defining the outer limits of the area to be searched. Usually placed at the four corners of the area, they should be visible for at least one mile. Empty fifty-five-gallon fuel drums attached to a three-quarter-inch line and a heavy anchor are a good choice. They should be painted fluorescent orange or red and white like peppermint candy canes. When rough seas make it more difficult to sight them, six- to ten-foot poles flying brightly colored pennants can be attached to the drums.

During any kind of electronic or surface search when divers are not actually in the water, large numbers of smaller buoys will be required for laying out search patterns (the lines that the boat must follow on each run to cover a specific area) and to mark a spot when something is discovered. The best buoys are the eight- to twelve-inch styrofoam floats used by fishermen on fishnets and lobster pots. They should be attached to quarter-inch line and standard building blocks weighing from ten to fifteen pounds. The line on all of these buoys should be considerably longer than the water is deep so that when the seas get rough the buoys will not be lifted and carried away.

When setting up a search pattern close to shore it is sometimes easier to place markers on the beach and use them as reference points than to lay out line after line of buoys. If one were undertaking a magnetometer search at intervals of, let us say, two hundred feet, poles with brightly colored banners would be erected on shore, also spaced at intervals of two hundred feet. The banners should be of different colors so that the person steering the search boat won't become confused and duplicate runs or miss any areas.

On each run the boat is steered to or from each marker at right angles and kept on course with the aid of a compass. Another method is to station a person ashore with a surveyor's transit or theodolite which is moved up or down the shore at predetermined distances for each run. The transit operator lines up his instrument on a course running at right angles to his position, keeping the search boat in sight and directing its movements on each run via a walkie-talkie. The man on shore makes certain the boat keeps on a good heading so that no areas are overlooked. The advantage of this method is that when a target is located by the search vessel, the transit operator is notified and can immediately establish the spot's precise location by moving his instrument to permanent landmarks on the shore and taking bearings from them to the buoy dropped marking the spot.

In recent years several electronic positioning devices have come on the market, such as the Mini-Ranger and Auto-Tape. Using a computer printout, these devices tell you your exact position at all times in relation to beacons you must set up ashore or on offshore towers or buoys. To get back to any precise position at a future time you must set up the same transmitting beacons in the exact places again. These systems also enable you to make your search pattern runs without using any buoys. Some even give indications of drift caused by currents or the wind. Their only restrictions are their rental or purchase costs, which are prohibitive for anything but a professional operation.

Buoys left on sites have a nasty habit of disappearing. Some are accidentally cut by passing boats and others break loose in heavy seas. Even with the most elaborate electronic equipment, a considerable amount of time is usually required to relocate the exact position of a site, provided it was accurately plotted in the first place.

One way to make it easier to relocate a spot is to use submerged buoys which can be spotted from the highest elevation on a boat when one has a rough idea of the location and the water is reasonably clear. A more involved and expensive method is to use Underwater Beacon Transponders, which have an operational life of several years, depending on the size of the battery power source. Some of these units, as small as a baseball, can easily be concealed on the bottom. When a boat returning to the general area of a site uses sonar it can home in on the signal transmitted from the beacon.

There are several techniques for establishing the perimeters of a search area or plotting the positions of a target when working within sight of land. Measuring with an instrument from a rocking boat is not an accurate way to get precise bearings, but in many cases, when out of sight of land, the searcher has no choice. He should twist his body to counteract the boat's movement and to keep his instrument on a horizontal plane. Compass bearings taken from at least three landmarks or points on the shore is the most widespread method of establishing position. Each point from which bearings are obtained should be at least 30 degrees from the others and it is a good idea to take at least three sightings on each point and use the mean of the three. The bearings are then plotted on a chart and can be used to guide the boat back to the same spot.

I prefer using the Weems Position Finder, a simple and inexpensive instrument. It is a three-armed protractor with a position-finding sighting device. Three points are selected ashore and bearings are taken from each through the sighting device and one of the arms, which are then locked to the protractor. After all three bearings have been taken, the whole unit is laid on a navigational chart of the area until the end of each arm points directly to the same points on the chart as those from which the bearings were taken. A mark is then made on the chart where the other end of the three arms intersect to indicate the position of the boat.

Sextants are chiefly used by navigators on the high seas to establish positions through latitude and longitude, but they can also be used for finding positions and distances from shore. At least three landmarks should be selected and the sextant then used to find the degree of angle between two of these points at a time. These angles

Diver setting up an underwater location transponder; a device used to relocate a site when surface buoys are not used.

are plotted on a chart indicating the position of the boat. Even though it is simple to then measure the distance on the chart between the position of the boat or site and the shore, one should verify the accuracy of the angles by also using the sextant again for determining the distance. If the height above sea level of a particular landmark is known, such as a lighthouse or tower, by using the sextant in a vertical plane it is possible to obtain the angle between the highest point of the object and the water level. This can be equated to a distance by referring to the tables found in all navigational books.

There are simple, inexpensive instruments called Range Finders which are not as accurate as sextants in fixing distance between objects ashore and a boat but which can be used without knowing the elevation of the landmark one is sighting.

When working offshore, out of sight of land or any navigational aids such as marker buoys, it is not possible to attain the same degree of accuracy in establishing a precise position even if one is a master navigator. Using a sextant to establish latitude and longitude is only accurate to within several hundred yards and this can only be reckoned by those with long experience. Yachtsmen used to rely on Radio Direction Finders which establish a relative position by obtaining the compass bearings of three or more shore stations which are then triangulated on a chart.

For example, if a boat is about fifty miles from each radio station, the final fix will only be accurate to within a quarter of a mile. A LORAN set is the best way, by far, to establish a precise position. Good units cost around $500 but are well worth it. Anyone can learn how to operate this positioning instrument with a couple of hours of instruction. It can be used throughout most areas of the world and has an accuracy factor of within three hundred yards. I used a LORAN set while working on a shipwreck in the Bahamas, more than forty miles from the nearest land. Even though we generally returned to the site at night, when the sun came up in the morning we were always anchored right on top of the wreck.

Even better than a LORAN set for precision are the new satellite navigation systems that have an accuracy of less than ten meters. LORAN can only be used in areas where this system is in use, such as all waters of the United States and Canada. Elsewhere in the world one must rely on the satellite navigation system, which is in use worldwide. They cost about four times as much as a good LORAN set.

Since almost all New World shipwrecks are in water fifty feet deep or less, the first method of search, when the water is reasonably clear, should be visual. There are several techniques for searching for a site visually, some much more expensive than others. If through research the target has been narrowed down into a small area, divers with snorkeling or scuba equipment can do the job. However, if the area is large, an aerial search will be more efficient as a start.

In searching extensive areas from the air both light small planes and helicopters offer advantages and disadvantages. I find a single-engine, high-wing plane such as a Cessna 172, with the doors removed, a practical choice. The searchers should wear Polaroid sunglasses to eliminate reflections from the surface of the water. The time best suited for aerial search is between 10 a.m. and 2 p.m. on a clear day when the sun is high enough for deep light penetration into the water. When a promising area is sighted, the plane circles it several times for confirmation before a buoy or other marker is dropped. Since a plane, unless it is a seaplane, cannot land to investigate a promising place, it is a good idea, if feasible, to have a surface vessel work with the plane. The boat can be directed to suspected sites by radio and divers can immediately investigate. A boat makes the placement of buoys over a spot much easier. Without

Aerial view of a sunken building in the Bahamas.

the aid of a surface vessel it is often impossible to establish the precise position of a shipwreck, even when sighted from the air. This is especially true if the location is not near a noteworthy, easily recognizable marker such as a particular reef, island, etc.

If one is flying alone, the best method to fix position is the LORAN set, but they are rarely carried as standard equipment on small planes. Flying several timed compass headings from the site to stationary landmarks is another method. Another is to use the aircraft's OMNI set, a type of radio direction finder, but neither of these two methods is very accurate.

Interesting underwater sites have been spotted fortuitously by planes crossing over water. During the summer of 1968 a pilot sighted something that did not look like natural formations in the water off both the western side of Bimini and off the northern end of Andros in the Bahamas. Archaeologists and geologists investigating both areas found manmade structures—two walls, over a quarter of a mile each, constructed of monolithic stones and resembling breakwaters off Bimini and vestiges of some fourteen buildings underwater off Andros. Although neither site has been excavated yet, there is speculation they may have been built by people who came from the Old World as early as 3000 B.C.

Although a helicopter with flotation gear can land on a suspected target so that it can be inspected at once by divers, it has a number of drawbacks. Expense is the most obvious. A small plane rents for as little as $50 an hour, but a helicopter costs from $300 to $500 per hour. The helicopter with its ability to hover over a spot might seem to be an ideal way to check out suspected objects at close range when diving is not possible, if it were not for the downdraft from its rotors which roils the water, obliterating visibility.

A more economical method of aerial search is by balloon attached to the stern of a boat. The balloon filled either with helium or hot air is towed through a planned search pattern, and as something of interest is spotted by an observer aloft, the balloon can be hauled down and the boat stopped while divers investigate. If a good target is located, it is always easier and more accurate to obtain a good position of the site from a surface vessel than from an aircraft. Using a balloon in Bermuda several years ago, Teddy Tucker located more than twenty interesting shipwrecks in seven days.

For the best results from an aerial survey the sea should be flat calm and the observer at an altitude of between one hundred and five hundred feet. From the air I have spotted not only exposed shipwrecks, both old and modern, wrecked planes, lost parts of missiles, cannon, anchors, ballast piles and scattered ballast but even wrecks buried under sand. On wreck sites that have a great deal of metal, such as iron cannon, the iron oxide from the metallic masses generally stains the surrounding sand a darker color.

Spotting a small, solitary coral reef or mound higher than the bottom sometimes indicates a wreck site. Small reefs sometimes start growing on part of a wreck exposed above the sand. Isolated mounds are formed when sand piles up around a wreck.

Aerial photography with special water-penetrating films and polarizing filters can detect sunken objects which may not be visible to an observer in the air. Films of this type must have high contrast for their speed and granularity and must be sensitized to coincide with the transmission window of water. In 1969 the GAF corporation, manufacturers of many types of aerial film, produced a new film for the U.S. Navy called Anscochrome D-500. This still, non-blue-sensitive, aerial color film was developed to record for hydrographic purposes ocean bottom detail in coastal areas. It has also proved excellent for locating underwater archaeological sites. However, the film is manufactured only in widths of 70 mm, which requires special, expensive cameras. Eastman Kodak sells a number of good, still, aerial films which can be used in standard 35 mm cameras. Their best black-and-white film for this purpose is Plus-X Aerographic and the best colored film is Aerochrome Infrared. Both of these films are manufactured for use in 16 mm motion-picture cameras. By setting the camera to take one frame at a time a large area can be economically photographed. After the film has been developed and processed it can be projected on a screen by a projector set to show one frame at a time. The main difficulty with aerial photography is that unless it is used near a coastline, which helps determine the relative location of a site or suspected site, it is difficult to gauge precise location.

In looking for a site, the searcher has no way of knowing at the outset whether it is buried under the sea floor, so the first step is a visual search. There are several ways to conduct such a project. I shall first describe the simplest and least expensive and then the more elaborate and costly.

If the water is reasonably clear and one has keen eyes and previous experience in spotting objects on the sea floor, a simple search with the observer standing in the crow's nest or on the highest point of a boat is often productive. As in an aerial survey, the sea must be mirror-smooth and Polaroid glasses worn. With this basic approach, I once located fourteen old wrecks on the Little Bahama Bank in less than three hours. A less effective way to search visually is with a glass-bottom boat which permits viewing only the sea floor directly under it. Glass-bottom buckets can be used only if a boat is moving at a snail's pace.

A method I used when I first started searching many years ago and which I still like whenever conditions allow is to survey an area while being towed by a boat. The searcher wears snorkeling equipment and holds on to a line attached to a boat as he is pulled across the search area, following a grid pattern to make sure the entire zone is carefully examined. The line is tied to a short length of wood, such as a broom-handle section, which is grasped with both hands. The line should be long enough so that the searcher doesn't inhale the boat's exhaust fumes and so he doesn't have his vision restricted by the boat's prop-wash turbulence. By twisting his body the searcher can bank off to one side or the other, as much as 45 degrees from the course of the boat, to inspect anything not directly in the boat's path. Whenever he sights something of great interest, he either drops off the line and dives to inspect it closely, or drops one of the small buoys he should always carry so that he can dive on it later. I have found more than seven hundred shipwrecks with this modest technique.

When a number of divers are available to search an area, obviously, a much larger area can be examined in a shorter time. Two boats are used with a line stretched taut, the length depending on underwater visibility and the number of divers. If a diver can see clearly for 50 feet, for example, he will be covering a 100-foot width of the bottom on each run. To allow for an overlap (always a wise precaution) each diver should be spaced at 90-foot intervals along the line. Under these conditions fifteen divers could search a quarter-mile-wide stretch of bottom on each run.

Usually when a diver is towed on a line the boat towing travels between 1 and 3 knots, depending on the underwater visibility and the strength of the diver's arms. There is quite a pull on one's arms and many divers are exhausted after a couple of hours. Towing an underwater sled eliminates the strain and enables the diver to be towed closer to the bottom when visibility is limited and in deeper water. The sled, resembling a snow sled, is towed by a line from a surface vessel. The diver, in scuba gear, lies flat on the sled behind a fiberglass window, similar to a wind screen, mounted on the front of the unit which is usually of a nonbuoyant material like aluminum. He can alter the depth and direction of the sled by manipulation of ailerons or vanes mounted near the window. Control is maintained by the diver who can either go into a dive or rise higher and level off the way a pilot in a plane can. By moving the ailerons individually or contrary to one another he can bank the sled off in any direction. The window reduces the drag on the diver's body to such an extent that these sleds can be towed as fast as 10 knots. But be careful; a sled can be dangerous when used by the inexperienced in a reef or rocky area where there are hazardous obstacles.

There are power-towing devices, known as sea scooters, which allow a diver to search the sea floor without being connected to a surface vessel. The diver holds on to such a unit with both hands and is pulled through the water at three times normal swimming speed, pointing it in the direction he wants to move. They are relatively inexpensive, lightweight and can be used as deep as 150 feet. They are especially practical for searching around reefs or shallow water or where it would be hazardous for a boat to maneuver. Their only drawback is that the longest they can operate is two hours, after which the batteries require from eight to twenty-four hours of recharging. However, extra sets of batteries can be kept on hand to avoid loss of time.

A more sophisticated and rather expensive self-contained underwater vehicle called the "Pegasus" can carry a diver at 3 knots. He lies on the unit as on a sled and actually "flies" it through the water. It has a navigational module similar to the dashboard of a light plane, enabling the operator to follow a prescribed course and know his depth at all times. In addition, a magnetometer can be mounted on it to locate metallic deposits hidden from sight.

Powerful lights for searching in dirty water are available and cameras can be attached for photographing a site, especially when a mosaic is required. The "Pegasus" has the same battery-recharging limitations as the scooters.

A number of firms manufacture open, or "wet," submarines which carry one or two divers in scuba equipment. However, they offer no advantage over any of the above self-contained underwater vehicles other than some protection against sharks. Like scooters, they can only cruise for two hours at 3 knots before recharging.

When shallow water is too murky for efficient visual search, and if the area has a relatively flat sea floor without protruding rocks or reefs, the cable sweep method can be effective. It has been used for thousands of years and can cover quickly a large area. For optimum results two vessels with a heavily weighted steel cable strung between them are used. The length of cable determines the width of area covered on each sweep. With each pass several miles of sea bottom can be searched at a time. When an obstacle is snagged, both boats back down over it reeling in cable until the cable hangs almost vertical and the vessels are side by side. A buoy is then dropped and the cable pulled off the obstacle.

The Pegasus, a self-contained underwater vehicle for searching visually for underwater sites.

This system can also be used when looking for shipwrecks in lakes and rivers. Since wood is better preserved in fresh water than salt, they present larger targets than at sea. Most of the shipwrecks discovered in the Baltic and North seas have been found by drag lines. In some cases only one boat was used pulling a stout line with a quantity of grappling hooks attached. The most recent discovery of note was that of an unidentified galliot, dating between 1700 and 1710, found in 120 feet of water near the Borstö Islands in the Baltic. The ship, found intact and upright, conforms to the wildest Hollywood fantasy: Her masts were standing, and in the icy gloom of the main cabin Swedish and Finnish divers discovered the skeleton of a tall man, enameled snuffboxes, pocket watches, bottles and even much clothing. Plans have been made to raise this ship and preserve her like the *Vasa*.

Echo sounders, called fathometers by boatmen, are used to establish water depth, a contour of the sea floor, and locate schools of fish. Under certain conditions they can also be used to locate underwater archaeological sites. Sonic pulses are directed downward in a narrow cone and are then bounced back to the surface, revealing on a screen a profile of the bottom contour and any protrusions. Unless the search area is small, this is slow and impractical since the boat must pass directly over something to reveal it on the echo sounder screen. This requires narrow search lanes. Furthermore, unless the sea floor is fairly flat, without outcroppings, it is difficult to distinguish between a ballast pile and a natural rock formation. However, when used in conjunction with a cable sweep it can help give a rough idea of a snagged object. If it turns out to be a fairly complete wreck, a good instrument would reveal its outlines. A fathometer can also be efficient in defining the limits of a site in which all, or most, of the material from a shipwreck or sunken settlement projects above the sea floor.

Sidescan sonar, developed in World War II to detect submerged submarines, is the best way to locate sunken objects projecting above the bottom. It has the advantage of not missing anything, as the cable sweep might. A cable could slide right over a smooth object without snagging. Sidescan covers large areas in a much shorter period than the echo sounder. It operates on the same principle, but the sonic signal is directed obliquely toward the bottom, and a good instrument can cover an area twelve hundred feet wide on each pass over deep water if the bottom is flat or has only a gentle slope. In shallow water of fifty feet, up to five hundred feet can be swept at a time. Thus, if a boat is moving at 10 knots, one square mile of sea floor can be covered in little over an hour. Unlike visual search systems, which are affected by bad weather, dirty water and darkness, the sidescan unit can be operated around the clock. The silhouette of any protruding object is recorded on graph paper and shipwrecks or walls of sunken buildings are easily distinguishable from other objects.

This system was successfully used by Dr. Harold Edgerton of M.I.T. to locate the *U.S.S. Monitor*, the Civil War ironclad lost in 1862 off Cape Hatteras, North Carolina; as well as in discovering the *Titanic* lost in almost three miles depth of water in the mid-Atlantic. It also led to discovery of the American Revolutionary War privateer *Defense*, which sank in 1779 in Stockton Harbor, Maine. In this case no traces of the ship's wooden hull remained, but the sonar detected several small cannon and a rectangular, mortared brick structure believed to be the fireplace where all the ship's cooking was done. In 1953, the beautiful bronze bust of a goddess, probably Demeter, was brought up in the nets of a fisherman near Marmaris, Turkey. He had been fishing for hours before hauling in the nets and had only a general idea of where it had come from. The University of Pennsylvania Museum in 1967 sponsored an expedition to find the area from which the bronze had come. They used sidescan sonar and found an early Roman amphora carrier in 280 feet of water. The site was identified and photographed from the museum's submarine, *Asherah*. During the summers of 1971 and 1972, Peter Throckmorton and Dr. Edgerton conducted a search off Greece in an area where more than one hundred ships were lost during the Battle of Lepanto in 1571. Using both sidescan sonar and a proton magnetometer, they located a number of the wrecks from this battle and later periods.

Magnetometers and sidescan owe their invention to World War II, when they were developed in 1942 to detect submarines. They are probably the most important search instrument used by the professional underwater archaeologist and the professional treasure hunter to locate sites in the Western Hemisphere. They can be used in shallow or deep water, in looking for buried or exposed wrecks. Until a few years ago a good unit cost well over $15,000 and some cost as much as

$30,000. Today a number are on the market for as little as $500, but they are far less sensitive than the more expensive models.

A magnetometer measures the strength and variations of the earth's magnetic field. The earth's rotation sets up a magnetic field around it, with the magnetic poles approximately coinciding with the geographic poles. Large local variations in the strength and direction of this main field are caused by concentrations of iron in the rocks and sediments in the earth's crust. The amount of variation is controlled by the size, depth and iron content of the material. Even smaller variations, technically "anomalies," are caused by man-made iron objects such as cannon or anchors found on shipwrecks.

There are four types of magnetometers, each working on a different principle: the rubidium, the caesium, the differential fluxgate and the proton. Best to use in looking for shipwrecks or sunken settlements is the proton magnetometer because it is most sensitive to gradients in the earth's magnetic field produced by localized concentrations of ferro-magnetic material.

The instrument consists of three basic components: sensing probe, control unit and power supply. The sensing probe is designed to be towed behind the search vessel from a cable connected to the control unit on the vessel. The probe is extremely stable and can be adjusted to run at predetermined depths by controlling the speed of the vessel or attaching weights to it. The unit will operate at full efficiency regardless of geographic location; it eliminates problems resulting from orientation of the earth's magnetic field and unlike other types of magnetometers the proton magnetometer is unaffected by ignition interference from the boat's engine and atmospheric conditions. Like the sonar instruments, it can be run continuously under most sea conditions.

In shallow water searches for large targets such as cannon or anchors, the sensing probe is pulled on the water's surface, usually at between 5 to 10 knots. However, where the amount of ferrous metal may be small, as on a ship that carried bronze cannons, which do not register on the magnetometer, or in the case of a ship that might have lost all its anchors in another area before wrecking, the sensing probe must be pulled close to the sea floor and the width of each search lane narrowed considerably.

A target like a Civil War blockade runner, which may have had as much as one hundred tons of iron used in its construction, can be

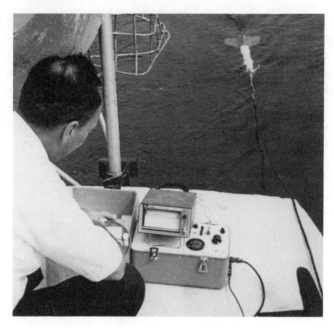

A magnetometer being used to locate concentrations of ferrous matter underwater. The sensor head is being towed behind the boat.

detected at from 400 to 600 feet. An older shipwreck site with a large number of cannon and anchors may be detected from 250 to 300 feet away if the iron objects are confined in a small area. However, if the wreck has been scattered and the large ferrous articles broadcast over a large area, each piece will probably be detected individually at a maximum range of 100 feet. In cases where a shipwreck has only small ferrous items such as cannonballs, tools, weapons and bits of rigging, the location will be detected only if the sensing probe passes within 30 to 40 feet of the site. If very small items are widely scattered, the probe must come within 10 to 15 feet to detect them.

During the past twenty years magnetometers have been used to locate hundreds of shipwrecks and other types of submerged objects such as airplanes or pieces of military equipment. On the east coast of Florida and in the Florida Keys treasure hunters have found more than five hundred shipwreck sites in the past ten years alone. The magnetometer is not practical for use in an area like the Mediterranean, since ancient ships carried little ferrous material.

I used a proton magnetometer to find the *Maravilla* on the Little Bahama Bank. We spent four months conducting a thorough magnetometer survey in the summer of 1972. We covered thirty-five square miles, averaging a quarter of a square mile per day. Usually when looking for a Spanish wreck searchers space each run about two hundred feet apart in the hopes of locating a cannon or anchor, since the sensing probe is detecting off to both sides as it is being towed. Various treasure hunters had covered this same area previously without finding the site. From my research I was sure the wreck was in this area. Consequently, I decided to space each of our runs at only one hundred feet, which meant the probe would pass within fifty feet of every object in the search area and could detect ferrous articles much smaller than cannon or anchors. I knew that the *Maravilla* had carried only bronze cannon which would make her difficult to find. Even though she was buried under twenty-five feet of sand, we were able to find her and twenty-four other wrecks as well, seventy-six anchors, some with chains, and even many odd items such as a fisherman's tackle box.

Many sites buried under the sea floor have little or no ferrous material on them, such as ancient shipwrecks and sunken buildings. None of the search methods described will reveal them. The only sure way to search for such a site is with a special sonar

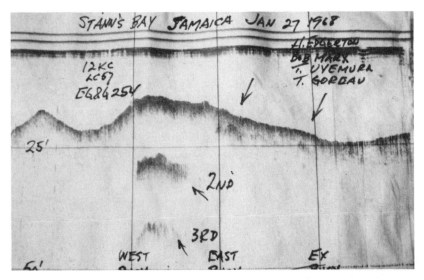

Sub-bottom profiling graph showing the remains of one of Columbus' ships, which was lost in St. Anne's Bay, Jamaica, and located in 1968. The dark shadow beneath the surface of the sea floor is the wreck. (Credit: Dr. Harold Edgerton.)

instrument, the sub-bottom profiler. Two of the best available are the "Pinger" and the "Boomer," both designed by Harold Edgerton. They have been used as the chief search tools on dozens of underwater archaeological sites all over the world. The sub-bottom profiler works on the same principle as other types of sonar, except that by using a lower frequency signal it can penetrate through the sediment interfaces and produce a profile of objects buried in the sediment or beneath it on bedrock. As in the case of the echo sounder, this instrument must pass directly over a buried object in order to detect it. The unit shows not only a profile of buried objects but reveals their size and shape, how deep they are buried, the depth of the water, and the thickness of different types of sediment lying on the bedrock.

Although the sub-bottom profiler generally gives good results in mud or silty bottoms, they are unable to penetrate deeper than ten feet into the sand. If a shipwreck is buried deeper, it will not be detected by a sub-bottom profiler.

During January and February of 1968, I was fortunate to have Dr. Edgerton run sub-bottom sonar surveys at both Port Royal and St. Anne's Bay in Jamaica. Most of his efforts were devoted to surveying and mapping Port Royal. A series of shore points, all about ten feet apart, were located, numbered and plotted on a map. Buoys were spaced about ten feet apart in lines running offshore. Then the survey boat with the sub-bottom profiler made runs at a constant speed. Since the site was almost a mile long, this sonar survey took about three weeks. The results were excellent. From the hundreds of feet of sonar-recording paper, and with the aid of several draftsmen, we produced four large charts covering the entire site and showing the precise positions of hundreds of walls of the old buildings as well as of several shipwrecks. An important feature of this survey was that it defined the extent of the whole site.

The sub-bottom profiler can also locate a buried wreck when its approximate position has been determined. One of the most famous ships in British naval history was the *Mary Rose*, which sank in Portsmouth Harbour in England in 1545. Research established she was in an area of about twelve hundred square feet, but attempts to locate her through visual and magnetometer search failed. A sub-bottom profiler produced a three-dimensional seismic sonar profile which proved to be the *Mary Rose* under ten feet of harbor mud.

Of the hundreds of ancient shipwrecks discovered in the Mediterranean, few were found through scientific methods. Most were accidently located by fishermen, sponge divers and sport divers. Since little original documentation exists on these wrecks in comparison to those of the past five hundred years, archival research plays a negligible role in their discovery. Countless ancient wrecks still lie in the silent depths waiting to be found either fortuitously by fishermen or by someone using any of the above methods.

The Mediterranean has three distinctly different types of areas where underwater archaeological sites are found. Most of the coastal areas of the lands bordering the southern and eastern Mediterranean are sandy, with a gradual sloping continental shelf similar to the East Coast of the United States. In these areas most of the shipwrecks and sunken settlements are in relatively shallow water and can be sought in the same way wrecks are sought in the Western Hemisphere. Magnetometers are not helpful in looking for wrecks more than five hundred years old because they have little ferrous material on them. Cannon were not carried and anchors were of stone, lead and wood.

In the northern Mediterranean, from Spain to Turkey, steep rocky coasts are typical, forming almost vertical cliffs one hundred to two hundred feet tall along the shoreline. In these areas shipwreck sites are of more archaeological interest than those lost in the shallower waters of the southern Mediterranean because they are normally found in better condition and are somewhat easier to excavate. In the deeper water the ships and their cargoes were not subjected to the degree of destruction by waves and currents as in the shallows, and their remains are generally less scattered. However, it is a great deal more difficult to locate a wreck in deep water than in shallow, and if the water is too deep a wreck cannot be easily excavated.

Most shipwreck sites in the northern Mediterranean will be fairly close to the coast and will have some visible traces unless they were lost in areas where rivers deposit a large volume of sediment into the sea. The typical ship loss would probably have occurred as follows: Because of bad weather or faulty navigation, a ship struck against the rocky shore and either her seams opened or one or more holes were torn in her hull, causing her to fill with water and sink. As she settled, gravity shifted her cargo to the part of the ship pointing down, and once on the bottom she listed to one side or the other, depending on the slope of the sea floor and how the cargo shifted. In most cases the bottom would be rocky and the ship probably lasted twenty-five to fifty years before borers devoured her wooden hull. The cargo would remain more or less as it had been stored but might be camouflaged by marine growth. If the bottom were mud or sand, the weight of the ship and cargo might have forced the lower section of the hull into the sediment where it could be found today, preserved.

The best method of search in areas of rocky bottom is visual. The irregular bottom prevents effective use of sonar and the cable sweep and, as mentioned, magnetometers are not helpful in looking for ancient wrecks. In some zones pinnacles of jagged rock, called "secs," rise precipitously from the bottom to within several feet of the surface. Many ships have torn out their bottoms on these pinnacles and sunk nearby. In some of these areas the sea floor is relatively flat and sandy so that use of sonar or a cable sweep search could be used.

A scuba diver is severely limited in the time he can search the bottom visually on these relatively deep sites. Unless a search area is small, diving is not practical.

Good seamen can generally pick out places where shipwrecks occurred. Cousteau and his team proved this on an expedition in 1953 about which he wrote: "To find Aegean wrecks we followed the old trade routes. Any reef or cape that looked treacherous to us may have been fatal to the ancients, so we dived there. At every spot we found the litter of an old ship and, on several, signs of two or more."

When it is necessary to cover visually an extensive area in deep water there are several techniques to select from. The least expensive is a Towvane, a self-contained diving chamber capable of searching in depths to six hundred feet. One or two observers can comfortably be towed in it and can control their elevation over the sea floor with ailerons mounted on both sides of the chamber. When a target is sighted they notify the surface by telephone and a buoy is dropped. Another system good in deep water is closed-circuit television. A television camera, with strong lights if the water is dark or dirty, is mounted on a small platform, similar to a sea sled, and towed through the water like a Towvane.

The "Poodle" was the most sophisticated submersible vehicle developed to locate deep wreck sites. Dimitri Rebikoff, an early pioneer in underwater archaeology and photography, invented it to find ancient wrecks off the French Riviera. Similar in shape to the "Pegasus," it is controlled from the surface by remote control via a tether cable. It carries both sidescan and sub-bottom profiling sonar, a magnetometer, a wide-angle, distortion-corrected-lens television camera, various types of still and motion picture cameras, lights and its own self-contained navigation system. Rebikoff built a model with hydraulic grab-arms to collect samples from deep water sites.

Manned submersibles or submarines have also been used successfully on several deep-water archaeological sites but their cost is prohibitive and they require a tremendous amount of maintenance. However, of some one hundred submersibles built for the oceanographic industry, many are not used. Perhaps, some might eventually be donated for underwater archaeological work.

The third type of Mediterranean shipwreck site is one far from a coast and in deep water. I shall discuss this in Chapter 8 dealing with the future of underwater archaeology.

Once research has been done and a search results in the probable location of a site, the spot must be investigated by a diver, by an observer in a submersible, or through closed-circuit television. In shallows where the water is clear this is easy if some vestige of the site is visible on the surface of the sea floor. It is slightly more difficult if the underwater visibility is poor, in which case one of the following methods can be used.

The most efficient method of zeroing in on a likely target is with a hand-held sonar unit, no larger than an underwater camera, which can locate objects up to two hundred feet away. A diver descends to an area where a buoy marks a spot worth examining closely and sweeps the surrounding area in a 360-degree arc, until the sonar unit emits a beep which indicates the direction of an object protruding above the sea floor. The closer he gets to the object, the stronger the beep. A model called "Scuba-Eye" has an illuminated scope to show the distance between the target and the diver.

Another method good in either clear or turbid water is the circle sweep. After the search boat reaches the vicinity of a likely target, a heavy anchor is dropped on a line. Another line is also attached to some part of the anchor. If the search is to be visual, this line is marked at intervals so the diver knows how far to space each circle he will make. If the underwater visibility is only five feet in each direction, each mark on the line should be spaced about eight feet apart. The marks can be made by knotting or tying a piece of cloth to the line. The diver starts by swimming a complete circle around the anchor holding the first mark, then moves out further in progressively larger circles until the target has been located.

A faster method, when the target is large, is for the diver to swim out to the far end of the search line, holding it taut and swimming a large circle, the circumference depending on the length of the line. Once the target is snagged by the line, the diver, still holding the line taut, swims back toward the anchor until he runs into the target. He quickly drops a small marker buoy which serves until a larger buoy can be dropped from the search vessel.

In areas such as rivers or streams where there is a strong current, the best way to locate a target is with the traverse sweep search. The anchor and line are dropped up current of the likely area and the diver operates in the same manner he would in executing the circle sweep search, save that to avoid fighting the current on each sweep he swims a pattern in a relatively flat arc, which increases in size the farther he moves from the starting point near the anchor. After each sweep he drops back a bit farther until he reaches the next marker and then starts on another sweep in the opposite direction.

It is, of course, far more difficult to identify a buried target. A precise area must first be narrowed from a generally promising area. The best way to do this if the site has any metal, either ferrous or nonferrous, is to use an underwater metal detector which senses the presence of all metals. The diver holds this portable instrument in his hand, swimming over an area until he locates a target. On sites containing ferrous metal located by a magnetometer, the magnetometer can pinpoint the site. A diver must wear no ferrous metal himself. (A scuba tank must be aluminum.) The sensing probe is pulled slowly over the bottom, the diver making sure it doesn't catch on any obstructions. When the person monitoring the control unit on the surface sees the target has been found, he signals the diver by jerking the cable and the diver then buoys the spot.

If a sub-bottom profiling sonar unit is available, so much the better, especially when no metal exists. If one is not available, as is likely, there are two less sophisticated methods. In mud or silt a long metal probe, usually a quarter of an inch thick and as long as necessary to penetrate the sediment, can be effective. The diver simply pushes it into the bottom until he strikes something solid, either bedrock or his target. With a little practice it is possible by either feel or sound to determine if the object is stone, wood or metal. Using a probe in Cadiz Bay I once found nine shipwrecks in four hours, all in harbor mud from six to eighteen feet deep.

In sand which is compact, the probe is more difficult to use unless the sand is no more than a few feet deep or the target is fairly close to the surface of the sand. In looking for an object under more than four feet of sand, an air probe should be used. It is also useful where the mud is hard and difficult to penetrate with a probe. I usually use a 20-foot length of 1-inch diameter galvanized iron water pipe, the kind plumbers use. On one end I attach a hose connected to a surface air compressor which sends down a continuous stream of air that blows away the sand or mud around the mouth of the tube and facilitates its penetration. After something solid is struck, the same method as used with the metal probe will indicate what type of material it is.

Once a buried target has been pinpointed, it must be identified by collecting sample materials. If a target is exposed, it is easy. If it is buried under only a few feet of sediment or sand, a small test hole can easily be dug by hand using the ping-pong paddle method or a scuba tank. By turning on the air in a scuba tank and directing its flow, a small hole can be dug rapidly. This makes it unnecessary to use more complicated equipment, although a small water or air jet can be used.

If the site is deeply buried, several other methods can be tried. The most effective I have found is the use of a coring tube. This is practical not only in mud or silt but also on sandy bottoms and even in soft coral growth. The coring devices used by marine geologists are generally driven into the sea floor by explosives or equipment operated from a surface vessel. Those used in underwater archaeology can be much simpler, like the one I used to find the two Columbus wrecks in Jamaica, 4-foot sections of 4-inch diameter iron tubing. One diver placed one end of the tube over the sea floor, holding it vertically while another drove it into the sediment by hitting the top of the tube with a sledge hammer. As each section sank into the sediment another was attached. We continued until we hit bedrock at twenty feet. Before the coring tube was pulled up by a lifting bag filled with air, a rubber plug was inserted into the top of the tube to maintain suction in it so that the sediment and any artifactual material it might contain would not fall out as the tube was freed from the sediment. Either aboard the boat or ashore I recovered the sample in the tube by simply removing the rubber plug. I held the tube at a 45-degree angle and shook it lightly, backing away with it as the contents came out. Thus, we ended up with a twenty foot long core of sediment and other material. In this manner we recovered not only a rewarding variety of archaeological samples, such as wood, glass, flint, iron nails and tacks, small ballast stones, animal bones, ceramic shards and even beans, but determined their stratigraphical depth as well. No doubt, artifacts can be destroyed in this procedure, but we had to risk it on that site to eliminate the greater danger of exposing the ship's long-buried wooden hull and so as not to disturb the archaeological context of the site. We had learned from historical research and the Edgerton sub-bottom profile that the hulls of both vessels were remarkably well preserved beneath the protecting sediment, and since we were not prepared to excavate the site at that time it would have been unforgivable to expose the ships to destruction by borers or other forces.

If a coring tube is used in coral growth, the bottom of the tube must have a keen cutting edge which must be frequently sharpened. Each tube should not be longer than four feet so that a diver can stand on the sea floor and pound the tube into the sediment with more power than if he had to do it while swimming over the bottom.

To dig a small test hole on a target site which is buried two to six feet, a small airlift or hydrolift can be used. I have operated both of these without the use of even a small boat on sites located close to shore. The compressor for an airlift and the water pump for a hydrolift were mounted on a platform floated on a large piece of styrofoam or the large inner tube of a truck tire. This is an especially good method in shallow rivers and streams.

If the target is deeper than six feet, a larger airlift requiring an air compressor carried on a boat should be used. If the sediment is fairly hard and the target not too deep, this isn't too formidable an undertaking. However, when the sediment is soft and silty, much larger test holes have to be made because the sediment continually caves in. At Port Royal I found areas where the sediment was so fine and soft that in order to make a test hole to reach an object twenty feet down, I had to make one with a diameter of sixty feet or so at the top, narrowing to a diameter of only a few feet at the bottom. It took almost eight hours to make such a hole with the size of airlift I used.

I eventually overcame this problem. I used five sections of concrete water pipe, 4 feet in diameter and 5 feet long. After driving the first section as far down into the sediment as possible, I began digging out the sediment inside the pipe and as I went deeper the pipe sank. When it sank below the level of the sea floor I attached another length of pipe and continued in this way until I reached the target. The only problem with this technique is that it is impossible to retrieve the pipes without excavating a large hole around them, which can be as time-consuming as digging the 60-foot diameter hole in the first place.

I have since learned a simpler method involving a long metal tube instead of using a water pipe. Its diameter should be a few inches wider than the airlift tube. This method is quicker and safer than using water pipe. The diameter of the test hole is smaller, requiring less time to make but giving equal results. The metal tube is easier to handle than the unwieldy water pipes, and instead of the diver having to operate the airlift inside the pipe, as I did at Port Royal, he remains on the sea floor operating the airlift as it and the metal tube sink deeper into the sediment. The diver does not face the risk of having the pipe collapse, trapping him under tons of sediment.

To determine beneath the sea floor stratigraphical levels at which small items are uncovered and pumped up into the airlift, the diver simply measures the length of the metal tube remaining above the sea floor and subtracts it from the total length of the tube. From a boat the metal tube can be removed from the sediment with lifting bags or lifting equipment such as an anchor winch. Although this is better, at times the water-pipe system is the only answer. The airlift will suck up only small artifacts, and on a site where the target may be an empty sunken building, it will have to be identified through visual observation by a diver who must reach it.

5

<hr>

Excavation

Excavating an underwater site properly requires a great deal of planning, skill, patience and knowledge. It must be done right the first time; there is no second chance. One must be committed to a high standard of performance, including the obligation to execute a scrupulous excavation according to plan, and be fully aware he has the opportunity to contribute to knowledge about the past. Even the treasure hunter must appreciate how much more meaningful are the artifacts he seeks if he has regard for the context in which he finds them. Each site tells a unique story, each artifact has a unique history and once destroyed are irreplaceable.

Once a site of underwater archaeological interest has been pinpointed and as much research done on it as possible, excavation can begin. The area should be tested to determine which approaches waste the least time and effort. Sites vary in size from refuse sites or middens a few yards square to scattered shipwreck sites or sunken settlements spread over several square miles. No one should undertake a project for which he does not have adequate resources, experience, competent help and funding. A project should be scaled to suit its means. By planning thoroughly and adhering to plan, unless data turns up which makes change imperative, even a small section of a site can be excavated in a creditable way. It is better to work slowly and carefully on a small area than to risk destroying an entire site through hasty, careless work.

The amount of money available will determine the scale of the excavation. In selecting personnel for an underwater excavation it is important that each diver be fully qualified and that he bring an additional skill to the team. He might be a mechanic, artist, draftsman, archaeologist, photographer or geologist. Some expeditions have teams of a hundred but many accomplish a project with only three or four participants.

Selection of the most efficient and safest diving equipment is of paramount importance. Choice of equipment will depend on depth of site, type of site and bottom, distance from land, and water visibility. On deep-water sites a portable recompression chamber to treat cases of the bends should be carried aboard the vessel from which the excavation is conducted or, at the least, be available on shore. A doctor versed in diving medicine is an essential member of a team working in deep water.

Excavation tools are chosen to do the most efficient job without endangering either the divers or the site. If the excavation is to have any scientific validity, constant attention must be paid to accepted archaeological practices, so that through mapping and recording the maximum amount of archaeological data is obtained.

Three workers would be a minimum number on an excavation. Two divers should always be together on the bottom in case one has a problem such as entangling his regulator hose on an obstruction. The third person is in the boat or close by on shore to run the excavation equipment, to record artifacts and other material recovered and to help the two below if they are both endangered—which could happen if the hole they were digging collapsed over them. In general such a small team would only be used on a shallow-water ceremonial or refuse site.

When working on a shipwreck site in shallow water at least six persons are essential, all qualified divers. Two teams of three divers each can alternate working on the bottom and topside. While one team is on the bottom the other is fully occupied on the boat with many assorted and never-ending tasks—running the diving and excavation equipment, moving the boat to new positions, raising the items recovered and recording them. In the warm waters of the Caribbean one team usually works the first half of each day, the other the second half. However, in cold water it is often necessary to alternate teams every hour or so to allow the divers to work efficiently and comfortably. A diver with numbed fingers will accomplish little. When the site is deeper than thirty-five feet and the decompression factor must be taken into account, the time each team can spend on the bottom will be dictated by the diving tables.

At sites deeper than 80 feet much larger teams are required. The more divers, the more quickly the work will be done. If the site is 80 feet deep, a diver can spend only 70 minutes underwater without decompressing for a long period. If two-man teams are used and each work day is eight hours, at least 14 divers are required. At sites 160 feet deep, where divers can spend only about 20 minutes bottom time, forty-eight divers are required for an eight-hour day.

It is important to select not only the best diving equipment for a particular site but to have a sufficient quantity of replacement gear. Scuba regulators frequently break down because sediment gets into them during the course of an excavation; weight belts are lost when a diver has to take them off to swim to the surface with a heavy object; and gloves tend to disappear at an alarming rate. Since the divers are usually either lying or kneeling on the bottom, rubber suits wear out rapidly, especially on a rocky or coral bottom. The most common complaint is the breakdown of air compressors. Both compressors used as a source of breathing air and those that run excavation tools require a high level of maintenance. The safest practice is to bring at least two of each type, with a generous supply of extra parts such as spark plugs, air and fuel lines and fittings, and chemicals for the filters that purify breathing air.

The standard tools used on a land excavation include picks, shovels, trowels, a variety of brushes, sifting screens, buckets or baskets and wheelbarrows to haul overburden away. On some professionally conducted excavations bulldozers have been used to strip away a deep deposit of sterile overburden. None of these is necessary on an underwater site. Those which are effective vary, depending on the nature of the site and the amount of funds available.

In some cases unorthodox tools have been useful. In 1865, the Confederate ram C.S.S. *Neuse* was scuttled and burned in the shallow Neuse River near Kingston, North Carolina. After it was accidently discovered by a fisherman, a group of citizens of Kingston began salvage operations in 1961. Due to swift currents and a lack of visibility, divers could not be used to excavate the ship. Airlifts were used on a few attempts, but the holes they dug filled with mud immediately. Finally, a cofferdam was constructed around the site, and the water and mud overburden were removed with a combination of pumps, dragline buckets and shovels. The hull, reassembled, and artifacts recovered with it were placed on permanent exhibit. Underwater archaeology is still in its infancy and there will continue to be an evolution in techniques and novel but productive tools and methods to meet the peculiarities of each site.

The standard, most frequently used tool in underwater archaeology, on both shallow and deep sites, is the airlift. It consists of a metal or semirigid plastic tube into which a continuous stream of compressed air is ejected through one or more holes near its bottom, depending on the diameter of the tube, which also determines the volume of air required. An air hose delivering the required amount of air is connected to a surface compressor. The size of the hose and air compressor are determined by the tube's diameter and the depth of the excavation.

The airlift works on the principle that when compressed air is forced into its lower extremity, the air rises rapidly up the tube, creating suction that sucks up bottom sediment and small artifacts. There should be a control valve on an airlift tube so a diver can control the air entering. When removing overburden, the airlift is run at full speed to remove as much sediment as possible. However, when a zone containing any fragments or artifactual materials is reached, the power of the suction must be reduced to permit the diver to extract these items before they are sucked up the tube or damaged by striking against it. When small objects such as coins, buttons, musket balls, etc., are sucked up, the spill from the top of the tube is directed into a catch-basin screen either underwater or on the surface or onto a barge or boat containing a screen. The air pressure used in an airlift must be at least one atmosphere greater than the surrounding ambient water pressure.

On the next page is a chart indicating the diameter of the tube and hose required at various depths and the amount of air pressure and volume of air needed to work efficiently.

Aluminum tubing or PVC plastic pipe, both widely used for irrigation, are the best materials for the airlift tube. The minimum length for an airlift tube is about fifteen feet, but there is no limit

Airlift diameter	Hose diameter	Maximum depth to be used	Air volume in cubic feet per minute	Air pressure in pounds per square inch
3 inch	1/2 inch	40 feet	20–40 CFM	50 PSI
3 inch	1/2 inch	65 feet	30–50 CFM	75 PSI
3 inch	1/2 inch	90 feet	40–60 CFM	100 PSI
4 inch	3/4 inch	40 feet	30–50 CFM	50 PSI
4 inch	3/4 inch	65 feet	40–60 CFM	75 PSI
4 inch	3/4 inch	90 feet	50–70 CFM	100 PSI
6 inch	11/4 inch	40 feet	75–100 CFM	50 PSI
6 inch	11/4 inch	65 feet	100–125 CFM	75 PSI
6 inch	11/4 inch	90 feet	125–150 CFM	100 PSI

to its extension. If one is working in 20 feet of water and simply wants to excavate and deposit the spill behind in an already excavated area or a sterile area, a 15-foot tube will do. If the site is two hundred feet deep and the excavator wants to deposit the spill on a surface vessel, a tube two hundred feet long can be made, usually by attaching 20-foot sections. The valves and fittings to attach the hose to the bottom of the tube can be bought in any hardware or plumbing-supply store. The hose should be attached about four to six inches from the end of the tube. The hose can be any type of low-pressure hose, similar to a garden hose, but one that will resist kinking. The compressor model is contingent upon the amount of pressure and volume required. One can be bought for as little as several hundred dollars. When a small, 3-inch diameter airlift is used in about thirty feet of water, a standard paint-spraying compressor will do.

Under no circumstances should an airlift be used with a diameter of more than 6 inches. Too large an airlift is unwieldy and hard to control, and a great many artifacts are destroyed or lost. This occurred at Port Royal in 1959 during a six-week excavation conducted by a group more interested in attracting publicity for their finds than in trying to save the fragile objects. They used a 12-inch diameter airlift powerful enough to snap a man's arm if it were sucked into the tube. Hundreds of seventeenth-century artifacts were smashed.

During my excavation of the sunken city I used a 4-inch diameter airlift with satisfying results. On the bottom of the tube I attached two wires, crossing each other, to keep all but the smallest artifacts such as pins, buttons and tiny pottery fragments from going up the tube. These tiny items landed on a barge where two men stood watch to recover them the moment they landed on the screen. The bottom of the tube should not be placed directly in contact with the sediment but held about four inches off the bottom so the diver, spotting objects as they are uncovered, can quickly jerk the tube higher to reduce suction. Thus, he extricates the objects before they are sucked up or caught against the bottom of the tube.

The advantage of the airlift over other types of excavation tools when working on muddy or silty bottoms is that the spill or fallout from the top of the lift can be directed and carried away by the current, keeping underwater visibility at a reasonable level. At Port Royal rarely was there any underwater visibility, and at best it was no more than a few inches. Even there it was helpful to have the currents carry off the

An airlift being used on a shipwreck off Australia. The basket on the bottom left contains coral-encrusted artifacts. (Credit: Western Australian Museum.)

sediment pumped to the surface so that it did not settle back on unexcavated areas. Another method can be used to ensure that the spill doesn't cloud the water too much or sink on unexcavated areas. The bottom of the tube is attached near the sea floor by several lines tied to it which are anchored on the bottom. The tube is held vertical by floats attached to its top. The air is still forced into the bottom as before, but a flexible hose, the same diameter as the tube, is attached to the mouth of the tube. The diver holds the end of the hose and can excavate some distance away from the tube with this "vacuum cleaner" arrangement, the spill coming out at the desired fixed point.

The airlift cannot be used effectively in water less than fifteen feet deep because the differential between the atmospheric pressure on the surface and the water pressure on the bottom is not sufficient to create much suction in the tube. Nor is the airlift useful on sites widely scattered or buried under deep, sedimentary deposits. In these situations work that might take years with an airlift could be done in a fraction of the time by another tool, the prop-wash. Depending on its size and the depth of the site, the prop-wash can be as much as one hundred times more effective than an airlift. However, it does have a number of restrictions and is not suited to all types of sites.

The prop-wash, also called "blower," "blaster" and "mailbox," was invented early in this century to blow away sediment covering oyster beds in Chesapeake Bay. In 1962, treasure salvors working on the 1715 wrecks off the Florida coast, accidently discovered its effectiveness as an excavation tool. Confronted with murky water, the divers devised a prop-wash to push clear water from the surface down to the bottom where the water is much dirtier and darker. To their great surprise, they found it was a much better excavation tool than the airlifts and hydrolifts they had been using.

This tool is simple and inexpensive to construct, and easy to operate. It consists of an elbow-shaped aluminum or stainless steel tube several inches larger in diameter than the boat's propeller diameter. The tube is attached to the transom of the salvage vessel in such a way that the wash of the propeller is forced into the tube and deflected toward the sea bottom. Generally, the upper end of the tube is attached from one to three feet behind the propeller. A wiremesh cage covers the propeller area to protect divers from being sucked into the propeller. On twin-screw vessels, two prop-washes can be used side by side. The length of the prop-wash will depend on the diameter of the tube. A small prop-wash on an outboard engine is usually about three feet long. On larger boats, such as those with propellers as big as four feet in diameter, the tube is usually six to eight feet long, and half this length is used in the section of the tube running horizontally from the propeller to the elbow.

When you use a prop-wash the vessel must be kept stationary by placing four anchors out at 90 degrees from one another. The two running off the stern are most crucial since they receive the greatest strain when the prop-wash is in action. The anchors are also used to reposition the vessel before a new area is excavated. If the vessel is to be moved to port, for example, the two starboard anchor lines are slackened and the two port lines are used to pull the vessel to the desired location. Then, all four lines are tightened and made fast. If the vessel must be moved ahead, slack is let out on the two anchor lines farthest aft and those forward are hauled on to move the boat. Depending on the length of the anchor lines, the vessel can be moved over large areas on a site without having to bring up the prop-wash and move the vessel with her own engine.

The elbow-shaped device on the stern of the author's salvage vessel is an excavation tool known as a "prop-wash," which can remove vast amounts of sediment off of a site in minutes.

After the boat is in the correct position, its engine is started and the propeller speed controlled to blast away sediment. The speed will, of course, vary with the depth of the water and amount of sediment to be removed. The wash of the propeller deflected downward creates a whirlpool action that forces water to the bottom at a terrific velocity which rapidly blows away the sediment. It is so powerful that it can cut through coquina and even some coral. Its effective depth depends on two factors: the size of the propeller and the highest velocity at which it can run. A small prop-wash on an outboard engine is effective only down to fifteen feet. The wash from a propeller two to three feet in diameter can blast down as deep as thirty-five feet and one four feet in diameter can be used up to fifty feet. My salvage vessel has a propeller five and one-half feet in diameter and it has worked effectively in seventy feet of water. This is about the maximum depth to which any prop-wash can be used, no matter how great the propeller diameter or how powerful the boat's engines. In twenty feet of water a prop-wash two to three feet in diameter can excavate in the sediment a hole twenty feet in diameter and fifteen feet deep in only a few minutes. A larger prop-wash can excavate a hole in fifty feet of water to a diameter of fifty feet and twenty feet deep in the same time.

The key to using a prop-wash effectively lies in controlling its speed—running at high speed to remove overburden and knowing when and how much and for how long to slow it when a stratum containing any vestige of artifactual material is reached. Through experience I have learned that to remove twelve feet of sand from over a shipwreck, I must run the engine so that the propeller turns at 1,200 revolutions per minute for exactly three minutes. Then, I reduce the speed to 400 rpm and send divers down to work under the prop-wash while it runs slowly and exposes artifacts. At this speed the prop-wash will remove approximately one inch of sand per minute and the divers have time to find all the artifacts before they can be blown away. If the prop-wash is not properly controlled, many artifacts are destroyed or blasted into other areas where they may be lost. I have seen a six-pound cannonball blasted over fifty feet from its original position when a prop-wash was run too fast. Some prop-washes are so powerful they help remove ballast stones from over a wreck. However, this is not recommended since often mixed in with the ballast are many items of archaeological interest which would be lost.

When a section of a site has been reached in which there are fragile or very small objects such as coins or jewelry, excavation with the prop-wash should give way to another method which gives the diver more control. More than once, I have been working under a prop-wash which uncovered coins while running at the slowest speed possible. Even so, I was unable to collect everything before it was blasted away. There are several good ways to excavate in such a situation, either by fanning the sand by hand or using a small airlift or hydrolift.

Stopping the prop-wash or slowing it down takes only a second, but since only the divers on the bottom usually know when it should be done, they must have a way to send a signal topside. I use a weighted line which hangs down to the divers and is connected to a horn on the boat. I use the same system for sending other messages to the surface. In this way the need for going up and down all day to ask for a lifting basket for a heavy artifact, for tools or cameras, is eliminated. A steady long pull on the horn is my signal for immediate assistance.

As the prop-wash excavates a hole, sediment is thrown or blasted out of it, settling on unexcavated areas. This accumulation of

Author's wife recovering gold and silver coins from the wreck of the Maravilla.

overburden must first be removed before starting a new hole. With a big prop-wash it can be done quickly. Excavating the *Maravilla* in the Bahamas we faced this problem. Most of what remained of the ship's cargo and the negligible traces of her wooden hull rested on solid bedrock under twenty-five feet of sediment. The site covered an extensive area and the only way to get to the wreck was with the big, powerful prop-wash. The water was fifty feet deep and each hole we made had a diameter of about fifty feet at the top and twenty-five feet at the bottom. The sand blown out of a hole piled up like dunes, sometimes fifteen feet high, around the perimeter. Consequently, each time I moved the boat to start a new hole, this sand had first to be blown away. It usually shifted right back to the hole it had come out of. This amounted to moving sand from one spot to another in order to reach the site. If I had been working in an area of mud or silt bottom, most of the lighter sediment would have been borne off by currents.

The prop-wash roils the water, especially when the bottom area is sediment or mud. However, divers on the bottom always enjoy good visibility because the propeller sucks in clear surface water and pushes it to the bottom. The surface water is warmer, too, and makes the diver's work more comfortable.

An air jet is an excavation tool used in rare instances. It is nothing more than a hose connected to a surface compressor which forces air at high pressure into it. The diver holding it directs it to blow away sediment. The strength of the air pressure dissipates so rapidly on the bottom that the jet can only move the sediment a few feet away. It is useful, however, in very shallow water to remove small amounts of sediment from such places as shallow coral reefs or potholes. The same hose and air supply used on an airlift can double as an air jet.

A water jet is similar, except that water instead of air is pumped down at high pressure and used to blow away sand or sediment. It is a great deal more powerful than the air jet. A small, high pressure pump, costing a few hundred dollars, makes an inexpensive excavation tool since it can be run from a small float on the surface and doesn't necessarily require a boat. The working end of the hose is fitted with a special nozzle with small jets feeding part of the water flow backwards to counteract the tendency of the hose to recoil, flinging the diver about. The nozzle should have a valve with which the operator can control the water pressure.

Diver using a hydrolift in a shallow river. The spill is fed through a sluice box to recover small artifacts. (Credit: Richard Anderson.)

This is a specialized tool, used only in limited circumstances. A water jet can remove sediment faster than an airlift, but there is always the risk that valuable archaeological material will be blasted away as well. It is the only tool capable of digging tunnels under a ship that is going to be raised as were the *Vasa* and *Cairo*. In very shallow water during excavation of sunken buildings where an airlift or prop-wash cannot be used, the water jet can be used with caution. It decreases underwater visibility so drastically that it can't be effective unless there is some current to bear the turbid water away.

A hydrolift, also known as a transfer tube, underwater dredge or gold dredge, was first developed to aid divers recover placer deposits of gold which gathered in crevices on river bottoms. It has a limited function; in very shallow areas it might be the only effective excavation tool and it is useful in making test holes where sediment is no more than six feet deep. The hydrolift consists of a six-foot length of metal or plastic tube, like that on an airlift, and it is four to six inches in diameter. At the working end about a foot of the tube is bent like an elbow in a 90-degree angle. At the apex of the outside bend a water jet from a surface pump is attached. This jet is pointed straight up the centerline of the tube and forces the high-pressure water to flow along the length of the tube, creating what is known as a venturi effect, causing sediment and small objects to be sucked through the length of the tube and discharged several feet away. The spill should either be directed to fall into a screen basket, so that small artifacts can be found, or a diver should be stationed at the exhaust end of the tube to search for artifacts as they spew forth. The hydrolift can remove only one quarter as much sediment as an airlift with the same diameter tube.

The most difficult shipwreck site to excavate is one embedded in a coral matrix, like the Spanish merchantman *Matanceros* sunk in 1739, which I excavated on the coast of Yucatán. On this site the only effective excavation tools were sledge hammers and chisels to chop out the coral and extract artifacts. We usually tried to cut out pieces the size of a basketball or larger which we raised aboard the salvage vessel and later broke apart to free the artifacts they contained. In

Divers using hammers and chisels to dig artifacts out of hard coral on a shipwreck site in the Caribbean. (Credit: Walter Bennett.)

many instances we had no idea of the contents of the conglomerates until they were opened. From one twenty-pound coral clump we extracted more than two hundred individual artifacts. In most areas, parts of artifacts could be seen embedded in the surface growth, so we dug there, sometimes as deep as five feet, until there were no more artifacts. In some places the top three feet of coral had nothing, but beneath were artifacts. Large things like pewter plates and wine bottles were carefully and patiently extracted from the coral growth on the bottom because it would have been too difficult to dig out and raise a large enough section of coral to include them. During the third year of excavation on this wreck, I used three pneumatic hammers which proved quite effective. In the case of a wreck like the *Matanceros* there was no question of being able to preserve the wreck itself. The site was of no archaeological value, and our concern was to recover artifacts without damaging them. The largest pneumatic hammer was used to excavate cannon and anchors. It was 3 feet long and had an 8-inch cutting blade. Two divers were required to wear an extra fifty pounds of weights each to hold it and control the recoil. The medium hammer was only 12 inches long, with a cutting chisel 6 inches long and 2 inches wide and was used for cutting the basketball-size chunks of coral containing smaller artifacts. For excavating fragile items like brass medallions or crucifixes, the smallest pneumatic hammer, with a chisel only 4 inches long and three-quarters of an inch wide, was used. All three were standard models used in masonry work. They had no special adaptation for use underwater, although to prevent them from rusting, we immersed them in an oil bath when not in use. A standard air compressor like that used for an airlift provided power, and they were connected by the same kind of hose used on an airlift.

The overall area of the *Matanceros* site was no larger than a football field, and yet, in spite of the thousands of man hours put in over a period of years by hundreds of divers chopping into the coral, the wreck was never completely excavated. This was the most challenging and difficult wreck I have ever seen or heard of. Other wrecks fixed in coral have been easier to excavate because, in most cases, a large portion of the wreck was actually buried in sand pockets on a reef and those parts under coral were in much softer growth than that at the *Matanceros* site, so that high-pressure water jets could blast the coral apart. Explosives have been used to free wrecks from coral growth but this is reprehensible in any kind of underwater work dealing with possible archaeological material.

The most important hand tool a diver carries is a diver's knife. It has myriad uses and is particularly useful in digging around an object to speed its exposure by another excavation tool. It can pry loose objects which are attached to bedrock, ballast stones or the ship's hull. Crowbars, chisels and hammers are handy, but must be used with care. A variety of scrapers help remove coral growth from heavy objects before they are lifted to the surface. In areas where marine vegetation flourishes a sickle may be helpful in clearing an area. To recover very small things such as flecks of gold dust and tiny gem stones small tweezers or hypodermic needles are useful.

Anyone participating in an underwater excavation must be aware of what to expect. Recognition and identification of artifacts which have long lain under the sea is not simple. Many a diver has tossed away what looked like a coral-covered dark shell and lost a piece of eight that was badly sulfated and cemented to coral. The leader of an excavation has the responsibility of making sure his divers know what to look for and how to handle what they find. Small, fragile items should be placed in a jar or plastic bag and hand carried to the surface; larger items can be placed in buckets or baskets of wire mesh. Large, bulky or heavy items can be raised by pulling them aboard the vessel by lines or with lifting bags.

Lifting bags, often resembling parachutes, come in many sizes, some capable of lifting two hundred pounds and some able to raise two tons. They are attached to an object, air is injected into them, and they rise to the surface. They have to be controlled to avoid having the bag hit the bottom of the vessel overhead, in which case the air might escape and the heavy object tumble down, endangering the divers. The most common way of raising large artifacts or pieces of material is with 55-gallon fuel drums. The drums are sunk and attached by steel cables or lines to the heavy object, then filled with air until they rise to the surface. Using compressed air and fuel drums salvors operating from a small boat have been able to recover large cannon and anchors. Once on the surface, drums and objects are towed to shore, where they can be lifted out of the water.

The ballast pile of a wreck should never be dismissed as of no interest. Since many worthwhile artifacts are found mixed in with ballast stones, the most time-consuming and back-breaking chore on

Divers using a small lifting bag to raise a small grappling anchor off the sea floor.

any wreck excavation, that of moving the ballast rock, must be done thoroughly. The best way to attack a ballast pile is first to excavate all adjacent areas and then move the rock into those areas. Sending ballast rock to the surface in baskets can take months and is not really necessary if it can be moved to an already worked-over area. The most efficient way to move the ballast is with a large metal box of strong material about 10 feet wide, 6 feet long and 4 feet deep. It can be filled with ballast, lifted and moved to another area. The bottom of the container should be made so that by loosening a fitting the bottom will open and the ballast will spill out. If the surface vessel doesn't have the capability to lift such a weight, which might be several tons, smaller containers can be used and moved with the aid of lifting bags. More divers are hurt when ballast is being moved than at any other time during an underwater excavation.

Before excavation can begin a site is surveyed to determine the overall area in which material of archaeological import lies. Once the extent of a site is known, a decision can be made as to how to excavate it, or even if it can economically or realistically be excavated. The survey would also indicate where to begin and with what equipment.

In one instance failure to make a survey cost an expedition in the Bahamas a great deal of time and money. The salvors spotted a wreck site from a small plane, sighting a large number of cannon on a sandy bottom. They assumed the wreck was buried in the sand and accordingly outfitted their salvage vessel with airlifts and a prop-wash. To their dismay, they discovered that the sand was only several inches deep and that the wreck was cemented in a thick, coral matrix they couldn't excavate with the equipment they had brought.

Knowing how a site is laid out is essential in deciding where to start work. Where the spill from the excavation will be deposited must be taken into account, as well as which areas might yield the most data or artifacts. In Florida, salvors must obtain a pinpoint lease from the state government before doing any excavation. If a salvor is unaware of the limits of the site he is interested in, he is apt to find himself with a lease for an area which leaves out the most important part of what he is after. Generally a lease is given for an area consisting of a circle with a half-mile diameter. On several occasions a salvor has been frustrated at having found a

Diver placing an eigthy-pound silver bar into an iron lifting basket.

promising site only to have the best part of it lie in an adjacent area granted to someone else.

The first step in a survey is to mark all visible traces of the site. I generally do this by carrying small buoys with me underwater as a small boat follows me. After I buoy something, I immediately surface and tell the recorder in the boat what it is. He has a chart on which he plots the information. In this way even if the buoys disappear the objects can be found.

The next step is to locate all concentrations of metal. This is especially important when there are no visible traces of a wreck. A good magnetometer functions well at this when used in the same way it is to pinpoint a target. The relative sizes of the anomalies recorded give some indication of what the buried object might be: large anomalies are often cannon, anchors or iron ballast; moderate anomalies might be weapons, piles of cannonballs or large pieces of rigging; and small anomalies are usually such things as spikes,,tools, cooking utensils or solitary cannonballs. A metal detector can be used in the same way and is helpful because it detects the presence of nonferrous metals. This information is plotted on the chart and the estimated size of a buried object is included.

Generally enough information regarding the extent and nature of the site can be gained through a combination of visual, magnetometer and metal-detector surveys. However, on some sites that are completely buried and contain little or no metal, it would be necessary to use a sub-bottom profiler, a metal probe, an air probe or, in areas of coral growth, a corer. On the two St. Anne's Bay Columbus shipwrecks I used an air probe with good results: it not only established the perimeters of the site but confirmed the depths given by the sub-bottom profiling sonar, at which the wrecks lay in the sediment.

Reference points are set up to facilitate the mapping done on a survey. Buoys can be used to form a square or a rectangle, if the site is oblong. Their precise positions must be found by taking bearings on shore points or in some other way, and these bearings are plotted on a chart. Each time an object is sighted or detected, a surface buoy is placed to mark the spot, and the man in the survey boat takes compass bearings on all four reference buoys. When this information is plotted on the chart it will not only identify the outline of the site, but indicate the position of objects in relation to one another which may give some idea of the disposition of whatever is on the site.

Diver using a small, hand-held metal detector on a shipwreck site buried under coral growth.

As on a land site, the primary obligation of the archaeologist is to record all details of a site before and during the excavation. The techniques used to record will differ from site to site depending on financial resources, size of site, type of site, and the estimated volume of archaeological data and artifacts, nature of bottom, water visibility and the time available (whether the entire site will be excavated or only a small section of it). Failure to faithfully record one's findings reduces an excavation to a salvage operation and strips it of any claim as an underwater archaeological project. Once worked on, a site is destroyed, and it is only through the written reports, charts, maps and photographs of the expedition that knowledge can be shared with archaeologists, historians and the future. There are underwater archaeologists, George Bass among them, who believe that simply recording the cargo on a shipwreck site and the remains of the vessel's hull is more important than raising any of it. This may be true in cases when a ship had a homogeneous cargo such as hundreds of marble columns or thousands of the same type of amphora, but when the cargo consisted of many types of material, it should all be raised for comprehensive study before a report on the site can be written.

Many modern-day treasure hunters seldom map a site. They consider it too time-consuming and feel that any information gained would be of no use to them. They err in this, because by mapping and recording during both the survey and the excavation information about the site is revealed in addition to its outline. The pattern which pieces of a wreck make on a site can give clues to how it was sunk and why. This is important when trying to determine whether or not the wreck was salvaged previously. For example, a wreck that has remained intact for a long period is more likely to have been salvaged than a scattered one. A wreck lying on the sea floor or buried in shallow sediment was also probably salvaged soon after being lost and again later through the centuries. A wreck buried deep was probably covered over before it could have been salvaged.

It is important to map a wreck site to ascertain the size of the ship. If its approximate tonnage, size and number of cannon coincide with the record of a particular shipwreck, the wreck can be identified. Identification can also be made by measuring the length of the keel of a wreck, estimating the amount of ballast, or

An underwater archaeologist recording data on a Byzantine wreck off Turkey. (Credit: University of Pennsylvania Museum.)

recording the position of the ballast and cargo if the wreck is not badly scattered. Most shipwreck sites in the Mediterranean and some in this hemisphere retain, more or less, the shape of the original ship when the ballast and cargo remained as they were. When this has happened it is possible to distinguish between a ship of several hundred tons and one of a thousand.

Mapping or plotting the locations of major artifacts can aid salvors in other ways too. From the disposition of the various items recovered, the salvor can determine which end of the ship is the bow, which the stern. The largest anchors were normally carried on the bow of a ship, and if a ship remained fairly whole after sinking, finding these large anchors establishes the bow position.

However, this is not always true since anchors were also carried astern and sometimes several were stowed in the hold as spares. If a ship threw several overboard off her bow before wrecking, only those on the stern or in the hold may remain on the site, confusing the issue. Salvors more interested in material gain than in making a contribution to archaeology are eager to distinguish the bow from the stern because the most important treasure carried on old ships was stored in the stern castle. In many cases the most likely areas in which to find treasure on a wreck which is not too widely scattered can be determined by mapping the locations of even the smallest artifacts found. The ship's officers and the wealthier passengers lived in the stern castle. This is the area in which fine pewterware, good silver, personal items and the like are found. It would not be safe to assume that every silver plate or pewter ewer came from the stern, however. Items showing no signs of use, such as scratch marks on plates, could have been carried elsewhere in the ship as cargo.

Nothing is more frustrating than to take a first look into a newly dug hole and find a beer can thrown overboard from the salvage boat several days before when a hole was dug on the same spot. This is what happens when there is a lack of systematic mapping and excavation. Such a waste of time and duplication of effort can be avoided by keeping precise records. Unfortunately, many treasure salvors do not, but rely on intuition to decide where to excavate. This kind of hopscotching around means they often miss the best areas altogether. When a wreck is worked patiently and systematically it is a simple matter to keep track of what has already been done. Professional treasure hunters cannot, perhaps, be expected to use the more refined recording methods used by underwater archaeologists, but they can, at the very least, lay out all of their finds at the end of each day, take photographs of them, and record the locations in which they were found. Although the above procedure constitutes a rather primitive means of mapping a site, it would assist them and, more important, give a rough idea of information about the site to an interested archaeologist. In addition, the treasure salvors themselves would gain more from the excavation if they had some feeling for exactly what the ship they are working on was and some understanding of it in a historical context.

When I was mapping the *Maravilla* site on the Little Bahama Bank, I was compelled by the nature of the site to employ a system of mapping which might not meet with the approval of professional archaeologists. The site covered a large area. The ship had broken in three pieces, and the stern and main section lay more than two miles from the bow section, which we were then excavating. Even the bow section had been badly broken up and scattered over an area 600 by 900 feet with only a few traces of the wooden hull still left. Normally I would have used the grid system, but neither that nor any other orthodox mapping system was possible since the wreck lay under twenty-five feet of sand. I considered removing all the overburden first and then erecting a grid, but this would have taken years and, even then, been impossible because there is a never-ending movement of sand on the bank due to the strong currents running on it.

I decided on the following method after a thorough survey. Buoys were placed at twenty-foot intervals around the perimeter. They served as reference points both for mapping and systematically excavating this portion of the site. The excavation began in the northeast corner and progressed on a north-south heading until we reached the southern extremity. Then, we moved twenty feet farther to the west and started moving due north until the northern extremity was reached. This system ensured that we would cover every inch of the bottom. We assigned a code number to each hole dug, and the chart was marked accordingly. The overburden was removed and artifacts and bits of the wreck were exposed on the bedstone bottom. With a wide-angle lens on a still camera I was able to photograph everything in situ before anything was removed from the hole. When a large object such as a cannon or anchor was uncovered, buoys were attached directly to them and their positions reckoned by taking bearings between the buoys and several buoys on the outer perimeter of the site. Since each hole had a diameter at the bottom of about twenty-five feet, everything raised had to come from within a twelve-and-a-half-foot radius from the hole's center, the position of which we had already fixed. We recorded the major artifacts recovered from each hole, and at the end of the day were able to plot their relative positions on a chart. Later, ashore, after the photographs were developed showing what we had uncovered in each hole, I was able to produce a more accurate chart of the site and a good photographic mosaic showing the whole bottom as if it had all been exposed at the same time.

All measurements taken on underwater archaeological sites are based on the metric system, which is used for all measurement just about everywhere now except in the United States. It is easier to use, and reducing measurements taken in meters and centimeters on the bottom to plot on a chart can be done more accurately than when using feet and inches. The two basic pieces of equipment for recording are a clipboard and a grease or graphite pencil. A piece of formica makes the best clipboard. A hole can be drilled in a corner of it so that a pencil can be permanently attached. Measuring tapes or rules should be made of material not affected by salt-water corrosion.

The earliest mapping methods used on underwater archaeological sites relied on tape measurements and underwater compasses to establish the horizontal relationships between objects. Later, grid frames were introduced which are used in making vertical measurements in addition to horizontal calculations. However, a grid system can only be used efficiently on a site covering a relatively small area and should only be used when vertical measurements are relevant, which is rarely the case on Western Hemisphere shipwreck sites. In addition, the precise recording of every single item and fragment found on a badly scattered site is not essential.

The first step to be taken in the excavation of a shallow-water shipwreck is to establish a datum point, or reference center, from which all subsequent measurements will be taken. It should be located in the center of the site as determined from the preliminary survey. To make sure this point remains constant buoys should not be relied on because they are subject to shifting or loss. The best method is to drive a long metal pipe as far down into the sediment as possible. This can be done with an air probe, and after the pipe has reached bedrock the air hose is detached. The pipe should be painted yellow, which is highly visible, and have one or more brightly colored banners. As each artifact is recovered, its location in relation to the datum point can be established by using an underwater compass and its distance from the datum point can be measured. A small plastic tag with an identification number is attached to the object before it is raised. All this data is marked on a clipboard and later, after the object has been properly identified, transferred to a chart of the entire site.

A system developed by Mendel Peterson, formerly of the Smithsonian, can be used. It is based on a metal azimuth circle marked with the 360 degrees of the compass, which is mounted on a rod and driven into the center point of a site, becoming the datum point. Using an underwater compass, one lines up the azimuth circle with magnetic north. A chain or line is connected to the center of the circle and distances are marked off along its whole length. When the chain or line is stretched to an artifact, beam, etc., one diver records the bearing on the azimuth circle to the object and another diver measures the distance from the datum point. This information is recorded on a clipboard along with the object's tag number and later plotted on the site chart. This device is compact and inexpensive.

If the site covers a very large area, such as several square miles, it is gridded off on the site chart into many sections and a datum point is established in the center of each section as it is excavated. The size of each section depends in great part on the underwater visibility. If there is unlimited visibility of some two hundred feet, each section can be three hundred feet by three hundred feet; the datum point would be in the center, and all mapping done in a hundred-and-fifty-foot radius from the datum point.

Trying to map a site in murky water is at best very difficult and sometimes impossible. If the site is relatively close to shore, divers can place buoys on the major objects, and bearings can be taken from them to shore points. If this is not possible, a surface buoy placed in the middle of the site can be established as a datum point. Bearings and distance from this point to the surface buoys which mark the objects can then be taken by compass and measuring tape.

As mentioned before, taking compass bearings from a rocking boat is neither easy nor accurate. Whenever possible, bearings are taken from shore to the buoys placed on each object to be plotted. The

Diver using the azimuth circle for recording the position of finds made on a site. (Credit: Mendel Peterson.)

bearings should be taken with a surveyor's transit or theodolite, which are more precise than a compass. Radio communication is necessary between the man on shore and the vessel.

At Port Royal, I used shore markers erected by the Jamaican Survey Department and plotted on special grid charts for my use. When major finds were made, one of the team on shore reckoned the precise position of the object by taking compass bearings from three or more shore markers to the top of the airlift tube, which protruded vertically above the water right over the location of the discovery. Since stratigraphical information was of importance on this particular site, the vertical depth of the recovered item was simultaneously established by determining the length of the airlift tube remaining above the water. Taking the length of the tube, the water depth and the state of the tide into consideration, I could later compute the stratigraphical depth of an artifact and plot onto the grid charts this factor, with the horizontal position of each object.

In clear water in the Mediterranean, underwater archaeologists often prefer using a system of triangulation for plotting positions of objects excavated. Although this is a more accurate means of measurement, it requires a larger number of workers and is much more time-consuming. A simple device called a plane table, similar to a surveyor's transit, can be used. It has two units: a form of underwater drawing table and a sighting device. The sighting tube is of plastic or metal pipe, about 10 inches long and 2 inches in diameter. Two wires are stretched at both ends of the tube, crossing each other and resembling a telescopic gunsight without magnification. The sighting device is mounted on a base plate and a mark is made on the front end of the plate corresponding to the line of sight of the device. A pipe or something connected to the bottom of the base plate is fitted into a hole in the middle of the drawing table in such a way that it can rotate 360 degrees. An azimuth circle or protractor marked off in degrees is then attached or painted on the top of the table so that the sighting device and base plate are enclosed inside of it.

In normal operation three plane tables are used at once. They are placed in a pattern forming a triangle and their precise positions are established and plotted on the site chart. North on the azimuth circle is lined up with magnetic north on an underwater compass before the table is weighted down so it cannot be moved during the operation. A diver with a range pole, usually a plastic or metal pipe 2 meters long and graduated in sections of 10 centimeters using alternate red and white paint, positions himself directly over

A plane table being used in triangulation or plotting of finds made on a site.

the object to be mapped, holding a numbered identification tag. The operators of the three plane tables then sight onto the range pole and the bearing from each position is obtained by noting where the mark on the base plate either points to or touches the azimuth circle. The number tag is then attached to the object and the diver moves to another object and the process is repeated. When the information is plotted on the site chart, it will give the accurate position of everything mapped.

Providing that both the table and sighting device are perfectly level, this method can also furnish the datum height or elevation level of objects in relation to one another or to a fixed horizontal level for the whole site. At the same time that each operator is sighting to establish the horizontal position of the object, by recording where the cross hairs line up on the range pole, the elevation level can be ascertained. To calibrate this information one must know the depth of the water, the precise depth at which the sighting device was used, and the measurement on the range pole so that the difference between the top of the object and the line of sight of the sighting device can be established.

Another way to find the datum level of an object is with the AquaLevel, which is a simple device operated by two divers. A transparent plastic hose about half an inch thick, the length to depend on the extent of the site and the clarity of the water, is the main tool. One diver fills it with air and the air-water interface of one end of the hose is held by a diver on the object selected to be the datum level, generally the highest object on the site. The hose, which is buoyant because of the entrapped air, forms an arc, and the opposite end of it is held by another diver holding a range pole vertically over the object to be measured. The position of the air-water interface on the range pole then indicates the elevation difference between the two points. This system is especially useful when trying to map the contours or curvature of a ship's hull.

Rarely is wood found on shallow-water shipwrecks, except parts of the ship's bottom and parts of her ribs and planking up to the turn of the bilge. Accurate measurements of these portions are useful for historians and should be made whenever possible even if they appear fragmentary. Mendel Peterson used a special device for this with success on a number of shipwreck sites off Bermuda. He describes it as follows:

Utilizing the keel, or keelson, of the ship and the foundation, a cantilever frame is attached by self-leveling brackets. A theoretical plane is then established with a sighting device [plane table] and datum rods are set at each corner of the site with permanent marks recording this plane. These remain in place during the whole measuring operation index on the datum rods. The cantilever frame is then set at the standard height established by the sighting device. Attached to this frame is a rack in which ride at six-inch intervals measuring rods scaled in inches. This rack is set over each ship's timber starting at one end and progressing along the ship's remains. At each timber the rack is leveled with the beam [of the ship] and anchored. The measuring rods are then lowered to contact the frame of the ship and readings taken directly from the rods. In this manner the curvature of each ship's frame is established. If the ship has ceiling on the frames, the measurements of the frames are taken at the surface of the ceiling and its thickness is taken into consideration in making the readings. After the inner curves of the frame are read, the ceiling is removed and the curves of the outer edges of the frames are read by measuring to the inner surface of the planking alongside each timber. If the ship has no ceiling, these measurements may be made as those of the inner curvature of the frames are read. All vertical

A gunport from a Dutch shipwreck that sank in 1628 off the coast of Australia. Note the good state of preservation it is in. (Credit: Western Australian Museum.)

measurements are thus made from the theoretical plane established at the beginning of the operation with the sighting device.

Frederic Dumas, the noted French underwater archaeologist, developed a device for measuring in three dimensions. This tool can be used on a site in which both horizontal and vertical measurements are desired throughout the course of an excavation when different stratigraphical levels are reached. An instance of this would be a deepwater Mediterranean shipwreck site in which the ship's remains are still in situ and the cargo some feet off the bottom, such as an amphora carrier containing a number of layers of amphorae.

Dumas's device consists of a square metal frame, 3 by 3 meters, with graduated sides marked off in centimeters. The frame is mounted on adjustable legs. A horizontal bar, also graduated, slides across the frame at right angles to two sides and to this is attached a graduated rod with a vertical motion, serving as a plumb line. This rod can be moved back and forth across the bar as well as up and down. After it is placed over an object or section of the site, the entire device is made precisely horizontal by means of a spirit level and its position recorded. When the tip of the vertical rod is positioned so that it touches an object,

Diver using a device for measuring the size and shape of ship's timbers on a wreck site in Bermuda. (Credit: Mendel Peterson.)

three measurements are attained at once. The elevation of the object is reckoned from the position of the rod touching it, and the horizontal position is obtained by recording where the rod is positioned on the horizontal bar and where the horizontal bar is positioned on the two sides of the frame. After one square area has been recorded in this manner, the frame is swivelled on one leg and the process repeated. This is probably the best system to use when there are a limited number of workers on an excavation project.

When sufficient funds and personnel are available and the time factor is not crucial, the use of the grid system to record cannot be bettered on both shipwreck and sunken settlement sites. No other method can furnish more archaeological data. The grids are laid out in squares, generally 3 to 5 meters on each side and subdivided by wire or stout cord into smaller squares of a meter each. Each grid has four adjustable or telescopic legs mounted at its corners, so the squares can be arranged perfectly horizontal on an irregular bottom. The best material for making the grid frames is three-quarter-inch PVC tubing. All members forming the square frame are calibrated into known subdivisions using varying colors of paint, and all four corners of the frame bear an identification code, normally a letter and a numeral. The total number of grid squares depends, of course, on the overall extent of the site.

The grid-square system is effective on sites like Mediterranean deep-water sites, or even shallow ones, where the upper part of a shipwreck is visible on the sea floor or where a wreck is buried under no more than a few feet of sediment. It is not feasible on sites like Port Royal which are more deeply covered over. I attempted using it there, but as soon as I dug down a few feet into the sediment, the grid square moved out of position and slid into the deeper section. When a prop-wash is used as an excavation tool, a grid pattern can only be set up using heavy chain firmly anchored to the sea floor because the lightweight grid squares normally used would be blown out of position by the prop-wash.

Bass and Throckmorton were the first to use the grid system. This was on a Byzantine shipwreck located in 120 feet of water at Yassi Ada, Turkey, in 1961. The site was only 30 by 70 feet but was covered thickly by seaweed which they had to remove with wire brushes. Once the site was cleared, each visible object (in this case all amphorae) had a plastic numbered tag attached. The men attempted to use the plane-table system but it failed because it required too much coordination between the divers, and the water became too murky as they moved about. They then tried Dumas's measuring device, but found it too clumsy in trying to maintain a horizontal position on a bottom paved with amphorae.

They then covered the site with 3-meter grid squares on which wires 10 centimeters apart were strung like a tennis racket. It took the team more than two weeks to place the grid framework. Then, relays of divers in two-man teams armed with clipboards, pencils and carpenter's rules made measurements and drawings of what they observed in each grid square. The drawings and data were turned over to an architect, who plotted the information on an overall chart of the site. After each section of the wreck had been measured and plotted, the amphorae were removed. Only about one hundred of the more than one thousand amphorae on the wreck were raised. The others were moved to a zone off the site. During the last few weeks of the season, they used two airlifts and uncovered a small area of the site to determine if any wood from the hull had been preserved and were pleased to discover that some had.

Bass was not satisfied with the methods used that summer. He felt making the underwater drawings had been too time-consuming, so he devised a new system, using underwater photography. The following summer they spent the first month constructing a scaffolding of angle iron over the whole wreck area, stepped to accommodate the slope of the bottom, with squares spaced 2 meters apart, each leveled horizontally. Two portable photographic towers of light metal, each 13 feet high, could then be bolted to each grid. A camera mounted on the tower took photographs from the same elevation and angle, so that the inherent distortion remained constant and could be compensated for accordingly. The photographic records were transferred to a scale drawing and provided accurate measurements.

Improvements were also made in the airlifts. The previous summer the discharge end of the tube was attached to the surface barge with the result that everyone aboard was continually wet from the water gushing aboard. The discharge end was now held down some 50 feet below the surface, with a wire basket on top which funneled down into a cloth bag. The current carried away about 95 percent of the mud and sand and anything larger, such as a sea shell or small artifact, was deposited in the bag. When it was full, the bag was changed and brought to the surface for examination. Team members spent hours each day going through the muck. Occasionally they found interesting artifacts as well as some gold coins. When each of the gridded areas had been accurately plotted and all visible material removed, the airlifts were used to excavate to a lower stratigraphical level. Normally they went down only a few inches at a time, recording and photographing new material as it came to light. The actual excavation of the site, with divers using the airlifts, accounted for one half of the total one thousand man-hours spent on the bottom.

After all of the cargo had been uncovered and removed, they began finding traces of the ship itself. The wood was so fragile that they used their hands gently to fan away the sand, resorting to the airlift only when there was a pile of sand to remove. The wood tended to float off once free of the sand because the iron nails which once held it had long since corroded. To keep the wood in place so it could be tagged, photographed and later brought to the surface, bicycle spokes were used to pin it to the bottom.

Although underwater photography had cut short the time spent measuring and drawing on the bottom, it only gave a two-dimension plan, and the divers still had to spend a lot of time recording elevations with a weighted meter tape. That winter Bass read a report by Dimitri Rebikoff concerning his experiments with underwater stereophotography, in which he claimed that a shipwreck could be accurately measured photogrammetrically.

The third season on the Byzantine wreck began with Bass and an enlarged team experimenting with the new method of photogrammetrically mapping and measuring the wreck to end the need for divers to make measurements or drawings underwater. A bar was held horizontally over the site, attached to two floats held at a constant height off the bottom. A stereo camera, weighted so it hung level from gimbals, was slid along the bar by a diver who snapped a series of overlapping pictures. The resulting photographs were then matched as stereo pairs, and when their parallax differences were measured with a micrometer, the distance of any object under the bar could be calculated. Thus, both planimetric and elevation measurements were obtained without the time-consuming hand measurements.

The excavation of the site went slowly because of the fragility of such ancient wood. Bass had hoped that the entire wreck might be

Diver surfacing with two Greek amphoras found at Byblos, Lebanon. Although the water was quite dirty, the use of a wide-angle lens permitted this photograph to be taken.

uncovered during the season, but they found the wreck extended farther up under the sand slope on which it had come to rest than they had previously realized. Most of the summer was spent removing this new deposit of sand, which was so thickly bound together by seaweed roots that it had to be hewn out in large blocks with knives and carried away by hand. Four iron anchors and quantities of amphorae were uncovered in this new area. While teams of divers concentrated on fanning away the sand covering parts of the ship's hull, others worked near the stern of the wreck with airlifts. In this area they recovered five pitchers, two cooking pots, eight oil lamps, fragments of glass bottles, a stone pestle, lead fishing weights, a lead sounding weight and thirty copper and five gold coins. They also found an additional one-hundred-fifty nondescript concretions which yielded axes, a hoe, a shovel, a billhook, knives, hammers, files, dividers, brace bits, chisels and other tools.

By the middle of the summer they realized that enough of the ship's wood was left to be able to reconstruct the ship on paper, timber by timber, to above its waterline. In places where the ribs were missing, they could still trace them from the remaining nail holes which had left rusty deposits in the sediment. After all of the wood had been uncovered, tagged and photographed in situ, it was at last raised from the site. Since it was so fragile, the wood was not lifted as the amphorae had been, but with a wire basket, 18 feet long and capable of holding the largest of the ship's timbers. After gently placing the wood in the basket, divers in tennis shoes walked the basket up the slope to an island about a hundred yards away and 120 feet above the site. The wood was placed in specially constructed water tanks on the island for examination and preservation.

The monumental task of reconstructing the Byzantine ship on paper fell to Frederick van Doorninck. With unbelievable patience he was able to piece together all data and brilliantly recreate most of the ship from the keel to the deck beams. When he was through, history had been well served and they had the first accurate picture of such a ship. She was between 60 and 70 feet long, had a beam of about 17 feet and was capable of carrying 50 tons of cargo. In appearance the Byzantine ship closely resembled the ship built by Ulysses as described in the *Odyssey*. The final step in the construction of Ulysses' boat had been to fill it with brushwood. This long puzzled scholars who wondered what purpose it served. On the Byzantine wreck they discovered that brushwood had been placed inside the hull to protect the hull planking from heavy cargo.

Bass was still not completely satisfied. He wanted to find wrecks in which still more of the original hulls were preserved. He was sure that such wrecks lie in depths beyond divers' reach. As a result of surveys Throckmorton had made in Turkey and Greece, Bass knew that fishermen had brought up many artifacts snagged in deep water. The problem was that they pulled the nets for several miles on each drag and couldn't be sure of exactly where they snagged anything. Bass felt the problem of locating these deep wrecks could be solved with a small submarine. Grants from the Office of Naval Research and the National Science Foundation financed a two-man submarine, the *Asherah*, which was launched in May 1964. It was 16 feet long, weighed four and a half tons, could reach a depth of 1,000 feet, cruise at 4 knots and remain submerged for 35 hours. It was equipped with six viewing portholes and two powerful 500-watt strobe lights to provide sufficient light for two stereo cameras. The *Asherah* had the maneuverability of a fish provided by two side-mounted electrically powered propellers, which could be rotated separately or jointly. Thus, it could go straight up or down, forward or backward or hover in one spot like a helicopter.

When Bass and the team returned to Yassi Ada in the summer of 1964, the divers used airlifts to excavate around the outside perimeters of the Byzantine shipwreck site to make sure they hadn't missed anything and found only a few ceramic shards. While the divers were doing this, Bass decided to test the *Asherah* by mapping the visible remains of a Roman shipwreck, several centuries older than the Byzantine wreck and lying only 200 yards from it in 140 feet of water. This wreck also had a large cargo of amphorae, stacked in rows and seemingly undisturbed. Bass and another team member watched as the powerful strobe lights flashed rhythmically while the *Asherah* made only two passes and mapped the entire wreck. The photographs were developed that night and sufficed to make a complete and accurate map of the whole wreck area. Although 56 hours of laboratory work were needed to analyze the photographs and calculate the elevation measurements, the little submarine had accomplished in less than a day what had taken nearly twenty people three months to do on the Byzantine wreck.

The submarine was used to search in deeper water for the shipwreck site from which a fisherman had snagged a bronze statue

The two-man submarine Asherah, *with two stereo cameras used for mapping underwater archaeological sites. (Credit: University of Pennsylvania Museum.)*

of a Negro boy. Neither that summer nor the following did they find that site, and Bass concluded side-scan sonar would be the only way to locate it.

The Byzantine wreck had taken four summers to excavate at an approximate cost of one hundred thousand dollars. Bass felt that the next excavation he undertook, which was to be the Roman wreck mapped by the *Asherah*, would have to be completed in one season and at half the cost of the other. This meant squeezing more hours of work on the bottom in each day and getting more work done in those hours. One way to accomplish this was to have more divers and have them spend more time underwater each day. Since the Roman wreck lay in 140 feet of water, 20 feet deeper than the other, the diving time would normally be reduced. Bass looked into the various techniques for prolonging time underwater such as the use of mixed gases, underwater habitats and submersible decompression chambers, but they were all too expensive. He finally decided to have each diver make one dive per day of 50 minutes' duration, not including decompression time before surfacing. A diver would have to make stops of 3 minutes at 40 feet, 19 minutes at 30 feet, 26 at 20 feet and 62 at 10 feet.

The *Asherah* greatly reduced the amount of time previously spent in mapping and measuring, but there remained the tedious work of uncovering the wreck and cargo. The airlift worked efficiently, but once the divers reached the level of the ship's hull on the Byzantine wreck, they had to fan away sand by hand and it had all settled a short distance away. Piles of sand accumulated on the wreck in various spots and had to be swept away. Thus, the same sand was undoubtedly moved a number of times. To avoid this while working on the Roman wreck, Bass planned to make a large trench around the entire wreck using a big, 12-inch-diameter airlift mounted on a trolley on rails running around the site. Hydrolifts and water jets would be used to move the sand off the wreck into the trench where it would be sucked up by the airlift and carried away by the current high above.

Another phase of the operation that had been slow during excavation of the Byzantine wreck was removal of the amphorae. Since they were usually filled with sand or mud and quite heavy, a diver could rarely move more than five or six in the course of a dive. To resolve this, he devised a flatbed vehicle on four wheels, which could hold as many as a hundred amphorae and was pulled by a cable running to a winch on the nearby island. However, when they tested this system it was unworkable; because of the combined weight, the vehicle and the amphorae sunk deeper into the sediment, reducing underwater visibility. They replaced the flat bed with a large basket which could hold 20 amphorae at a time; when full, it was raised to the surface by a lifting bag.

Bass with a crew of forty-five arrived in June of 1967 and his improved methods of operation worked so well that in less than a month most of the cargo of amphorae had been removed and the wood of the ship's hull began to appear. The condition of the hull was far better than that of the Byzantine wreck, both the inner hull lining and outer hull planks attached to solid ribs. The divers were excavating along the hull, where they expected to find the ship's cabin and galley, when they made an astonishing discovery: resting right on top of the cabin and galley section of their Roman wreck were the remains of another, more recent, ship, probably Islamic and dating from the fourteenth or fifteenth century. They had to immediately shift their attention to the new find and with airlifts and metal detectors they traced it and found it almost reached the area where the Byzantine ship had lain. Thus, three shipwrecks, spanning centuries, had come to grief and settled almost on top of one another.

The following summer Bass concentrated all his efforts on finding a deep-water wreck using side-scan sonar. In the area where the bronze Negro boy had been found, they located a wreck in 285 feet of water. The *Asherah* was used to identify the site, which turned out to be a Roman merchant galley. To date, it has never been excavated because of its depth and the cost of such an operation.

George Bass was fortunate in being able to raise substantial sums, such as the $750,000 it cost to build the *Asherah*, for his work off Turkey. He is an exception in a field where most projects are carried out on limited budgets. Many underwater archaeologists, like Nicholas Flemming, can only spend several thousand dollars for each month of excavation. They must invent new and economical approaches to their work, improvise equipment and often rely on volunteer help. Instead of making grid squares of aluminum or angle iron, one can make them of stout cord or even cheap rope. Instead of mounting stereo cameras on expensive submarines, the first method Bass used of mounting cameras on the horizontal bar over the site works just as well, even though it takes more time. Since each year underwater photography is being employed in new and different ways to record pertinent archaeological data on sites, everyone working on an underwater site should have a basic working knowledge of photography.

Underwater photography had its beginning in 1893, when Louis Bouton, a Frenchman, took the first pictures under the sea. Today, the chief activity of most sport divers is underwater photography. Cameras range in price from twenty dollars to five thousand. Some cameras are encased in waterproof housings and others have been specially built for underwater. Most of the photography required on a site can be done with the Nikonos, a small, compact, underwater 35-mm still camera manufactured by Nikon and widely used all over the world by divers. It costs approximately six hundred dollars. On sites where the grid system is used and the squares are perfectly square, a 35-mm camera will not work because the film produces a rectangular negative. Instead a camera, such as the Rolliflex, which produces a $2^1/4$ by $2^1/4$ negative, should be used. A special housing called a Rollimarine is available to enclose this camera, but it is a great deal bulkier than the Nikonos and difficult to maneuver with underwater. The choice of film depends on light conditions. Black-and-white film is generally the best for recording or mapping because prints cost far less than color.

Daylight can penetrate sea water to great depths, at least in transparent waters in the Caribbean and Mediterranean. Dr. William Beebe, during one of his dives in the bathysphere, found daylight reflecting off the sea floor in 1,600 feet of water. Even the cleanest sea water appears somewhat cloudy because of suspended plankton or mineral particles. To overcome this cloudy effect, the camera should be used as close as possible to the subject and with a wide-angle lens in most cases. A rule of thumb is that if the underwater visibility is sixty feet, one should not shoot a photograph more than one-fourth this distance, or fifteen feet, from the subject.

The best time to shoot underwater pictures is on a clear, non-windy day between 10:00 a.m. and 2:00 p.m. when the sunlight most deeply penetrates the water. The blue-green color of the water acts as a filter, absorbing colors at the red end of the spectrum. At only ten feet below the surface red is considerably reduced in intensity. Orange and yellow are the next colors absorbed as the water gets deeper. For black-and-white photography this is not much of a problem, but in using color film, one should partially compensate for the lack of warm colors by using a red filter over the camera lens. However, below thirty feet the filter is ineffective because red is totally absorbed by the water.

The type of day, angle of the sun, depth of the subject, turbulence of the water, amount of material and type of sea bottom all affect choice of exposure. Cameras with automatic exposure control are simple to operate, but for better results, an exposure meter ought to be used and a reading taken close to the subject before backing away to snap the picture. It is always a good idea to bracket each photograph by taking one shot a stop slower and one a stop faster than the meter indicates.

Underwater objects appear slightly magnified and seem to be one-fourth closer than their actual distance. This means that a lens of normal focal length will produce a slight telephoto effect underwater. If the camera has a range finder or ground-glass focusing like the Rolliflex, the correct focusing scale can be set underwater as it is on land. However, in using a camera without a range finder, like the Nikonos, one must set the focus for about three-fourths the actual distance between the camera and the subject to eliminate the magnification effect underwater. For example, in photographing a cannon eight feet away, the camera focus is set at six feet.

When underwater visibility is limited it may be necessary to use artificial light. All underwater cameras are adapted for either use with flash bulbs or electronic strobe units. However, the light fall-off from artificial lighting underwater is great because of the water density and, for all practical purposes, lighting should not be more than twelve feet from the subject. If a photograph must be taken from a greater distance, a light source such as a slave strobe unit can be placed closer to the subject. Powerful lighting units connected to surface power sources are most effective in such cases.

Reasonably good underwater photographs can even be taken on sites where there is poor visibility. Photographs have been made when visibility was measured in inches or was nil. In 1959 Louis Marden was doing photographic coverage for the *National Geographic* at Port Royal. Unable to get any shots at all because of the opacity of the water, he constructed a large glass box, 12 feet wide, 10 feet high and 6 feet deep. After filling it with clear fresh water, he sunk it next to the walls of various sunken buildings and by shooting through it he was able to get good pictures. Frederick Dumas devised a similar system for photographing in dark turbid water. He fashioned a transparent, truncated pyramid whose top facet is at a slightly wider angle than the lens of the camera. Its height and width are sufficient to cover a reasonable area of the bottom. The top and bottom portions are of glass and the sides of light, transparent, unbreakable plastic. It is filled with clear water on the surface, sealed, carried down and positioned over the area to be photographed. This method was used recently with rewarding results on a lake site in Switzerland: the bottom of the pyramid was 2 meters square to fit over grid squares of this size which were used on the site.

Film is one of the least expensive tools used on an underwater archaeological project. A photographic record of everything uncovered should be made while the objects are still in situ as different stratigraphical layers are reached. Photography is a fast way to record the position of elements on a site and if properly used can be accurate.

While working on the site of a Greek shipwreck in the Bay of Cadiz some years ago, I mapped the entire site covering 120 by 60 feet in two days. The wreck had been uncovered during a severe storm and her cargo of amphorae and miscellaneous objects was exposed on the bedrock bottom. The wreck site lay on a north-south axis in 30 feet of water and the visibility was about 80 feet. I first strung out taut lines running east and west over the site at an elevation so they almost touched the highest points on the site and spaced them about 10 feet apart. Numbered plastic tags were attached at 5-foot intervals along the lines, so each photograph could be identified and fitted together to make a mosaic of the entire site. For less than ten dollars I constructed an angle-iron photographic tower about 15 feet high, on which a wide-angle lens camera was mounted. From this elevation each photograph I shot covered a width of 15 feet and overlapped the grid lines on both the top and bottom of the picture. The tower was moved from position to position, always overlapping some of the area in the previous shot. I covered the whole site and when the photographs were blown up and cropped to fit each other, they made up an excellent mosaic record of the site.

A photographic mosaic of a shipwreck site, especially when it is in a compact area or is one on which some parts of the wooden hull remain, can be useful in trying to determine the type, size and sometimes the nationality and identity of the ship. Experts on old ship construction can deduce a great deal from an accurate photographic record of this type. Mosaics can be made during different phases of the excavation, but the most important will be those taken when the site has been completely uncovered and the anchors, cannon, ballast, wood and other remaining features and objects can be seen in relation to one another. A fast and efficient method of making a site mosaic and one which is not too expensive, is to use a *Pegasus*, or some other type of underwater vehicle like a scooter, with a pulse camera mounted on it. A pulse camera is one that can be set to take photographs automatically at preset intervals. Regular cameras can be fitted with a device which permits automatic interval shooting. The focal width of the camera lens and the clarity of the water will determine the elevation above the site from which the photographs should be taken and the total number required. In making a complete mosaic of a Spanish galleon wreck site which encompassed an area 200 by 100 feet, only fourteen individual photographs were required. This was because of good underwater visibility and the depth of the site, which averaged 30 feet, so that the pictures were shot with a wide-angle lens 25 feet over the site.

Hand-held cameras can be used to make a mosaic, but they must be held at a constant elevation over the site by a diver who swims a

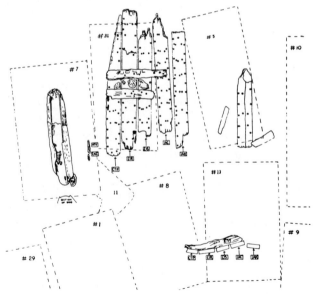

Drawing made of the remains of timbers on a Roman shipwreck located off Italy. (Credit: Peter Throckmorton.)

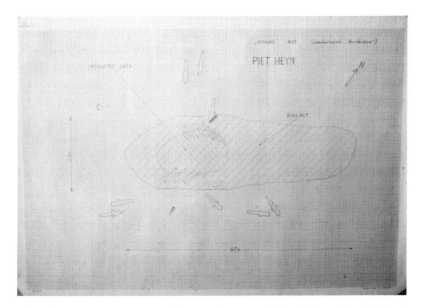

Excavation sketch of the remains of the Hollandia, *which sank in 1627, off Salvador, Brazil.*

straight course. If not, the mosaic will not be accurate and the photographs will be difficult to piece together. A vehicle like the *Pegasus* eliminates the difficulties a diver on his own would encounter, since it has a complete navigational system and can be flown at a constant depth and maintained on a straight course.

If a hand-held camera is used to photograph objects on the bottom from close range (less than ten feet away), the photographs will have some distortion unless the camera is held exactly vertical over the subject. This is no easy feat when a diver is swimming and trying to hold a position. However, by attaching a plumb line with a weight from the side of the camera, the diver can note when the line stops swinging and almost touches the object and then shoot.

When underwater photographs must be made on a horizontal plane of objects which protrude relatively high off the bottom, such as walls or other structures or a ballast pile, some of which stick up as high as fifteen feet, the photographer always shoots with the sun at his back to eliminate shadows on the subject. This can be done by selecting a time of day when the sun is in the right position or by using artificial light.

6

Dating and
Identification

The dating and identification of objects recovered from an underwater archaeological site is challenging and time-consuming. Many sites, especially those in harbors and bays, are badly contaminated, presenting special problems. At Port Royal, for example, objects less than fifty years old were recovered at a lower stratigraphic depth than those from the 1692 earthquake. This happened because for hundreds of years ships had anchored on the site; their anchors plowed the sea floor, dredging up long-buried objects and allowing things on the surface of the bottom to fall into the furrow. Salvors worked on some shipwrecks years, or even centuries, after the vessel was lost and their debris, bottles, clay pipes, crockery, etc., mixed in with older items. On ceremonial sites in lakes or springs, the heaviest objects usually sink through the soft silt to the very bottom, whereas lighter articles like pottery or bones stay on the surface or close to it.

Trying to establish a date or identity of an artifact through reference books and papers is sometimes helpful, particularly for items about which a great deal has been published, but one must often turn to other sources. Even with a library of several thousand books and scientific reports on history and archaeology, I realized long ago I

174

would never be able to identify and date the thousands of assorted items I have found on underwater sites. To avoid error, I consult specialists for verification.

When dealing with artifacts about which little or nothing has been written, I rely solely on the help of experts. In some cases even they are unable to identify something. For some subjects there is a lack of expertise or interest. Ship's pumps, fastenings, lead shipping seals and sewing thimbles are examples of things about which little has been written. This is especially true of items which changed little in form from era to era.

There are thousands of experts on subjects ranging from the identification of buttons to ancient monolithic structures such as are found in sunken cities. Most of these men and women are happy to help identify and date objects recovered from underwater. In most cases a descriptive letter accompanied by several good photographs with the scale shown is enough to send to such a person. However,

Brass button from the uniform of an artillery officer, c. 1690.

if laboratory analyses are necessary, as in the case of a ballast stone or a bone sent to a geologist and paleontologist, then the object must be carefully packed and sent with a detailed letter to the expert who has agreed to examine it.

The first people to get in touch with are those at local and state museums and professional archaeologists at universities and colleges. If they are unable to help, they generally suggest an expert who may. The Smithsonian Institute in Washington, D.C., has specialists in almost every field associated with objects found on underwater sites in the Western Hemisphere. Many other institutions have resource people who may assist in identification. These include the Peabody Museum in Cambridge, Massachusetts, with specialists in pre-Columbian artifacts from Central and South America; the Corning Glass Museum in Corning, New York, with specialists in historical glassware; the Colonial Williamsburg Foundation, Williamsburg, Virginia, with specialists in Colonial artifacts; and in England, the British Museum, the Victoria and Albert Museum and the Science Museum, all in London and able to provide information on most artifacts of European origin. Many countries have national museums staffed with experts who can be consulted about indigenous objects. Often a letter to the director of the Smithsonian in Washington will get one started in the right direction. If the Smithsonian does not have the information one seeks, they can indicate who might.

Before discussing the identification and dating of items by means of their physical appearance, I shall mention the various scientific methods that can sometimes be used to determine origin or age of articles found underwater. Few of these methods can be used by the archaeologist himself. They require scientific expertise and special equipment. Consulting a specialist in no way detracts from an archaeologist's work. He remains responsible for interpreting the results of any scientific analyses of material he has excavated and for fitting the entire picture together.

Recently when an archaeologist excavated a spring in Florida containing human bones more than ten thousand years old, he consulted a number of specialists. Paleontologists examined the bones and were able to provide clues about the physical appearance of the people who once lived there. Botanists, through microscopic examinations of seeds found in the spring along with pollen samples and other surviving vegetable matter, helped to build a picture of the flora ten thousand years ago, and zoologists examined all recovered faunal material to identify the coexistent animals.

On submerged settlements of early man, the only way recovered objects can be dated is through scientific laboratory methods. The age of an object which was buried can be calculated in two ways: by dating either the object itself or the geological stratum in which it was embedded. Until recently, sedimentary strata were dated by comparison of fossilized fauna with similar finds elsewhere. With the introduction of radioactive dating such as the Carbon-14 process, there is less of a margin of error or uncertainty. Other new and highly sophisticated techniques have been developed such as spectrography, x-ray defraction and x-ray fluorescence, which can analyze precisely the composition of trace materials and classify the object's age and origin. Raw materials were seldom imported in the first days of civilization; men made do with what was around them. The workshops of antiquity specialized, each manufacturing particular items which can today often be identified. As techniques developed from generation to generation, a chronology was established which can be used to date the artifacts and find their origin.

Radiocarbon, or Carbon-14, dating is the most widely used method of chronometric dating. It was introduced and gained acceptance among archaeologists in the late 1950s. It can only be used on organic material such as wood, bone, peat, charcoal, shell and plants, and is not too accurate or helpful in dating items less than five hundred years old. This method was conceived by the nuclear physicist W. F. Libby, who discovered that all organic material absorbs Carbon-14 from the earth's atmosphere until it dies and that this absorption ceases and disintegrates at a known rate with the passage of time. By measuring the amount of Carbon-14 remaining in a piece of organic material, scientists can determine the length of time elapsed since it died. Only small samples are needed for analysis. If something was discovered in water, it must be kept wet until the tests are made. Many universities have facilities for Carbon-14 dating and a number of commercial laboratories also do it. The average price per sample is approximately a hundred and fifty dollars and the procedure takes from two to six weeks.

The older the sample, the more precise the date will usually be. For something dating from 11,000 B.C., the date established will have a plus or minus figure of 550 years. Yet, for objects dating between 2,500 and 300 years there is a plus or minus factor of 150 years. In using this system to date material only a few centuries old, there is too great an uncertainty to make it worthwhile. Recently I submitted a wood sample from a shipwreck and received a date of 1520, plus or minus 150 years. This meant the wood could date anywhere from 1370 to 1670, which was no help at all. Perhaps in the case of a suspected counterfeit artifact a Carbon-14 test might be valuable in establishing whether the item, a bone tool, for example, was modern or not. When Carbon-14 is used on objects many thousands of years old, the plus or minus factor is of little significance. In the case of a shipwreck, the date established by this process may bear no relationship to the actual date of the shipwreck. The vessel may have been decades old; some were used as long as fifty years. The ambiguous date would relate to the time the tree was cut. There are many instances when a ship was constructed from the timbers of an even older ship. Other articles such as bone or charcoal found on a wreck are preferable as samples since they date to within a few years of the loss of the ship.

A more definite method for determining the date and origin of wood samples is through the relatively new science of dendrology. Experts in this field cannot only identify the kind of wood and its country of origin, but in many cases even narrow it down to what part of a country the wood came from. This information is an aid in establishing where a ship was built and was one of the ways the two Columbus wrecks in St. Anne's Bay were positively identified. Dendrologists are also able to date most wood samples precisely by dating tree rings. The ring pattern of a tree reflects climatic conditions prevailing during its life span. Catalogues of tree-ring patterns have been compiled stretching back for thousands of years. For ships built in Western Europe this method has restricted application. It can only be used if the origin of the wood is known, since the climate fluctuated so much over the centuries that the ring patterns for various regions are quite different. In the United States the best source for this type of wood analysis is the Dendrology Laboratory of the University of Arizona.

Botanists can help identify the origin of vegetable material found on an underwater site. I recovered several black beans from a test core on the Columbus wreck site which botanists were able to identify as a type grown only in Spain. On another occasion a botanist identified several tobacco leaves I found on a shipwreck as coming from Venezuela, thus helping me identify the shipwreck. Geologists are often able to identify the place of origin of ballast rock. Knowing where a ship's ballast stones are from, one knows in most cases where the ship was from, provided they were not picked up in a foreign port.

Zoologists can identify animal, fish and fowl bones. While excavating a shipwreck near Jamaica, I found a great many fish bones mixed in with the ballast. At the time I assumed they were either from local fish that had died or, much more likely, the remains of meals eaten by the ship's crew. The latter case proved correct when a marine zoologist identified a selection of bones as a North Sea herring. This information combined with the great number of Dutch objects on the site identified the wreck as a Dutch merchantman.

Scientists specializing in metallography can use atomic absorption spectrography and other means to determine the exact origin of the minerals and metal alloys in metal artifacts or objects such as ore pieces. This will not necessarily establish the nationality of a sunken ship, but can help. This is especially helpful when metal fastenings were used in a ship's construction, since fittings were normally manufactured near the source of the raw materials, which, in turn, was near the shipyard. If a ship carried a cargo of pig iron or silver bars, copper or fool's gold, metallographers can determine their origin.

The Corning Glass Museum has conducted extensive research in methods of identifying and dating glassware. Throughout history, various methods have been used to make glass, and through scientific analysis the place of manufacture of most glassware can be traced. Several years ago, Dr. Robert Brill of the Corning staff developed a way of precisely dating glass recovered from the sea. By counting the number of layers of weathering crust on a glass fragment under a powerful microscope, he can establish how long it was underwater. I have submitted a number of samples of glassware from dated shipwrecks to him and his findings have always been accurate to within a year or two.

Ceramic and clay items like building bricks which were kiln-fired can be dated by two methods. Thermoluminescence is a process based on the fact that radioactivity from certain isotopes is trapped in the clay until the object is fired. The firing releases the electrons in a thermoluminescent glow. When the clay cools, the electrons are again trapped but continue to increase with the process of decay, and the number of electrons released increases with time.

By measuring the number of electrons remaining in the clay, its date can be fixed fairly accurately.

Archaeomagnetic dating, the other method for dating clay, is based on the knowledge that the intensity and direction of the earth's magnetic field varies over the years. Clay contains magnetic minerals such as hematite and magnetite and when it is heated or fired these minerals will assume the direction and proportional intensity of the magnetic field that surrounds them and continue to hold it after cooling. By measuring these quantities, the age of a clay piece can be reckoned if the changes in the earth's magnetic field are known for the location where the piece was fired.

In some instances, such as when samples are collected during the initial survey of a site, it is desirable to identify and date objects quickly. One might not have access to a large reference library or be able to wait weeks or months for a specialist's reply. The remainder of this chapter, therefore, is a rough, incomplete guide to the identification of certain objects commonly found on underwater sites.

Many problems are associated with properly identifying and dating a site, however, a shipwreck site is by far the easiest. The more material one finds, the better the chances for establishing a positive identification and date. Artifacts contaminated on a site after a wreck can cloud the issue. The first thing recovered from a site in the Florida Keys during a recent excavation was an anchor from the second half of the nineteenth century. If the salvors had relied on dating the shipwreck from the anchor alone they would have been mistaken because the wreck turned out to be a seventeenth-century ship. The anchor must have snagged on it and been abandoned some two centuries later. In another instance, I was asked to investigate a shipwreck discovered by fishermen near Málaga, Spain, on which they reported seeing a large marble statue. The statue was of Roman origin, but the rest of the cargo as well as the ship itself turned out to be from the latter part of the nineteenth century. Apparently the statue was on its way to Spain for sale.

Identifying the origin of cargo on a shipwreck is not always a clue to the vessel's nationality. The bulk of goods brought from Spain to the New World were not of Spanish manufacture but from a dozen other countries. The *Matanceros* shipwreck site is a good illustration. Although Spain was at war with England at the time the ship sailed for the New World, over 50 percent of her cargo consisted of

British-made items. To further complicate the identification of the *Matanceros* wreck, the remaining cargo was French, German and Dutch and little of Spanish origin. Ships of other European nations also routinely carried mixed cargoes.

Discovering Spanish specie or bullion on a shipwreck does not prove the ship was Spanish. Spanish coinage was the chief currency used by all European nations with settlements in the New World. Even in the United States it was legal tender until the beginning of the nineteenth century. Spanish coinage was widely used throughout the rest of the world as well. Each year huge sums were shipped from Mexico to the Philippines to purchase Oriental goods to be shipped to Acapulco. The Philippines belonged to Spain until the end of the nineteenth century, and Spanish coins were traded throughout southeast Asia. Recently, a Dutch ship wrecked on the west coast of Australia in 1656 was excavated and 7,500 silver coins were found dated 1654 and 1655 from the mints in Mexico City and Potosí.

The nationality and type of a ship can sometimes be determined by finding out how big the ship was and the amount of armament or cargo she carried. During the first half of the sixteenth century, when the New World was called a "Spanish Lake" where few ships of other nations sailed, even some of the largest Spanish ships carried few cannon or none at all. Few traces of wrecks could be found if they carried no armament and their cargoes were perishable items like tobacco, cocoa or sugar. Generally, a Spanish galleon can be

Although these artifacts were recovered from a Civil War blockade runner located on the coast of North Carolina, all four items were manufactured in different European countries. (Credit: North Carolina Museum of History.)

identified by the large number of cannon it carried and its size, since the largest ships were only used for transporting treasure. All treasure-laden ships were not Spanish galleons; ships of other nations also carried Spanish treasure back from the New World. Finding a shipwreck which is large and has many cannon and hand weapons but little or no cargo most likely means the vessel was a warship. Warships of all nations were forbidden to carry cargo. British warships are easily identified because of the broad-arrow mark on the cannon, anchors and all the other items aboard. The origin of the mark is obscure, but from the second half of the sixteenth century until the end of the nineteenth century it was in regular use to denote all Crown property. Finding on a wreck only a few items so marked indicates they might have been taken from a British ship after capture or salvaged from a British wreck.

After consulting thousands of documents relating to the size and tonnage of ships of different types and nationalities, I have made the following table to assist in establishing the size and draft of ships in use throughout the world between 1500 and 1820. If one knows from a documented source that the ship he or she is interested in weighed 500 tons, it can be reckoned that when the correct wreck is found, the length of the keel should be, or give evidence of having been, close to 92 feet. One is unlikely to find a complete wreck but you may be able to estimate the former size of the keel. This information can be used in another way. Locating a shipwreck and finding that the keel was 120 feet long, one could figure that the ship was about 1,500 tons, which might aid in identifying it. The figures in the table are given in feet.

Ships were frequently sold or captured and their flags changed, so that determining where a ship was built does not, as a matter of course, establish its nationality. In 1593, owing to a scarcity of Spanish shipping, the king ordered the seizure of all foreign ships in Spanish ports so that a fleet could be outfitted for a voyage to the New World. Of the sixty-two ships in the fleet, only fourteen were Spanish-built. The rest came from twelve European countries including Greece and Sweden.

Generally, so little of a ship's wood remains on a wreck which has long lain in the water that it is impossible to try to date or identify the ship's origin from it. The spikes, nails, tacks and other metal fastenings are also of little help. Their shapes and sizes varied little through the centuries. Brass tacks recently found on a Roman

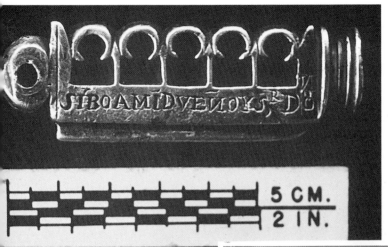

Silver pocket knife from a Spanish shipwreck that has its owner's name on it, which is very useful for identifying a wreck. ▲

Four Spanish silver Pillar dollar coins. These were first struck in 1732 and used throughout the world ▼ as currency, not just by the Spaniards.

Diver using an underwater scooter to search for shipwreck remains. ▲

Lead merchant seals like these three are very useful in dating and identifying a wreck site. These are Portuguese from the late 16th century. ▲

Diver removing ballast rock to expose two bronze cannon hidden beneath the ballast on a wreck off Mexico. ▲

After removing 15 feet of sand, the side of an early Dutch shipwreck is exposed off coast of Australia. ▼ (Photo courtesy of Pat Baker.)

Diver using a metal detector on top of a pile of ballast stones on a shipwreck in the Philippines. ▼

Gold, jewel-studded Kris handle found on a Spanish wreck in the Bahamas, which was originally made in Indonesia. ▶

Diver using hammer and chisel to extract artifacts embedded in coral growth on a wreck site. ▼

Author's wife Jenifer holding a gold scabbard tip, next to an iron cannon off Caicos Island. ▲

Diver using his hand to fan away sand covering silver coins located with a metal detector. ▶

Diver tagging sections of a ship's wooden hull before taking the wooden remains to the surface for preservation. ▲

This bronze ship's bell was just recovered by an ROV from a depth of 1,500 feet of water off the Florida Keys. It dates from end of the 16th century and is to date the deepest object recovered from a historical shipwreck site—in this case a Spanish galleon. ▼

Diver using an airlift to remove sand on a 17th century Dutch shipwreck—note intact wooden chest—off coast of Australia.
▲ *(Photo courtesy of Pat Baker.)*

Using an airlift to remove sediment off a 1st century A.D. shipwreck site in deep water off Israel's coast. ▼

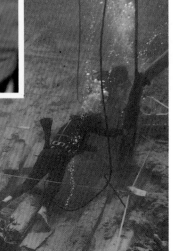

British and Dutch bottles and ceramic jars from a c.1825 shipwreck off Panama's coast. ▲

A Spanish olive jar, which is similar to the amphorae used during the Classical Period in the Mediterranean. These jars can be found on all Spanish wrecks from the time of Columbus up to the beginning of the 19th century. ◄

All of this equipment had to be flown in to conduct a wreck survey in the Indian Ocean. The small remote-controlled plane on the left carried a camera to help locate wrecks. ▼

Gold is generally found shining as seen here with a cannon in background. ▶

Diver attaching lines to raise a bronze cannon from a wreck site. ▼

Aerial view of a submerged building in a sunken city off the Bahamas. ▲

A French bronze mortar, a type of artillery used by ships when attacking forts. This one dates from mid-18th century and was found in ◀ *Cadiz Bay, Spain.*

Here, archaeologists use a theodilite to locate objects on a shipwreck by taking the angles and bearings of buoys attached to the objects. ▲

Roman frescos such as this help archaeologists understand how ◀ ancients ships were constructed.

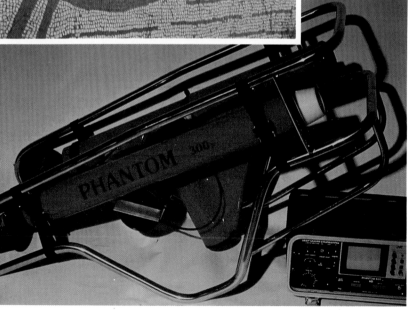

Remote operated vehicles (ROV's) such as this are used to locate, survey, and recover small objects from shipwrecks laying in thousands of feet of water. ▲

Chart of Cadiz showing an English fleet attacking the port in 1625. Such old drawings are sometimes useful in locating shipwrecks. ▶

A 19th century anchor with iron chain strewn around it on top on a reef in the Bahamas. Wrecks like this one can be located by visual search. ▲

Graph of a side-scan sonar unit showing an intact shipwreck in 2,000 feet of water off the Azores. ▶

Relative Ship Dimensions, 1500–1820

Tonnage	Length of keel	Width of beam	Draft
100	52	19	7$^{1}/_{2}$
200	66	24	9$^{1}/_{2}$
300	76	27	10$^{1}/_{2}$
400	84	30	12
500	92	33	13
600	98	35	14
700	102	37	15
800	104	37$^{1}/_{2}$	15
900	107	38	15$^{1}/_{4}$
1000	109	39	15$^{1}/_{3}$
1100	110	40	15$^{1}/_{2}$
1500	120	44	16
2000	152	60	18

Archaeologist tagging timbers on the wooden remains of an early 17th century Dutch merchant ship.

shipwreck of the third century A.D. were identical to those found on an eighteenth-century French warship. Treenails (wooden pegs) used to fasten the planking to the frame of a ship are of no help because they remained unchanged for almost five thousand years. If they were turned on a lathe rather than fashioned by hand, it indicates only that a wreck dates sometime after 1825. Nor will the types of wood used in a ship's construction provide a clue for instant dating or identification, since the type of wood used in different periods and locales varied a great deal, and depended upon what types were available at the time of construction.

The destruction by marine borers has been a major problem since the earliest days of seafaring. We know that most ships had a protective lead sheathing as early as 500 B.C., perhaps even earlier. It is not known for how long this lasted. The earliest proof of sheathing in more recent history was mention of a Spanish lead-sheathed ship in 1508. In 1567, the king of Spain ordered its application to cease, claiming the added weight made his ships too slow. In 1605, lead sheathing was again applied to ships sailing to the New World, but only to those going to Mexico to protect their hulls from the borers during the long months they wintered at Veracruz. Those sailing to other Spanish settlements were still forbidden to use the sheathing. Unable to use lead, the Spanish turned to protective compounds which were applied to a ship after it was careened and the planking burned a bit. The Spanish generally used a mixture of tar and lime. The French favored a combination of tar and animal hair, and the British a mixture of pitch, brimstone and brick or marble dust. In 1766, the British began to cover their ships' bottoms with copper sheathing. The French followed in 1775, but the Spaniards and Portuguese did not apply copper to the hull until the first decade of the nineteenth century.

Anchors are often baffling because their shapes and methods of construction changed so little over the centuries. The first type used, a basket anchor, was a double line attached to some form of basket which held enough rocks to secure a vessel. One line was attached to the top of the basket and lowered by it. The other was attached to the bottom so that when the vessel wished to get underway, rather than pull all the weight up, the second line was pulled, overturning the basket and dumping the rocks.

Anchors are one of the most common, and generally one of the first objects encountered on shipwrecks. My original intention in studying

Chinese stone anchor, c. pre A.D. 500, found on wreck site off Palos Verdes, California. (Credit: Larry Pierson.)

anchors was to provide sufficient data on anchors to enable underwater archaeologists to use anchors as a tool for identifying the approximate age and nationality of shipwrecks. However, after very careful study I now realize much more study is needed to produce even a preliminary guide to achieve this objective. Over the years I have inspected many shipwrecks worldwide but only in a few instances is there any certainty that the anchors from an individual wreck positively came from that wreck and not from an earlier or later period. Great caution must be exercised when using anchors to attempt to date a shipwreck. There have been many instances when anchors have been recovered from the sea, either by divers or when snagged on other anchors or cables and brought to the surface and used again, centuries after they were last in use. Even a date on an anchor, which is quite rare, is not necessarily accurate. An example of this is to be seen outside the Ships Museum in Amsterdam. The anchor dated to the late 18th century is actually an early 17th century anchor which was recovered from the sea, and the date was placed on it after it was introduced for use by the Dutch East India Company.

Another problem is contamination of shipwreck sites that contain anchors of later or earlier periods. Lost anchors do not necessarily indicate a shipwreck, as many were lost by snagging on underwater obstructions or when vessels had to get underway in a hurry and had insufficient time to raise anchor. During hurricanes or bad storms it was also the practice to cast anchors, and sometimes cannon, overboard to lighten ship and prevent it from capsizing. In many instances, contemporary or later salvors are also known to have thrown over anchors on shipwreck sites in order to carry more of the salvage materials on their vessels. A good example of this is a 1648 Dutch merchantman, lost near Memory Rock in the Bahamas, that has a 19th century anchor on top of its ballast pile. Beneath another section of the ballast were numerous 19th century spirit bottles. This seems to indicate that the site was worked by salvors, because the water was too shallow to be used as a normal anchorage.

Trying to establish the nationality or place of manufacture of anchors during the colonial period is difficult because of several factors. Too little data are currently available to enable proper identification of the place of manufacture. Furthermore, there was a great trade in anchors throughout this period; all nations were using anchors of foreign manufacture. During the 16th century the manufacture of anchors in northern Spain was a big business, yet a document dated 1557 states that most of the anchors on that years' outward-bound New Spain Flota were of foreign manufacture. Another document dated a few years later states that over 50 anchors had to be seized from visiting merchantmen in the port for that years' outward-bound flota. In 1606, most of the anchors used on Portuguese East Indies ships had been purchased in Scandinavia, and in 1678, an English ship with a large cargo of anchors destined for sale in Genoa was seized by the French off Ushant.

The number of anchors carried aboard ships varied for a number of reasons. Among the numerous reasons for the great losses of ships in the 1588 Spanish Armada debacle was the insufficient number of anchors on most of the Spanish ships: the majority had only one or two anchors. After passing through the English Channel and anchoring off Calais, the English used fireships at night and in the ensuing panic the Spaniards were forced to cut their cables in their evasive action, resulting in some ships left without any anchors for future use. Later, when rounding the British Isles on their return voyage to Spain, they met with bad Atlantic gales and were wrecked on the coasts of Scotland and Ireland because of insufficient ground tackle.

Until 1579, there was no regulation as to the number of anchors that Spanish ships must carry, but that year the King issued an order stating that ships over 100 tons going to Tierra Firme must carry five anchors and those going to Mexico seven. The latter ships required more because they wintered in Veracruz and had to brave the Gulf of Mexico "northers."

The first mention of anchor weights occurs in 1620, when a galleon of 500 tons carried seven anchors on a voyage to Veracruz: one of a ton weight, two of 1,800 pounds, two of 1,600 pounds, one of 450 pounds, and one of 350 pounds. In 1651, another document mentioned a Spanish galleon carrying nine anchors weighing a total of 16 tons on a voyage to the New World. In 1709, an order was issued that the total weight of anchors on all Spanish warships must be equal to five percent of the total weight of the ship.

The first French regulations were issued in 1634; merchantmen were required to carry four large anchors and warships at least six. One large French warship lost in the Caribbean near the end of the 17th century was carrying ten anchors at the time, while another, lost during the same hurricane, had only two available. This resulted in her loss when both cables parted and she wrecked on a reef.

In 1688, British warships were required to carry the following number of anchors: a ship of 2,000 tons, known as a first-rater, carried a total of nine anchors weighing 17 tons; a second-rater of 1,500 tons carried nine weighing a total of 12½ tons; a third-rater of 1,000 tons carried six weighting a total of 8½ tons; a fourth-rater of 700 tons carried six weighing a total of 5½ tons and a fifth-rater of 500 tons carried five weighing a total of 4½ tons.

Future study on the subject of anchors should reveal much more information that will give the underwater archaeologist more assistance in using the anchor as a dating and ship identification tool.

Cannon were first carried on ships in the mid-fifteenth century, during the Age of Discovery. When found on a shipwreck site, they are helpful in determining the size, type and approximate date of the ship, but not always its nationality, since cannon manufactured in several countries can be found on a ship. During the second half of the sixteenth century the majority of cannon carried on Spanish ships were made in England and Holland, and during the seventeenth and eighteenth centuries a large percentage were still of foreign manufacture. Aboard the Turkish ships in the Battle of Lepanto in

1571, more than 90 percent of the cannon were Dutch and Italian. Recently discovered on the coast of Japan, a Dutch ship which sank in 1626 carried twenty-four cannon, eighteen founded in Denmark, the rest in England.

Most bronze and iron cannon were struck with the date of their manufacture. Many also bear the coat of arms of the reigning monarch. English cannon were for the most part struck with a crowned rose and the king's initials, e.g., GR, for George Rex. These marks are still clear on bronze cannon found on underwater sites but seldom visible on iron cannon, eaten by corrosion. The first two bronze cannon I found on the Spanish galleon *Maravilla* were dated 1653 and bore the name of the founder, Johannes von Horst. In addition they had the elaborate coats of arms of Philip IV, the king of Spain, and of the Marquis of Leganes, who had paid for them to be made for the king's treasure ship. When no markings are visible, a cannon can be dated by its shape and other distinctive features. All European countries have artillery museums and their

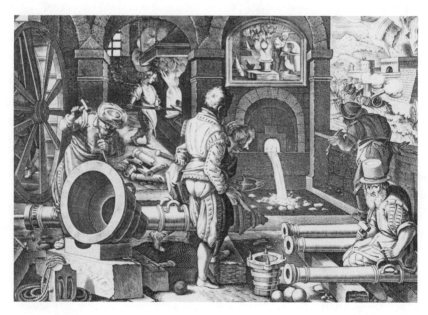

Contemporary drawing of a sixteenth-century cannon foundry in Holland. (Credit: New York Public Library.)

experts can generally date a piece within twenty years. In the United States the Smithsonian and the National Park Service have specialists who can help identify artillery pieces.

The ships on which Columbus made his voyages were armed with two types of cannon: Lombards and Versos, also called swivel guns. The Lombards were made of forged-iron strakes (continuous bands) running the length of the barrel and held together by iron bands spaced every four to six inches. The piece was open at both ends and a breech block loaded with powder was wedged against the back end of the piece after a ball was inserted. The Lombard, mounted on a wooden cradle, was carried on the main deck. It varied from six to twelve feet in length, weighed from five hundred to two thousand pounds and fired a stone ball between four and ten inches in diameter. Unlike any later cannon, this type of cannon had no trunnions (sockets for pivot pins). Lombards were used on ships of many nations between 1420 and 1560.

The Versos were either cast in bronze or made of iron in the same manner as the Lombards. Toward the end of the sixteenth century they were cast in iron as well. They were mounted on a pivoting frame and attached to the bulwarks of the ships. They varied in length from four to ten feet, weighted between one hundred fifty and eighteen hundred pounds and fired a stone or iron ball between one and a half and three inches in diameter. These small-caliber guns were mainly used to attack personnel on the decks and castles of enemy ships, rather than the hulls, which resisted the shock of such small projectiles. Versos were used between 1480 and 1750, but during the latter hundred years were chiefly carried on small ships as signal guns or used to quell mutinies.

As early as 1504 some of the larger Spanish ships sailing to the New World were carrying bigger cannon which were mounted on two-wheeled gun carriages. A merchantman sailing to Santo Domingo in that year carried one bronze Demiculverin, 11 feet long, weighing two tons and firing a 12-pound ball; four iron Serpentines, 8 feet long, two and a half tons and firing a 40-pound ball; one bronze Saker, 7 feet long, 1,200 pounds and firing a 6-pound ball, and three Versos of unknown size and weight but firing a 4-pound ball.

In 1552 a royal order was issued listing the armament all Spanish ships sailing to the New World had to carry. Merchant ships between 100 and 170 tons were required to carry: 1 bronze Saker, 1 bronze Falconet, 8 iron Lombards and 18 iron Versos; ships of 220 and 320 tons, 1 iron Demiculverin, 2 bronze Sakers, 1 bronze Falconet, 10 iron Lombards and 24 iron Versos; treasure galleons of between 400 and 600 tons were required to carry all-bronze cannon, 30 to 50 Culverins, 4 to 6 Demiculverins, 2 to 4 Sakers and 4 Falconets.

The Demiculverin fired balls weighing from 7 to 12 pounds, were 25 to 40 times their bore diameter in length and weighed between 3,000 and 4,000 pounds. The Sakers fired balls weighing from 5 to 10 pounds, were from 5 to 8 feet long and weighed between 1,700 and 2,400 pounds. The Falconets fired a 3- or 4-pound ball, were 30 to 36 times their bore diameter in length and weighed between 1,500 and 2,500 pounds. The Culverins, the main pieces used in fighting enemy ships, were made in many sizes and fired balls between 20 and 40 pounds. Their lengths were 30 to 32 times their bore diameter and they weighed from two to three tons.

About 1570 a scarcity of copper affected the manufacture of bronze cannon for Spanish ships and iron cannon soon replaced them, except on the main ships of a fleet or on the treasure-carrying galleons. The largest iron piece was called simply a cannon and fired a 40-pound ball, was 17 times its bore diameter in length and weighed about three tons. There were also demi-cannon, which fired balls weighing from 12 to 20 pounds, were between 12 and 20 times their bore diameters in length and weighed between 2,300 and 3,600 pounds. Smaller vessels carried smaller pieces and fired balls weighing from 2 to 15 pounds. Throughout the period of Spanish dominance of the New World, which lasted until the opening decades of the nineteenth century, these were the types of cannon on Spanish ships. Cannon on Italian ships were similar.

The principal cannon on English ships differed somewhat in size, weight, and size of shot. The following tables give statistics for those used during a 300-year period.

Of the above-mentioned English-made cannon, all were generally of bronze except those called cannon, which were iron. The number and type of cannon carried on English merchantmen depended not only on the size of the ship but on the availability of sometimes scarce cannon. This was true also of English warships until 1762, when the Admiralty issued an order specifying the number and types to be carried on their vessels. A first-rater of 100 cannon carried thirty 42-pounders, twenty-eight 24-pounders, thirty 12-pounders, ten 18-pounders and two 6-pounders. A second-rater carried twenty-six

Sixteenth Century

Name	Weight (in pounds)	Length (in feet)	Caliber (in inches)	Weight of Shot (in pounds)
Robinet	200	5	1¹/₄	1
Falconet	500	4	2	2
Falcon	800	6	2¹/₂	2¹/₂
Minion	1,100	6¹/₂	3¹/₂	4¹/₂
Saker	1,500	7	3¹/₂	5
Demiculverin	3,000	10	4¹/₂	9
Culverin	4,000	11	5¹/₂	18
Demi-cannon	5,000	9	6¹/₂	30
Cannon	7,000	12	8	60

Seventeenth Century

Robinet	120	3	1¹/₄	³/₄
Falconet	210	4	2	1¹/₄
Falcon	700	6	2³/₄	2¹/₄
Minion	1,500	8	3	4
Saker	2,500	9¹/₂	3¹/₄	5¹/₄
Demiculverin	3,600	10	4¹/₂	9
Culverin	4,000	11	5	15
Demi-cannon	6,000	12	6	27
Cannon	7,000	10	7	47
Cannon Royal	8,000	8	8	63

Eighteenth Century

Robinet	150	3¹/₂	1³/₄	¹/₂
Falconet	700	4¹/₂	3	3
Falcon	800	6	3¹/₄	4
Minion	2,000	7¹/₂	3³/₄	6
Demiculverin	2,600	8	4¹/₂	9
Culverin	3,200	9	4³/₄	12
18-Pound Cannon	3,900	9	5¹/₃	18
24-Pound Cannon	4,600	9	5⁴/₅	24
32-Pound Cannon	5,500	9¹/₂	6¹/₂	32
42-Pound Cannon	6,500	10	7	42

32-pounders, twenty-six 18-pounders, twenty-six 12-pounders, ten 9-pounders and two 6-pounders. A third-rater of 74 cannon carried twenty-eight 32-pounders, thirty 24-pounders, fourteen 9-pounders and two 6-pounders. A fourth-rater of 50 cannon carried twenty-two 24-pounders, twenty-two 12-pounders and six 6-pounders. A fifth-rater of 36 cannon carried twenty-six 12-pounders and ten 6-pounders, and a sixth-rater of 28 cannon carried twenty-four 9-pounders and four 6-pounders.

A new type of cannon, called a Carronade, was introduced on English ships in 1779. It was easily distinguished from those of earlier years by its large-bore diameter and length of only three to six feet. Carronades fired balls of 9, 12, 24, 32, 42 and 68 pounds. Those made prior to 1800 had low trunnions, and after 1800 the trunnions were centered. After 1825, however, many had no trunnions at all, but were mounted with lugs on the gun carriages. From 1800 on, the Carronade replaced most of the large-caliber cannon on ships of all nations.

The cannon used by all other European countries, from the beginning of the sixteenth century to the middle of the nineteenth century, were similar to English cannon and tended to be elaborately decorated, particularly those cast in bronze. The numbers and types carried aboard ships closely paralleled English practice. The Dutch, however, apparently always had sufficient materials to make bronze cannon, for even their merchant vessels carried mostly bronze pieces. Many Portuguese ships carried cannon that differed greatly in shape from any others manufactured in Europe and were actually founded in India or other Portuguese Far East possessions.

From the mid-sixteenth century on, the basic cannon projectile was the round shot, normally of iron, but sometimes of stone or lead. The size of shot used by a cannon was one-quarter-inch smaller in diameter than the caliber of the piece. Because there was no difference in appearance in the round shot of various countries, all one can tell from finding them on a wreck site—if the cannon are no longer there—is the caliber of cannon the vessel carried.

Bar shot and chain shot were primarily used during sea battles to destroy the sails and rigging of enemy vessels. The first mention of bar shot was by the Dutch in 1619. Some were made by attaching a 6- to 12-inch iron bar between two round shots. Others were made with two halves of a round shot and some with round disks. Chain shot was introduced by the Dutch in 1666. A chain replaced the bar of the bar shot. Two types of antipersonnel shot were also used: grapeshot and canister shot, sometimes called case shot. The earliest mention of grapeshot was in 1556 aboard English ships. It consisted of from twenty to fifty small cast-iron balls, one to two inches in diameter and held in place between two or more wood or metal disks connected to a central rod. The balls were lashed to the frame with cords or leather and the cylindrical projectile was covered with canvas and coated with wax, pitch or paint. The diameter of the projectile depended on the caliber of the cannon; its length was between six and twelve inches. Canister shot, introduced by the French in 1745, consisted of a thin cylindrical metal can containing such things as glass fragments, nails, tacks, musket balls and small pebbles. Another type called carcass shot came into use about 1650. It was an incendiary projectile, a hollow, cast-iron ball filled with combustible material. When fired, flames streamed out through small holes in the side of the ball. It was primarily used to set fire to the sails of enemy ships.

Myriad types of hand weapons have been carried on ships since man first sailed the seas, and it is a relatively simple matter to identify them and establish their approximate date and place of manufacture. It is a subject on which countless books have been written. Passengers as well as crew carried hand weapons to aid in defense should a ship be attacked. This was true no matter what the ship's nationality. Swords, daggers, boarding axes, pikes, lances and shields were basic hand weapons for thousands of years. Cutlasses, which were widebladed and shorter than swords, were used by seamen and

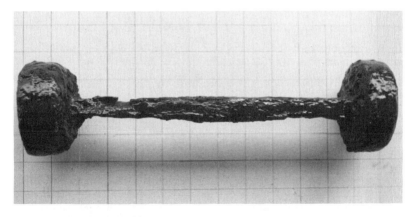

A bar-shot, c. 1690.

marines from the mid-sixteenth century on. Bayonets on firearms were introduced by the Spanish in 1580, but not adopted by the French until 1647 and the English in 1690. Full suits of armor were worn by officers and those who could afford them from the advent of the Middle Ages until about 1550. Armored breast plates and helmets remained in use until the end of the sixteenth century.

Crossbows were first used during the Middle Ages and were employed until the end of the sixteenth century. However, during the fifteenth and sixteenth centuries generally only small numbers of them were used because harquebuses and muskets were considered more effective. Matchlock harquebuses introduced in the fourteenth century were some five or six feet long, weighed as much as sixty pounds and fired a lead or iron ball ranging from half an inch to an inch in diameter. The firing mechanism of an S-shaped level pivoted to the stock near its center and forked at its upper end to hold the match. By pressing the lower end of the lever, the match was forced down into the flashpan and ignited the primer. The disadvantage to this weapon was the necessity of keeping the match lit or having some means to light it quickly. In 1517, a German invented the wheel lock, which replaced the match-lock. It consisted of two main parts. A steeltooth wheel was wound by a key to tighten a spring. By pulling the trigger, the wheel, containing a piece of pyrite or flint, struck the firing pan and ignited the primer. Another improvement on the firing mechanism was introduced toward the end of the sixteenth century when the flintlock superseded the wheel lock. In the flintlock, by pulling the trigger a piece of flint held in the jaws of the cock was released, striking against a piece of steel, sending a shower of sparks into the priming power pan. Although the flintlock was invented near the end of the sixteenth century, some nations did not use it for many years. In France it was not widely used until after 1670, but it continued as the firing mechanism on all firearms until 1820, when it was replaced by the percussion lock.

Muskets, introduced in 1521, were the biggest guns fired by a single man. Some were as long as ten feet and weighed over one hundred pounds. Because of the size and recoil of the large muskets, they had to be supported by rests. The average size of the ball was about one inch in diameter. They gradually decreased in size and by 1690 the average musket was about five feet long. From 1700 on, the name musket was used to identify any type of firearm shot from the shoulder. Carbines were introduced by the English during the second

The author coming ashore with a six-foot-long, coral-encrusted musket that he recovered from Port Royal.

half of the sixteenth century. Similar in appearance to muskets, they were much smaller and fired a lead ball less than an ounce in weight. Pistols were first used in England in 1521 and in most other European countries soon afterward. Actually, they were a smaller version of the harquebus. Lighter and easier to handle, they had been developed primarily for use on horseback, where a man had only one hand free. By the mid-sixteenth century, they were standard equipment for all ships' officers. The firing mechanisms on the muskets, carbines and pistols changed at the same time as those of the harquebus.

Hand grenades were used on ships as early as 1467 and remained in use until the mid-nineteenth century. They were fashioned many ways, but were usually round, made of metal, glass or ceramic, and filled with gunpowder. A small hole held the fuse, which was lit before the grenade was thrown.

One of the best objects for establishing a date of a shipwreck which sank after 1650 is a glass bottle. Bottle shapes changed frequently and a bottle can usually be dated within ten years of its manufacture. The life span of a bottle was short; generally, it was used and discarded. Glass had been invented by the Phoenicians about a thousand years before Christ. They made glass objects of many types and traded them throughout the known world. The Egyptians and other Mediterranean peoples also

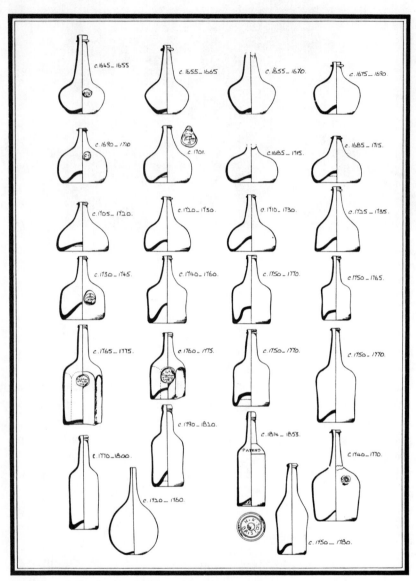

Drawings of glass bottles of different dates.

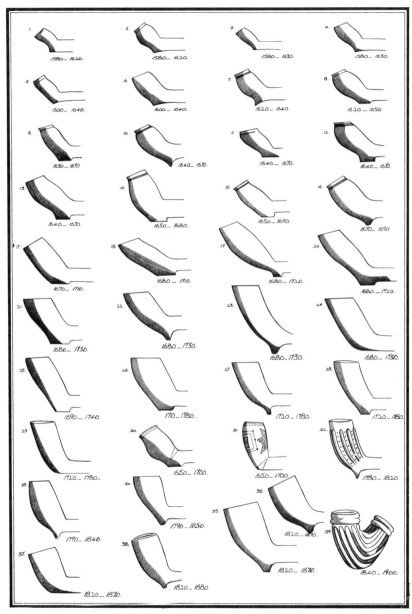

Drawings of clay smoking pipes of different dates.

produced glassware but during the five hundred years of the Dark Ages, little glass was produced. Even after this era, glass production was limited and at the time of Columbus' discovery of America, Venice was the only place in Europe manufacturing glassware, specializing in drinking glasses and decanters. Glass works were founded in Antwerp in 1550 and in London in 1557. Another was founded in Jamestown, Virginia, in 1608 but went out of business in 1624. A second American glass works opened in Salem, Massachusetts, in 1632 and made bottles to transport cider and spirits to the West Indies and England. After 1662 other glass works were opened in Germany, France, Spain and Holland.

Glass bottles that contained any liquor are generically referred to as "wine bottles." The first were those manufactured in Salem. Bottles were first made in England in about 1650. Other European nations did not manufacture wine bottles until well after 1700. At least 95 percent of all wine bottles found on seventeenth- and eighteenth-century shipwrecks throughout the world were made by the English, who produced them on a large scale to export all over Europe. Wine bottles manufactured in Holland are similar in appearance to English and American bottles. Those of other European countries, however, have distinct characteristics which make it possible to trace their origin.

Some bottles are marked with the date of manufacture and others also bear identification seals of those for whom they were made, e.g., the owner of a tavern. Bottles were always sealed with cork, which was held in place by brass wire until the end of the eighteenth century when copper wire was introduced. All bottles were hand-blown until the second decade of the nineteenth century when they were first manufactured in molds.

White clay smoking pipes are excellent aids in establishing the date, but not the identity, of a shipwreck. Almost all pipes were made either in Holland or England and exported throughout Europe. Pipe models changed continually and it is possible to place most pipes within ten years of the time they were manufactured, with the exception of a few made in Virginia and Jamaica. Pipes had a short life. They were fragile and were so inexpensive that they were almost as expendable as cigarettes today. Tobacco was unknown in Europe until imported from the New World after Columbus' discovery. However, it wasn't used until the last quarter of the sixteenth century.

The first mention of clay pipe manufacture was in 1573 in England and within a few years the smoking of tobacco was widespread in both England and Holland. By 1619 there were so many manufacturers of clay pipes in England that they incorporated into a guild. Dutch pipe makers formed a guild in 1660. Clay pipes were first made in Denmark in 1655 and in Switzerland in 1697, but nothing is known of when they were first made in other European countries. It is believed, but uncertain, that small numbers of pipes were manufactured in Virginia and Jamaica in the late seventeenth century, but it was not until about the beginning of the nineteenth century that they were manufactured in the United States on a large scale. Interestingly enough, although the Spanish colonies produced and sold tobacco to other European nations from about 1570 on, the Catholic Church forbade the use of tobacco by Spaniards until the beginning of the nineteenth century.

A number of peculiar features of clay pipes aid in dating them. When smoking first came into vogue in England and Holland, tobacco was expensive, since it was purchased from the Spanish. Thus, the bowls of pipes were small. After the English began cultivating tobacco in Virginia and exporting it to Europe, the cost went down and the bowls of clay pipes became correspondingly larger. The shape of the bowl changed through the years and makes it possible, in many cases, to date a pipe within twenty years of manufacture. Furthermore, a majority of English pipes were marked with either the initials or full name of the manufacturer on the bowl or stem. In England records list 3,400 pipe makers from 1600 onward and several good reference books on the subject are available to help identify the maker, place of manufacture, and date range of a particular pipe. Practically nothing is known about the markings on pipes made in other European countries until well into the nineteenth century.

The discovery of large numbers of pipes on a wreck usually signifies the ship was not Spanish, although some pipes have been found on Spanish shipwrecks. The use of snuff was widespread after 1700 and tobacco stoppers, made of brass or pewter for the most part, are first mentioned as being used in 1640.

Items made of gold, silver or pewter are usually easy to identify and date. At Port Royal, for example, I found hundreds of platters, bowls, spoons, knives, tankards, etc., and with only a handful of exceptions I was able not only to identify the place, date, and person who manufactured an object but in many cases also to trace the object to its former owner. Some pieces bore the full name of the owner, but the majority were stamped or scratched with the owner's initials. From historical records in the Jamaican archives I was able to match these initials with the names of seventeenth-century Port Royal residents. This, in turn, enabled me to determine the identity of the buildings I was excavating. I have been able sometimes to match objects marked with initials found on a shipwreck with the names of crew and passengers on the ship's lists. There is a particularly rewarding feeling when this is done.

The identification marks on gold and silver pieces, called hallmarks, were struck in the form of shields or cartouches, averaging about three-eighths of an inch in height and aligned in a row. The first hallmark denoted the place of manufacture, e.g., the crowned leopard's head was the mark of the London manufacturers, the anchor of those in Birmingham, and a plain crown of those in Sheffield. The second mark was a letter of the alphabet and denoted the year of manufacture. Every twenty-seven years they started the alphabet again employing different-shaped letters. The third hallmark signified that the object was of good quality metal; in England this was always a lion, and elsewhere in the British Isles other devices were used, such as the thistle in Edinburgh. The fourth hallmark revealed the identity of the maker and usually consisted of his initials. American made silverware of the seventeenth and eighteenth centuries bears only the maker's mark, so that these pieces can only be placed within the working span of the known craftsman. Silver plating on copper items was first done in 1743 but not used on a large scale until 1833, when electroplating was invented.

Only the very rich could afford articles of gold and silver, and as a rule only small quantities of such items are found on shipwrecks. Items made of pewter, first used by the Romans, were widely used by the vast majority of the upper and middle classes. There are different types of markings on pewterware made after 1500. A mark usually between one and two inches high, called a touchmark, identifies the maker. The touchmarks of over six thousand English pewter makers are recorded and published in reference books. The majority consists of a design: flower, animal, crown, etc., with the maker's name or initial around it. On many, even the place and date of manufacture are marked. Most pewter pieces were made in London and stamped with a crown Tudor rose. When the letter X is stamped below this mark, it denotes that the item was of extraordinary quality, usually made by a master craftsman. Many pewter articles bore hallmarks similar to those found on gold and silverware, but such marks were not authorized for use on pewter and were illegally struck. However, they serve the same purpose as on gold and silver pieces.

The English had a virtual monopoly on the manufacture of silver and pewterware and more than 95 percent of that found on ships which sank prior to 1850, no matter of what nationality, is English, except for jewelry. A small quantity of silver items, chiefly spoons, plates and cups, were made in France, Holland, Germany, Italy, Spain and Belgium. These countries produced a number of ornate pieces, but in general their pieces were not well marked and therefore difficult to trace unless the work of a master silversmith who made a commemorative or presentation piece. Large serving forks were used as early as 1300, but the use of forks to transfer food to the mouth is not mentioned until the latter part of the sixteenth century, when they came into widespread use among the upper classes. The lower classes didn't use them until about 1700. Cutlery used by the less wealthy until late in the eighteenth century was usually iron or brass.

The most common type of pottery found on shipwrecks is utilityware, in use for over five thousand years, which is made of a coarse, hard paste, normally red but sometimes gray or brown. The small amounts of glazed utilityware were generally green. This was the pottery used by the lower classes and was rarely decorated or endowed with characteristics making it easy to identify by date or place of manufacture. Smaller items such as plates, platters and bowls can be approximately dated by their shapes. If found intact or in pieces which can be reconstructed, their origin can sometimes be determined.

Amphorae were also made of this same material from clays indigenous to the area where they were made, so that it is possible to trace their origin through the type of clay. Their shapes were made to suit local taste, and over the years models changed enough so that approximate dates can be established. Millions were produced, since Greeks and Romans used these clay jars much as we use tin cans. From the time of Columbus onward, all Spanish ships as well as those of many other countries used a type of vessel resembling an amphora to transport liquids and other things. These vessels, known

Drawings of Spanish olive jars
and their necks.

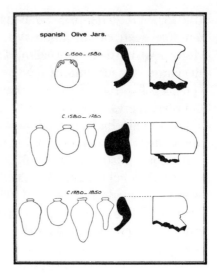

as Spanish "olive jars," were manufactured in Seville and the surrounding countryside and exported all over Europe and the New World. An approximate date can be calculated from the shape of the vessel and sometimes by a maker's mark. They were of utilityware, usually gray, ranging from two to six gallons.

Another type of jug often found on late-sixteenth- and seventeenth-century European wrecks is the round-bellied jug with a bearded man's face decorating the narrow neck and sometimes featuring armorial medallions on the body. They are stoneware, made of clay containing flint and fired at a high temperature. They are covered with a salt glaze and are usually brownish with a whitish-gray interior. They were probably first made in Cologne about 1540 and produced thereafter in Holland and Germany. They are commonly referred to as Bartmannkrug (bearded-man jug) or Bellarmine, after Cardinal Bellarmine, much hated by the Protestants. The face on the neck was said to be a caricature of him. They were exported in large numbers to England where they were called "graybeards" or "tigerware," after the common mottled-brown glaze over a grayish body. The jugs vary in size from one pint to five gallons.

Another common type of ceramicware found on shipwrecks is faience, or tin-enameled ware recognizable by its characteristically colorful, elaborate designs. It began as the maiolica of Italy during the Renaissance and manufacture spread to France, Germany, Holland,

England and Scandinavia. In Holland and England these pieces were know as Delftware, and in Spain and her possessions as majolica. Faience, or maiolica, was generally made of the same clay as earthenware. Pieces found on shipwrecks can usually be traced to their country of origin and sometimes the time of manufacture can be determined through the characteristic design painted on before firing. Many reference books help identify this kind of ceramicware.

Quite a lot of porcelain has been found on ships wrecked after 1560. Most porcelain pieces can be identified and dated fairly accurately. The distinguishing feature of porcelain is its hard, translucent body. All porcelain found on sixteenth-century wrecks and most of that on seventeenth-century wrecks is Chinese or Japanese. Innumerable reference works aid in the identification, including such literary sources as two letters of 1712 and 1722 written by Père d'Entrecolles, a Jesuit missionary in China. He described in detail the making of Ch'ing dynasty porcelain (1644–1912).

Little porcelain of European manufacture has been found on shipwreck sites. Porcelain was not manufactured on any scale until the beginning of the eighteenth century. The English first began producing small amounts about 1745, and the Dutch a few years later. The first European hard porcelain was made at Meissen in Germany. Early European porcelain, when it did not copy Chinese and Japanese styles, was baroque in form and decoration. Experts can easily identify European porcelain, most of which was German and French.

Coins can generally be used to date a shipwreck to within a few years of its loss. This is especially true when large numbers of coins are found bearing the same date or dates spanning a short time. There have been

A Spanish silver coin, the eight real or piece of eight. This one is dated 1684 and was minted in Lima, Peru.

cases when coins were found on a wreck a hundred years older than the shipwreck itself. A wreck must, of course, date from the same year, or later, than the latest dated coin on it. Coins were first introduced in Asia Minor about the middle of the seventh century B.C. and their use spread quickly around the Mediterranean and throughout the civilized world. These early coins were copper, brass, bronze, silver, gold and electrum (an alloy of gold and silver). The first coinage in the United States was of copper and made in Boston in 1652.

Close to 99 percent of all coins found on shipwrecks dating prior to 1850 found in New World waters are of Spanish-American mintage. I shall give a general description of these coins and the way they can be identified. There are many excellent numismatic books available for identifying and dating all other coinage.

Little is known about the earliest coins minted in the New World. Several documents mention that private individuals minted their own issues of gold and silver coins in Mexico City as early as 1528, but there is no record of their appearance or the length of time they were issued. In 1535 a mint was established in Santo Domingo where the copper maravedi coins were first produced. Almost nothing is known of these coins except that they were later minted in Mexico City, Panama City and other places and used on a small scale until the beginning of the nineteenth century. Very few bore distinctive markings such as dates, mint marks or assayers' initials. Some, dating from the second half of the sixteenth century and minted in Santo Domingo, had an anchor on one side and a fort on the other. Others, minted there in 1636, bore a fort on one side and two ships on the reverse. Occasionally, maravedi coins were minted in Spain, dated and shipped to the New World colonies for circulation. The known denominations of these coins were 8, 4 and 2 maravedis, but they were minted in other denominations as well. Their buying power small, they were basically used as change, like pennies or nickels. A silver one-real coin was worth 34 maravedis, and an eight-real coin, or piece of eight, was worth 272 maravedis.

Silver coins were first officially minted in Mexico City in 1536, in Lima in 1568, at Potosí in 1572, at Bogotá in 1622, at Guatemala City in 1733 and at Santiago (Chile) in 1751. It is believed they were also minted at Cartagena and Panama City for short periods at various times during the seventeenth century. The basic silver coin was the eight-real piece, which weighed an ounce. The other real denominations were the four-, two-, one-, half- and one-quarter real coins which were progressively smaller in size and weight.

Gold coins were first officially minted at Cartagena in 1615, at Bogotá in 1634, at Mexico City in 1679 and at Lima and Potosí about 1697. They were also minted for a six-month period in 1698 and, again, after 1750 at Cuzco. The gold coins are of the same size and weight as the silver and are in denominations of eight-, four-, two-, one and one-half escudos -called doubloons by other nations.

Although the screw press was used to mint round-milled coins in England as early as 1610, it was not used in Spanish America until 1732, when the first round coins were made in Mexico City. The Lima mint did not produce round-milled coins until 1752; the other mints even later. Prior to 1720 almost all gold and silver coins minted in the New World were not round but highly irregular, with no two perfectly alike. There were some exceptions. The silver coins minted in Mexico City during the first twenty or thirty years of operation were almost perfectly round, and over the years all mints turned out small numbers of flawlessly round coins in gold and silver, thought to be samples to show the king the mints' capabilities. The irregular-shaped pieces, called cobs, were made as follows: The molten metal was poured out on a flat surface in long, thin strips. When it cooled, pieces of the approximate size and weight of the desired denomination were cut from the strip and trimmed to their proper weight. The planchet was then placed between two dies and struck with a heavy hammer. Since one and sometimes both sides of the coin were not perfectly flat, the dies only marked the highest surface. Thus, the majority of the cob coinage did not have full die marks. In addition, because such incredible quantities of coins were minted each year, they were often carelessly marked, which accounts for many partial die marks. Coins made at the Mexico City mint prior to 1733 are poor in quality and less than 1 percent of the silver coins and about 15 percent of the gold found from this period show dates. Other mints appear to have exercised more quality control and more of the coins from them bear dates and full die marks. At Port Royal, of the more than twenty-five hundred silver coins found, ranging in date from 1642 to 1691 and from the Potosí and Lima mints, close to 98 percent were fully dated.

When dates are not visible on coins, there are other ways to date them approximately. The majority of cob coins had the shield or coat of arms of the reigning monarch on the obverse side, so the coin can be dated to the period of a particular king's reign. From 1772 on, the coins bore a likeness of the Spanish king. All coins were also marked with the assayer's initials and these can be matched with the period during which a particular assayer was in charge of a mint. The place in which a coin was minted can be determined by examining the mint marks on a cleaned coin. The letter L indicates the Lima mint, P is for Potosi, M for Mexico City, C for Cartagena, G for Guatemala, S for Santiago and NR for Bogotá. When the mint marks are not visible, the place of mintage can be determined by other characteristics of the die markings. Almost all of the Mexico City coins had a Jerusalem cross—a square cross with small balls on all four ends—as did some of the Bogotá and Cartagena coins. The Lima and Potosi coins bore a plain cross with the arms of Castile and Leon on their reverse. Even if only a small amount of the markings is visible on a coin, it is generally possible to identify its mint.

All gold and silver bullion minted in the Spanish New World possessions carried a number of marks which help establish their date, place of origin, and the identity of the individual owner of a particular bar. There are also other marks on them such as the bar number, its weight, the fineness or purity of the metal, the assayer's name, the assayer's bite (proof that taxes had been paid on the bar) and the shield or coat of arms of the reigning monarch. If the bar is not dated, the other marks may help reckon a date. This is not easy, however, and requires patient research in the Archives of the Indies

A seventy-two-pound silver bar with various markings on it, which are useful in identifying the place the bar was cast, the date, the weight, purity of metal, and the owner's name.

in Seville. If, however, one has a copy of a ship's manifest, he can easily identify a bar and determine if it is from the wreck he is after by comparing the markings with the descriptions of bars in the manifest, unless it is a bar that was being carried clandestinely, in which case it would not be listed.

Other artifacts help identify and date a shipwreck or other type of underwater site. They include a ship's bell, which may bear a ship's name and the date of construction, and personal items such as a snuffbox, pocket watch or hand-wrought belt buckle, all of which may have dates marked on them or the name and place of the craftsman who made them. Owners' names and ship names are also found on cannon, swords and firearms.

It is almost always possible to identify and date a site, but it may take longer than the search and excavation.

7

Preservation and Publication

One of the weakest aspects of underwater archaeology is the small number of preservationists and the lack of facilities to restore and preserve recovered artifacts. At present there are fewer than fifty people in this specialized field and no more than a dozen laboratories throughout the world where restoration and preservation work is done.

In the United States, only the Smithsonian Institute, the Metropolitan Museum of Art in New York, the University Museum of the University of Pennsylvania, the Institute of Nautical Archaeology of Texas A&M University, and the states of Florida, Texas, North Carolina, South Carolina, Virginia, New York, and Massachusetts have experts and the facilities to treat objects recovered from underwater. Other places where professional preservation work is done include the Port Royal Archaeological Laboratory in Jamaica, Parks Canada in Ottawa, the Institute of Archaeology in London, the Vasa Museum in Stockholm, Mary Rose Museum in Portsmouth, England, the Museé de Marine in Paris, the Riksmuseum in Amsterdam, the Maritime Museum in Haifa, Israel, and the Western Australia Museum in Perth.

The *Vasa* project has been the most ambitious restoration project thus far attempted in underwater archaeology. At the time the *Vasa* was raised, in 1961, there were no conventional techniques adequate to preserve such an enormous artifact. The ship was a proving ground for the development of new methods which are now accepted techniques. Although fresh water is a much better environment for the protection of materials than salt water, both wood and iron are affected by it to some degree and require preservation. About 90 percent of the *Vasa* was oak and the remaining 10 percent was pine, spruce, maple, walnut and beech. When the ship was brought to the surface all the wood showed signs of rot. It was necessary to protect it immediately from further deterioration and to prevent it from cracking during the time it took to dry out, when shrinkage would occur. While new methods were being worked on, the ship was enclosed in a large storage house and kept wet by an elaborate sprinkler system erected over it.

Preservation of the hull presented a special challenge. It was not practical to dismantle the complete ship and preserve it in sections nor was it economically feasible to immerse the whole thing in a massive vat with various chemical preservative agents. The sprinkler system was the best solution. To arrest the rotting, a soluble compound of seven parts boric acid and three parts of borax was mixed with fresh water and sprayed over the entire hull. After several months of this treatment the fungi that caused rotting were eliminated. To stabilize the wood and keep it from shrinking and cracking, the ship was sprayed with a solution of polyethylene glycol (PEG) and fresh water. This process was repeated hundreds of times over a period of five years until all of the wood had been completely permeated by the chemical concentrate.

In some fortunate instances even wood and iron are recovered from fresh water in an excellent state. This was the case when the U.S. gundalow *Philadelphia* was raised intact in 1935 from Lake Champlain after resting on the bottom more than a hundred and fifty years. Her wood was in good condition down to the splinters around the hole made by the cannonball that sank her. After the *Philadelphia* was dried out there was a bit of shrinkage on the surface of her hard oak timbers, but it was minimal.

On the other hand, when a British bateau sunk in Lake George in New York around 1750 was raised in 1960, her condition was poor. The oaken keel and ribs of the 32-foot-long vessel were in excellent condition. However, the pine planking was so soft it could be squeezed like a sponge because its inner cellular structure had deteriorated so badly. At that time the best-known preservative treatment was to impregnate the wood in an alum solution. After the boat was dismantled, the planks were immersed in a solution of one part alum and three parts distilled water. (Heating the water almost to the boiling point allows the alum solution to permeate the wood, and after the water is drained away the alum should crystallize and hold the wood's inner cells in place.) This worked well on other woods, but not on the pine planking of the *Philadelphia*. Fortunately it had recently been developed and was finally used to preserve the bateau.

On the *Vasa* almost all of the forged iron had disintegrated and only fragments of bolts and other fastenings remained. The cast-iron pieces had also deteriorated but to a lesser degree, thanks to the higher oxygen content of the metal. These items had retained their original shape and volume but were reduced in weight. If left to dry in the air, where rusting is rapid, they, too, would have disintegrated shortly. To arrest the crumbling, both forged and cast-iron objects were heated in an oven with hydrogen gas at 1,060 degrees centigrade, removing the injurious chloride compounds provoking the deterioration. The objects were then coated with a clear lacquer spray or a light layer of paraffin wax.

All other nonorganic material found on the *Vasa* and on other freshwater sites has required no treatment other than removal of a thin coat of verdigris from metal objects containing copper. This is done with a fine grade of steel wool, and the metal's original luster is restored with a metal polish. When organic materials such as leather or textiles recovered from freshwater need treatment they are dealt with in the same manner as artifacts recovered from saltwater.

A cardinal rule for anything recovered from underwater which requires preservation treatment is to expose it to air as little as possible. It should be kept wet, preferably in freshwater. This is not difficult to do with small objects which can be kept in plastic containers such as buckets and garbage cans. It can be more of a problem with larger objects, especially those as large as cannon or anchors. At sea, heavy, bulky objects can generally be left underwater until time to head for port. They can then be pulled aboard, covered with canvas, toweling

Enfield rifles recovered from a Civil War blockade runner are placed in freshwater until preservation treatment can begin. (Credit: North Carolina Museum of History.)

or some other absorbent fabric to prevent rapid evaporation, and hosed down several times an hour by a small water pump while the boat is underway. Once ashore there is still a problem, for it is usually too expensive to build a tank in which to store the object until it can be treated. If there is a body of freshwater or a stream nearby, the object can be put into it. If there is no such handy storage place, the best solution is to dig a hole in the ground slightly larger than the object, line it with a large sheet of plastic and then fill the hole with water after placing the object in it. When artifacts have to be sent long distances for preservation, the best way to safeguard them is to wrap them in wet rags, plastic and then ship them in an airtight container. Large items can be transported in wooden barrels or boxes containing moist sawdust.

When coral-encrusted metal objects are recovered from the sea there is a natural temptation to chisel away at the growth to see what the piece looks like. Giving in to this desire is a good way to inflict irreparable damage. If the object is brass, copper or lead, no harm may be done, but if of pewter, silver or iron, it may be badly hurt. There is often no way to tell from observation alone whether an iron concretion contains a solid piece of sound iron or nothing at all of the original metal. Such concretions should be examined by x-radiography before being broken apart. Medical x-ray apparatus will do the job. A white image on the x-ray negative indicates the presence of solid metal, whereas a black image reveals that the metal has already disintegrated. This method is also good for identifying all of the materials hidden in the mass. Obviously it is not practical to have x-ray facilities on a boat during an excavation, so it is a good idea to be patient and not attempt any cleaning of such concretions or conglomerates at sea.

Holding a magnetic compass close to a concretion is another way to determine if solid metal remains. If the mass causes the compass needle to move, there is solid iron. Even then, after removing the concretion, the object should be washed in freshwater so that ferric chloride will not form on its surface, turning into hydrochloric acid which attacks the metal. This acid causes cracks to appear on the iron and in a short time the outer surface falls away. If left to dry in the air over a long period, the corrosion process continues until the whole object crumbles into a pile of rusty powder. Even large items like cannon are not immune to this process. If an object is dried out in direct sunlight, the rusting can occur so fast that enough heat is generated for the object to disintegrate with explosive violence. Thus, once an object has been cleaned and inspected, it should immediately be put back in water until it can be properly preserved.

Some things found on saltwater sites, such as gold and platinum, are not affected by long underwater immersion and are recovered perfectly preserved. Most items recovered, however, have suffered

Coral-encrusted conglomerate containing many artifacts. (Credit: Empire Photosound, Inc.)

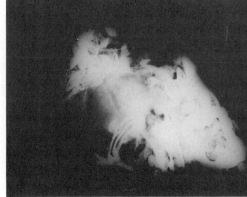

An X ray of the same conglomerate showing pins, needles, buttons, buckles, cuff links, and other items. (Credit: Empire Photosound, Inc.)

varying degrees of deterioration, and the purpose of this chapter is to introduce the underwater explorer to suitable restoration and preservation methods.

Most organic material, like wood, is immediately attacked by marine borers, fungi and diverse bacteria. The longer it is exposed to saltwater, the more it suffers. Some organic material disappears, but objects buried deep in silt suffer less and are sometimes discovered in excellent condition.

Of the various metals found on an underwater site, iron and silver undergo most change-because of electrolysis. Some metals and saltwater act together as a gigantic galvanic battery. The saltwater forms the electrolyte, and metals of two or more molecular weights become opposite poles with a current of electrons created between them. The galvanic current flowing between the different metals will attack those with the highest electrode potential and convert them to one of its compounds. Silver converts to silver sulfide and iron to iron oxide. The metals with the lowest electrode potential are preserved by cathodic protection. The effects of electrolysis on metal vary little whether the object is buried under sediment or exposed on the sea floor.

Objects recovered from the sea can be divided into three distinct categories: those, like gold and some stones, found in their original condition and requiring no treatment at all, or at most a brief immersion in freshwater to remove the salts; those suffering marked physical or chemical changes but which can be treated; those that have degenerated so far that they cannot be restored. In the last case, the remains of an object can be preserved by embedding it in plastic. In some cases nothing remains of the original piece other than a hollow form inside a coral-encrusted concretion which can be recorded through x-ray photography or by making a replica of it using the hollow form as a mold.

Hard gemstones and some semiprecious stones, cut or uncut, such as diamonds, sapphires, rubies and agate are not changed by long immersion in saltwater. Softer stones such as emeralds are often found scratched by the abrasive action of sand and other materials. Scratches should be removed only by lapidary treatment. The best method for removing coral growth from gemstones is to let the growth dry and in most cases it will fall off by itself. If not, judicious tapping with a soft object will be effective.

Stone usually survives intact, but softer types may be badly eroded. Several species of sea worm exude a calcium-destroying substance and burrow into limestone and some marbles, making a honeycomb network. Many of the marble sculptures brought up from sites in the Mediterranean have been eaten into, although usually only the portion exposed on the sea floor seems to have been affected. Badly deteriorated stone items should be washed in distilled water to free them of soluble salts, then allowed to dry thoroughly, and finally coated with either molten beeswax, epoxy resin or clear, flat lacquer. When lacquer is used it should be applied in several coats, beginning with a thin solution for maximum penetration and gradually thickening each successive application until the final coat is of normal concentration.

Ceramics, depending on the type of body and glaze, are affected in varying degrees by immersion in saltwater. Porcelain is least damaged, although its painted exterior may be eroded away. Because of its nonporous surface, it is rarely found with any adhesions of calcareous marine growth. When there is some growth it can be removed by delicate tapping with a rubber tool or by a bath in a 10 percent solution of nitric acid. Iron or lead oxide stains can be removed by a bath of 5 percent solution of sulfuric acid. When calcareous deposits and oxide stains are present together, the sulfuric-acid bath will remove both, following which a thorough washing in freshwater will remove all traces of alkalis.

Glazed pottery, covered with a waterproof vitreous layer, fares much better underwater than porous, unglazed pottery. If, however, the glazed layer is imperfect, soluble salts may get into the clay body of the ware and crystallize, forming efflorescence which causes the glaze to flake off. If the glazed layer is intact, the same methods used to remove calcareous deposits and oxide stains are effective. If the glaze is not intact or is flaking, which is the case with most of the maiolica and Delftware found, no acids of any kind should be used. The pieces should be thoroughly bathed in freshwater to remove the sea salts, then air dried and coated with several layers of clear plastic or lacquer spray.

No acids should be used on unglazed porous ceramics such as earthenware. Removal of deposits from unglazed pieces must be painstakingly done with small tools. Dental tools are particularly good for this. The pieces should then be immersed for several days in a number of freshwater baths to remove sea salts. To assure that they are free of water, they must be dehydrated in several baths of alcohol and then coated with a protective spray. This treatment is only suitable for pieces that show no sign of crumbling. Most ceramic pieces, whole or shards, require no treatment other than freshwater washing to remove sea salts.

Since the clay used for early smoking pipes is virtually indestructible, the pipes are found in excellent condition. Any calcareous deposits can be removed in the same manner as described for gemstones. Stains can be lifted by washing with a mild detergent and soft brush.

Repairing or piecing together ceramic objects and clay pipes is not particularly difficult, but it requires great patience and time. The surfaces must first be cleaned of any foreign material and then cemented together with glue, such as Durofix or Elmer's. While the glue is drying the pieces should be held together with tape or placed in a sandbox.

The change glass undergoes in the sea varies according to its chemical composition and the nature of the sediment it is lying on or buried in. Phoenician beads from the Bronze Age wreck off Turkey were of soft glass and seemed strong when first found, but when left to dry out, would suddenly explode into dust.

White-lead glass such as plate glass, wine glasses, tumblers and cosmetic or pharmaceutical vials are most often found free of calcareous deposits. They may have a thin coating of lead oxide, and sometimes iron oxide, when discovered in close association with iron objects. The following method is used to clean and preserve these objects: place them in a 10 percent solution of nitric acid for the time required to remove the lead oxide. If iron oxide is present, then use a 5 percent solution of sulfuric acid, followed by several thorough washings in distilled water. If, after drying, the glass still shows evidence of flaking, it can be coated with several layers of clear plastic spray such as Krylon. Optical glass is generally found well preserved, but occasionally pitted on exterior surfaces.

Most bottles postdating 1750 require little treatment. They are recovered well preserved because of their chemical composition. Sediment inside a bottle can be removed with a high pressure hose or, more safely, with a tool such as an icepick or wire. Exterior calcareous growth can be removed by tapping it gently with a rubber

Pieces of eight, before and after cleaning.

An artist making drawings of clay smoking pipes recovered from Port Royal.

mallet or by immersion in a bath consisting of 0.2 percent solution of sulfuric acid (one part of acid for every five hundred parts of water) lasting from several hours to as long as a week, depending on the amount of growth. The bottle is then washed in several baths of fresh or distilled water until the glass is free of alkalis. Litmus paper is the easiest way to test for alkaline presence. Upon drying, the surface of some bottles may look dull or develop a thin layer of pearly iridescence in spots. No further treatment is necessary, although the iridescence may eventually flake off on its own.

Preservation of badly decomposed glass is difficult. Unfortunately, most bottles predating 1750 are found in poor condition. If the glass is not impregnated in some way, it is likely that the exterior weathering crust will crumble away when it dries out, in hours or months, depending on the size and condition of the object. This was one of the most perplexing problems encountered during the Port Royal project. In consultation with Dr. Brill of the Corning Glass Museum, I tried to find out why wine bottles recovered from the sunken city were in a worse state than others of the same manufacture and date found elsewhere. The weathering crust on those at Port Royal was thicker than on other bottles of the same period. This made them more difficult to preserve. We theorized that the heavy concentration of bauxite in the harbor sediment was the chief cause. It may have created electrolysis with the lead component of the glass, causing the high degree of deterioration.

Through experimentation I discovered that the method which worked well on most bottles did not help preserve the more badly decomposed bottles found at Port Royal. After several months the glass began flaking under the protective lacquer, and in some cases, the bottles fell apart. To prevent this we followed the same procedure as already described, except that instead of coating a bottle with lacquer, we immersed it for a week or two in a solution of 50 percent distilled water and 50 percent vinyl acetate, which is the same material used in making bookbinding glue (marketed as Padding Cement). After removing the bottle, we wiped off the excess solution with a slightly damp cloth, then air-dried it in a cool place. After it was completely dried, we coated it with several layers of lacquer.

Convenient epoxy cements can be sparingly used to piece together broken glass objects. The most important step in cementing glass is to clean all surfaces to be joined. Care must be taken the first time, because, once set, the cement bonds are very strong.

All organic materials recovered from saltwater must be bathed in freshwater from two to four weeks, depending on size, to remove all sea salts before preservation treatment can begin. If possible, the bath should be of running water which will carry away the salts as they are leached. Large objects, like ships' timbers, can be placed in a freshwater stream, pond or river, if the water is not contaminated by industrial wastes. If a running-water bath cannot be provided, the bath water should be changed at least daily.

Organic materials such as sisal, hemp, textiles, beans and pods, tortoise shell, hair, leather, horn, bone and paper almost always disintegrate upon drying if not adequately treated. Occasionally items of bone or wood are found totally preserved because they lay near iron objects underwater and were saturated with iron oxide. In such a case they become mineralized and hard in texture.

Organic animal materials must first be thoroughly dehydrated in successive baths of alcohol to remove all water. The first bath consists of 40 percent alcohol and 60 percent water, the second 60 percent alcohol and 40 percent water and the third of 100 percent alcohol. The length of each bath is governed by the size of the object; i.e., an hour for a small leather fragment and several hours for a

Coral-encrusted iron artifacts—tools, padlocks, a key, knife, door knocker, and oar lock.

two-pound bone. Then the object is given two baths of xylene, the first lasting a week and the second four weeks. In the second bath, paraffin chips are added until a saturated solution of paraffin is obtained. After the object is removed from the second bath and allowed to solidify by air-drying, a small amount of paraffin crystals may remain on the exterior. These can be removed by heating the object in an oven until the crystals melt or they can be brushed off with a fine-bristled brush. Very fragile animal material, such as small or carved pieces of ivory or bone, can be preserved by embedding them in plastic after they have been dehydrated.

Vegetable material can be preserved by the alum and glycerin process. After the alum crystallizes and replaces the water in an object, it prevents shrinkage and preserves the original form. After all foreign matter has been removed, the object is put in a boiling solution of equal parts by weight of alum, glycerin and water. As soon as the object is placed in the bath, the container is taken off the heat source and allowed to cool slowly. The object should remain in the bath from one to two days, depending on size. After it has hardened and been air-dried, it should be coated with a solution of 50 percent turpentine and 50 percent linseed oil.

Wood is the most difficult, time-consuming, and expensive organic material to preserve. When waterlogged wood is allowed to dry out, the evaporation of water from its degenerated inner cellulose and lignin cells will cause the remaining outer cell walls to collapse from surface tension. The wood then warps and cracks, distorted beyond recognition. The aim in preserving wood is to remove all water without producing these damaging effects and to replace water with a substance which will strengthen and consolidate the object. At present, the best technique is the use of PEG, which slowly diffuses the water by harmless evaporation, at the same time replacing it with a synthetic water-soluble wax which solidifies at ordinary ambient temperatures. PEG is expensive and sold under the trade names of Polywax and Carbowax. It can either be used in spray form as it was on the *Vasa* or in immersion baths, suitable for small items.

The wood is first rinsed in baths of running water for several weeks. A metal container is then used for a bath of a 30 percent solution of PEG. This strength can gradually be increased by heating the bath to allow water to evaporate. The strength of the solution should be increased until it is 60 percent PEG as indicated by a hydrometer.

Objects weighing less than one hundred pounds should be kept for one week in the solution at 30 percent strength, another week at 40 percent, a third at 50 percent and then two to four weeks more at 60 percent. It is always safer to immerse an object for too long in a bath rather than too short a time. Larger objects may have to be in the bath for months or even a couple of years depending on their size and condition. After the wood has been permeated by the wax, it should be removed and heated gently by a radiated heat source. The excess wax can easily be wiped off with a rag dipped in alcohol.

Approximately 95 percent of all metal objects recovered from older shipwrecks are iron. This metal presents some of the knottiest preservation problems because it is so corrodible. In many cases cast-iron objects corrode into a crystalline form so that only powdered oxide remains. Wrought iron is not as easily corroded, probably because it has more nickel. The same applies to steel, which has even more nickel. The amount of metal remaining in an object can be determined by its weight, the use of x-ray photography, a fluoroscope or application of a magnet or compass. If the object has no magnetic attraction, it is quickly evident it is completely oxidized. This is often true of small objects found on sites in the Mediterranean more than five hundred years old.

The first step in the treatment of ferrous metals—iron or steel—is the removal of surface calcareous encrustations. However, unless a substantial amount of the original metal remains, it is unsafe to undertake this cleaning. On large objects these deposits can either be removed by gentle tapping with a rubber mallet or sand blasting under low pressure. Smaller items and delicate objects should be cleaned in an ultrasonic bath or chemically. Ultrasonic baths are easy to operate and can be bought for as little as one hundred dollars. The chemical process consists of a bath in a solution of 10 percent nitric acid and 90 percent freshwater, followed by several washes in freshwater to remove all alkaline traces.

To remove all corrosion and preserve the metal, two methods can be used, electrochemical or electrolytic reduction.

In electrochemical reduction, the object is put in a bath of 10 percent sodium hydroxide and 90 percent water and soaked for from four to eight weeks, depending on size. It is then removed and put in a new bath of the same solution, following which the entire object is covered with zinc chips or surrounded by zinc plates. Soon after the zinc is added to the bath the solution will begin to bubble. This will continue throughout the two to four more weeks the object is in the bath. Upon removal, it will be covered with a white coating which can be removed by placing it in another bath of 5 percent sulfuric acid and 95 percent freshwater.

Electrolytic reduction uses a direct electric current. The object is suspended by copper wires in an iron or steel vat, equidistant and some two inches from the bottom and sides of the tank. The wires are attached to stainless steel or brass rods laid across the top of the tank but electrically insulated from it. The rods are then connected electrically to the negative side of a direct current power supply of either six or twelve volts and the vat is also connected electrically to the positive side of the same source. The negative side is the cathode and the positive the electrode or anode. An electrolyte solution of 5 to 10 percent caustic soda in water is added to cover the corroded object. When the circuit is energized, an electrolytic process begins: hydrogen gas evolves, chlorides from the object flow to the walls of the vat and the corrosion will gradually disappear. As the treatment progresses, the electrical resistance of the object decreases, resulting in an increase of current flow, so the power supply must be equipped with a variable rheostat and an ammeter to keep the current within the proper range. The current required should be five amperes for each twenty-five square inches of the object's surface. Reduction of small objects may take several hours; large, several days or a week. Periodic washing will hasten the reduction. Items should be lifted from the electrolyte while the power is still on to prevent plating them with impurities in the solution.

After either method has been used, the ferrous object is next placed in a running-water bath for at least a week and brush-cleaned several times a day. Soft brushes are used for delicate objects or objects with bas-relief, and scrub or wire brushes on larger, non-delicate items where surface detail is not important. Then another bath, this time in distilled water, is given to the object for at least a week. If it is still not free of all chlorides and alkalis, alternate baths of boiling water and cold water are administered, each lasting about twenty minutes.

The water is then removed from small objects by heating them in an oven or furnace at 212°F for from eight to forty-eight hours.

Extreme heating of large, physically sound iron and steel objects like anchors, cannon, projectiles and tools seems to give better results than the lower temperatures. Use 200°F for the first two hours, increase at the rate of 300°F per hour until reaching 1,500°F, and hold for three to five hours; cool slowly to about 150°F before taking the object out and brushing it to remove scale.

The object must then be sealed from contact with air and moisture to prevent fresh corrosion. There are four methods to accomplish this, all of which should be used while the object is still warm from the drying process, with the exception of embedding it in plastic. Paraffin wax is the most widely used method. Paraffin is heated to 350°F and the object is either immersed in it or the wax is applied with a brush. Clear flat lacquers or clear flat plastic sprays can be used as well. Another method is to apply two or more coats of epoxy resin. This leaves a glossier finish which can be eliminated, if desired, by sandpapering and covering with a flat enamel paint. Clear plastic embedding is a tedious process by which the object is surrounded in a protective medium. A mold is used to encapsulate the object and one of several types of acrylic, such as Selectron 5,000, may be used. The plastic comes in liquid form and a catalyst or hardener is added, causing a chemical reaction which solidifies the plastic after a short time. To insure that the plastic will not crack as it hardens, only about an inch of plastic is added to the mold at a time. After each layer is hard, the process is repeated until the object is encapsulated. In the case of a cannon this might require a week of patient work. After hardening, the solid block of plastic is removed from the mold.

If a ferrous object has turned to oxide and further treatment is futile, an exact replica of the piece can be made instead. Through x-ray photography, the size and position of the deteriorated object inside the concretion can be established and this hollow area will serve as the mold. The surrounding concretion is cut in half with a diamond saw, the iron oxide is washed or scraped out and either synthetic rubber or plaster of Paris is placed in both halves of the mold, which are then placed together again until the substance hardens. If all the iron oxide is not removed, the replica will pick up a thin film of it which enhances its appearance, making it more realistic. Another technique involves drilling a hole into the concretion, shaking the oxide pulp out and injecting rubber or plaster of

A clump of silver pieces of eight held together by silver sulfide and coral growth; in the original shape of the canvas bag that once held them, but which has disintegrated.

Paris into the cavity. After hardening, the exterior concretion can be removed by grinding or breaking apart with hand tools.

Nonferrous metals are always recovered in far better condition than ferrous and are usually easier to clean and preserve. Some of the metals are found in such virgin condition that they require no more than a light once-over with fine steel wool and a polishing agent. Gold and platinum, for example, are almost always found as bright and shiny as the day they were worked. Occasionally, they will be tarnished due to close association with other metals on the bottom. This film is removed by soaking the artifact in a bath of 10 percent nitric acid and 90 percent water. The same bath can be used to remove any calcareous deposits.

The degree to which silver is affected by long immersion in saltwater depends upon the conditions surrounding it. A silver coin lying on the sea floor and not protected by electrolysis from other metals, even other silver coins, may be converted to silver sulfide. If this is so, nothing can be done to preserve it, although it can be embedded in plastic. When a silver coin or other small silver object is converted, it will weigh as little as one-fifth of its original weight, but may be two or three times its original thickness. Handling silver in this precarious condition requires great care, for when it dries it easily disintegrates into powder.

When silver has been protected by electrolysis it will survive intact, sometimes with only superficial corrosion which can be removed. Acid should never be used to remove any corrosion or encrustation. The electrochemical bath for preserving ferrous metals can be used, although it leaves a thick, black residue which requires a great deal of rubbing with solvents and polishes to remove.

The best method is the electrolysis reduction process. The semi-corroded silver object is made the negative electrode (cathode) and is placed between two plates of stainless steel or copper (acting as the positive electrode, or anode) in a plastic or glass container, such as an aquarium tank, filled with water and a 5 percent amount of caustic soda as the electrolyte. Electrical current, generally from a six- or twelve-volt battery, is the power source. The object is connected by copper wire to the negative pole of the battery, and the cathode plates are connected to the positive pole through an ammeter and rheostat. When current passes through the bath, hydrogen is evolved at the cathode, with the result that corrosion is gradually reduced. As the reduction progresses, chlorides are transferred from the cathode to the anode. The length of the process depends on the amount of corrosion to be removed. Generally about fifteen to twenty minutes is sufficient for a coin, thirty to sixty minutes for a spoon, and two to four hours for a plate or bowl. The object should be removed and periodically inspected until all corrosion has been removed. A light deposit of insoluble oxides and metallic powder remaining on the object can be removed under running water with a soft brush. To finish, the object is rubbed with a paste of water and baking soda and finally with a polishing agent.

A small electrolysis reduction bath is sold for less than $50. Called the Koin-Kleen and sold by D-Tex Electronics of Garland, Texas, it operates on a system similar to the one mentioned above but uses regular household 115-volt A.C. current. The electrolyte used is one teaspoon of citric acid (a harmless substance primarily used as flavoring in soft drinks) and half a teaspoon of table salt dissolved in each cup of water. A stainless steel electrode plate connected to the positive wire is placed in the solution on one side of a glass container and the coin is attached by an alligator clip to the negative wire and positioned on the opposite side of the container. The amount of current required is determined through experience and is regulated by a knob on the unit. I have successfully cleaned other small silver pieces such as buttons, buckles and jewelry as well. Gemstones in jewelry are not affected in any way by this method. The silver object is finally cleaned by the baking-soda and water paste and polishing agents.

In some instances, when a large number of silver coins are found together, the majority will be so well preserved that all they need is a bit of the paste and polish to rid them of a black silver-sulfide patina. At Port Royal the bauxite in the harbor sediment, which had such an adverse effect on glass, had a beneficial effect on silver; even solitary silver coins were brought up in fine condition. When large clumps of coins are found, such as were discovered on the *Maravilla* site where some of the clumps retained the form of the sack which once held them but had long since disintegrated, the coins inside the clumps are often as gleaming as the day they were minted.

Pewter is a dull silvery-gray alloy of tin with brass, copper or especially lead. Objects made of it are usually found fairly well preserved. Of the hundreds of items recovered from Port Royal, about 20 percent required little treatment. Rubbing with a soft cloth in water and a mild detergent removed a thin black film from the surface and luster was restored by the paste and polishing treatment. The remaining 80 percent was recovered with only a small amount of surface corrosion and occasionally small amounts of calcareous deposits. Both were easily removed by immersion in a bath of 20 percent hydrochloric acid and 80 percent freshwater, followed by washing in fresh running water for several hours. Then the surface was gently rubbed with a fine grade of steel wool to remove the black patina and the piece again placed in a bath of running water for another several hours. The final step was the paste-and-polish treatment.

On some sites, especially when pewter has not been buried in sand or sediment, it is found badly pitted and corroded. In some cases there is nothing to do but encase it in plastic as follows: A bath is prepared by dissolving a pint of lye in two gallons of fresh boiling water. When the piece is placed in the bath the container is taken off the heat and allowed to cool; ten to thirty minutes are usually sufficient to remove corrosion. Lye is caustic and care must be taken so it doesn't come in contact with skin or eyes. Next, the same procedure is carried out as for other pewter objects cleaned by the hydrochloric acid process. If the piece is bent out of shape, the best time to reshape it, normally with a rubber mallet very carefully used, is when it is taken from the lye bath and the metal is warm, soft and malleable.

Lead objects often suffer little in the sea, although they may have a thin coating of lead oxide which is easily removed in a bath of 10 percent acetic acid and 90 percent freshwater followed by a running-water bath for a few hours. Because of its softness many pieces are badly bent out of shape. Lead which has lain a long time in saltwater, however, is usually in poor condition. On the Grand Congloué Roman wreck, lead sheathing which once covered the ship's bottom was transformed into lead sulfate, and nothing could be done to restore it. If a lead object is only partially corroded, either the electrochemical or electrolytic reduction techniques can be used on it, followed by the same treatment given iron or steel. However, it should be noted that lead is slightly soluble in caustic soda, which is used in both reduction methods, so the object cannot be subjected to it for too long without losing fine surface detail.

Copper, brass and bronze are also little hurt by saltwater immersion. Calcareous deposits on large objects can be removed by tapping with a rubber mallet. Smaller pieces can be put in a bath of 10 percent nitric acid and 90 percent freshwater followed by the usual washing in running water. This bath will also remove the green patina always found on these metals. The patina can also be removed by careful use of fine steel wool. Some items made of these metals, if in the sea for many centuries, may also show superficial corrosion which can be removed by the electrolytic or electrochemical reduction methods.

Objects made entirely of magnesium, tin, aluminum, zinc, nickel, or other alloys in current use will not be found on sites predating 1850. Dealing with metals manufactured after 1850 gets very complicated and their preservation is outside the scope of this book.

The amateur underwater archaeologist, after taking a site apart has the obligation to "put it back together again" in the form of a thorough, honest and detailed report. Some particularly rich sites may merit a number of specialized reports on various facets of the excavation. However, a complete general report that makes an excavation a matter of public record is the culmination of any underwater project, no matter how small. The amateur may be tempted to undervalue his contribution. If his site seems to have yielded a meager amount of data, he may be so disappointed that he hesitates to write a report. However, it is possible that an archaeologist reading his report might find in it a missing piece to the picture of the past he is trying to reconstruct. It is through published reports of disciplined excavations that the professional archaeologist comes to value the contribution of the dedicated amateur.

Report writing isn't as exciting as excavating, but it is satisfying to see the random data, the myriad numbers and statistics take shape

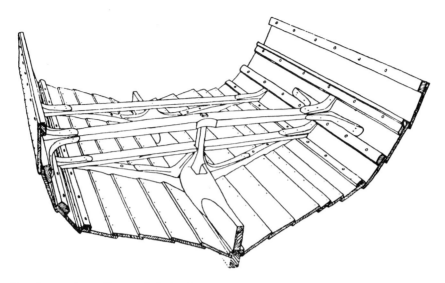

Drawings such as this one depicting how a Viking ship was once constructed, which information was obtained by careful recording during an excavation, should be contained in reports on archaeological excavations. (Credit: The Danish National Museum.)

and give coherence and meaning to one's hard work. Anyone can write an intelligent report. It doesn't take a literary bent to follow a basic outline covering the pertinent points.

A report should begin with the historical background of the site, even though it may have been researched after excavation was begun. In the case of a shipwreck, this includes where and when the ship was built, its size, number of cannon carried, type of cargo, number of passengers, route, cause of sinking, and anything else research discloses. In dealing with a sunken settlement site, the background of the site should be given in detail. There should be an indication of where and how research was done and a bibliography, if published reference materials were used.

The exact location of the site is given and described and how it was located, mapped, recorded and excavated, including a record of all equipment and techniques used. Problems encountered should be presented so that they might be avoided in the future.

It is important to locate the site precisely and to include maps or charts. In describing the site, weather conditions, currents, tides and underwater visibility should be taken into account. An overall plan showing the layout of the site is presented as well as drawings or photographs illustrating the site after it has been uncovered but before any objects have been moved. If the site is large, it may require many illustrations. Scale drawings or photographs accompanying meticulous descriptions of the most important artifacts are incorporated into the report. There should be a scale drawing or photograph of at least one of every kind of artifact found. If, for example, two thousand identical brass crucifixes have been found on a shipwreck site, a scale drawing or close-up photograph of one will suffice. If you find on an ancient wreck six types of amphorae which look almost alike, but are not identical, then a scale drawing of one of each type is included. As for coins, there should be a description of the numbers found, the types, their denominations, nationality, dates and place minted.

Describe all techniques in cleaning, restoring and preserving artifacts and note carefully for each cleaned artifact its form, size, weight, color, type of material and any other identifying characteristics.

Following the artifact inventory comes the meat of the report: the interpretations or conclusions derived from the project. In the case of a cargo ship, for instance, a statement regarding the origin of the various trade items carried aboard would be useful to historians interested in the extent of trade between nations during the period when the ship sank. If a ship carried a significantly larger amount of cargo than indicated on the manifest, a statement indicating this would add to historians' knowledge of contraband practices. When possible, information obtained from an underwater site should be compared with that from the excavation of a similar site. As an example, a Dutch wreck found in the Caribbean may have carried all-bronze cannon made in England but one found in the Indian Ocean may have carried all-iron cannon made in Sweden.

A report has value only when published and available to anyone interested in the subject. Many periodicals deal with archaeological material, but it is often frustrating for an amateur to try to get his report included in one of them since they generally prefer professional papers. This is true of such publications as *Archaeology, Science,* and *Scientific American.* Other journals sponsored by societies are sometimes receptive to creditable reports by amateurs, especially if they are thorough but not lengthy.

Journals most likely to be receptive to the amateur are state and regional historical and archaeological publications which, along with some archaeological societies and some universities, do not discriminate against the nonprofessional and judge a report on the basis of its value.

Since its founding in 1972, the *International Journal of Nautical Archaeology*, published by the Council of Nautical Archaeology in London, has published a number of reports by amateurs and will continue to do so.

If one is unable to have a report published in a scientific journal, it is possible to publish it oneself and have copies sent to those who might be interested. This can be done relatively inexpensively by offset printing or mimeograph. In such a case, use only scale drawings rather than photographs to keep cost to a minimum.

8

The Future

At the bottom of the Mediterranean lies the greatest untapped source of information about the ancient world; a deep, dark, silent storehouse of the past where a ship that sank five thousand years ago may lie next to the twisted hulk of a German submarine. Until recently, these ships lay beyond the reach, even the dreams, of marine archaeologists. Today exciting new developments promise to open a new realm to underwater explorers.

The normal sailing routes of the ancient world closely followed coastlines because ships steered from landmark to landmark. Often, however, they had to leave sight of land and make open water crossings, as when Phoenician ships sailed from the eastern Mediterranean to the colonies established in Spain and in the Azores, far out in the Atlantic. During tempestuous weather many of these ships foundered, and it is estimated that between 3000 B.C. and A.D. 1000 at least twenty thousand boats sank in the Mediterranean, most of them beyond the working depths of scuba divers. Since the sailing routes of the ancient mariners changed little over the centuries, it is conceivable there are areas where the sea floor is paved with shipwrecks spanning the history of mankind. If some of these ships are as well preserved as many scientists think, to locate and raise them intact would herald a revolution in underwater archaeology.

As mentioned earlier, one of the factors most responsible for the deterioration of shallow water shipwrecks is the marine borer, teredo navalis, commonly called shipworm. According to Dr. Ruth Turner of the Museum of Comparative Zoology in Cambridge, Massachusetts, and others, the teredo is not known to exist below six hundred feet. Specimens of waterlogged wood scarred by borers have been found in deeper water, but Dr. Turner believes they were infected before they sank. The basic requirements for survival of the more than one hundred species of borers are salt water, oxygen in the water, wood and the presence of some food in addition to the wood itself. In certain areas, at varying depths, there are layers where the water has a relatively low oxygen content. This may account for the absence of borers in deep water. In the Caribbean, such a layer is generally found at 1,300 feet and even shallower in other bodies of water. On the sea floor off the California coast, in most of the Black Sea and most of the Mediterranean abyss, for example, are anaerobic pools in which none

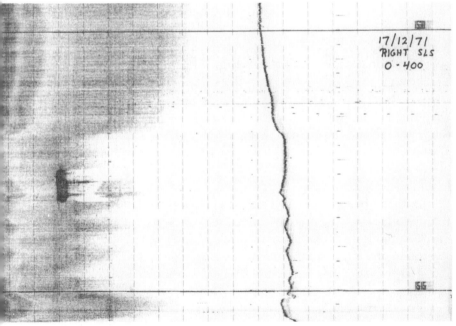

Recording graph from a side-scan sonar unit showing a completely intact shipwreck in 2,300 feet of water. Closed-circuit television revealed it to be a wooden sailing ship of the seventeenth century. (Credit: Scripps Institution of Oceanography.)

of the borers can survive. The Mediterranean, the most impoverished large body of water known, has the lowest sea bottom oxygen content in the world. Its entire supply of oxygen is expected to be used up within 1,000 years if not somehow replenished by nature. There is one genus of borer, Xylophaga, found as deep as 6,500 feet. Very little is known of its life or distribution; however, experts do not think it is as widespread throughout the world as the common teredo.

Other factors favor the preservation of shipwrecks in deep water. The bottom temperature is near freezing, decelerating or halting chemical reactions which would cause cellular damage to a ship's timbers and other components in warmer water. These wrecks lie beyond the reach of snagging nets, ships' dredging anchors and the forces of wind and waves. These intact ships would have their cargo stowed aboard and would be the most perfect kind of unpolluted historical capsule. In deep water the sedimentation rate is extremely slow, particularly beyond a few miles from shore. In the middle of the Mediterranean the rate of sedimentation is believed to be less than three inches per thousand years. Thus, a ship which has lain on the bottom for five thousand years would have no more than fifteen inches of sediment. These unburied ships should present excellent search targets, particularly for side-scan sonar or a drag cable sweep.

During the past thirty-five years there has been growing proof that these ships do, in fact, exist in the Mediterranean, intact and in remarkable condition. During a closed-circuit television search for the wreckage of a commercial airliner which crashed off the island of Elba in 1952, an ancient amphora carrier was accidentally discovered at a depth of 2,500 feet. Two years later a firm, studying the possibility of laying a pipeline across the Mediterranean from North Africa to the southern coast of France, reported television sighting of more than two-dozen ancient shipwrecks. In 1966, during the search for the H-bomb lost off the Spanish coast, the crew of the submersible, *Aluminaut*, sighted two cannon-carrying wooden ships in more than 2,000 feet of water. More recently, in 1972 a Japanese oceanographic vessel doing research off the coast of Lebanon reported finding six ancient ships in depths from 700 to 1,600 feet. In each case the wrecks were reported intact, just like the Hollywood fantasy wrecks.

In 1965, there was coincidental confirmation of the existence of intact ships in deep water in the Western Hemisphere. The shrimp

The submersible Aluminaut, *which has been used to locate deep-water shipwrecks in the Caribbean and Mediterranean. (Credit: Reynolds Aluminum Corp.)*

boat *Trade Winds* was hired by the Bureau of Commercial Fisheries to make a study to determine whether certain species of shrimp could be found in deep water in the Gulf of Mexico. While dragging nets about twenty miles south of the Dry Tortuga islands in one thousand three hundred feet of water, they snagged on an immense obstruction. It stopped the shrimper whose scuppers, normally eight feet above water, were almost awash. The captain backed over the obstruction and brought up his badly damaged nets. In them he found three complete Spanish olive jars, various pieces of metal and a large amount of wood, including a section of ornate railing and parts of a ship's rigging. He described the wood as being "as good as the day the ship was made," showing no sign of borers or rot. The olive jars, which had probably been kept on deck as water casks, date the ship as early seventeenth century. The shrimper made several passes over the wreck with the fathometer running. It indicated that the obstruction was ninety feet high on an otherwise flat sea floor where the depth increased only ten feet every thousand feet. Fortunately, the captain took good LORAN bearings on the site, primarily so he wouldn't snag it again.

I learned of this and in the spring of 1972 decided to try and relocate the site and inspect it with the help of the *Trade Winds* and Willard Bascom, the oceanographer. Bascom had designed and built a unit called the T.V.S.S. (television search and salvage system) for use on deep-water sites. The unit, lowered to inspect a site via closed-circuit television, incorporates lights, a still camera, narrow-beam side-scan sonar and a hydraulic grab-bucket capable of lifting up to five tons. By dragging a steel cable between our search vessel and the shrimp boat, we located and buoyed the site in less than four hours. The cable had snagged onto a large anchor, with its wooden stock still whole, but just as the cable reached the surface, the anchor broke loose and plunged to the bottom. We were prepared to use the T.V.S.S. to inspect the wreck but unfortunately it was impossible to anchor our vessel at the site or to lower the unit because of the strong current caused by the Gulf Stream which flows past the site area at a rate of 4 knots. Recently, I turned over the location and data of this interesting site to a firm specializing in deep-water exploration, and they are currently preparing to go after this shipwreck.

Back in 1955, Edwin Link decided the answer to locating and excavating deep-water shipwrecks lay in enabling divers to work at these great depths. At that time diving was as advanced as aviation had been in 1925, but Link was determined to meet the challenge. His plan involved the use of mixed breathing gases, such as a combination of helium and oxygen, rather than the nitrogen and oxygen mixture in the compressed air used in standard scuba diving. He envisioned divers living in an under-

The Television Search and Salvage System, which can locate and salvage shipwrecks in depths up to 5,000 feet.

SMITHSONIAN'S
JOHNSON-SEA-LINK

The Johnson-Sea Link submersible, capable of carrying divers to depths of 2,000 feet and permitting them to lock-out and undertake work on the sea floor at that depth. Credit: Smithsonian Institute of Oceanography.)

water shelter, or habitat, which would permit them to work on sites as deep as one thousand feet. His ideas were the forerunner of the U.S. Navy's SEALAB program conducted between 1964 and 1968. Under the sponsorship of the Smithsonian Institution, he designed and built *Sea Diver II*, launched in 1959. He then began designing underwater chambers and experimenting with mixed-gas and saturation diving. On September 6, 1962 (two years before SEALAB I was initiated), Link's chief diver, Belgian Robert Sténuit, spent 26 hours at 243 feet in a chamber off Villefranche, France, making several excursions out of it as well. As a result of this experiment, the U.S. Navy convinced Link to become involved in its Man in the Sea Project and to work on the Deep Submergence Group, which took up so much of his time that he had to postpone his goal of getting divers down on deep-water wrecks.

In June, 1964, Link conducted an important experiment off the Berry Islands in the Bahamas. Robert Sténuit and Jon Lindbergh, son of the aviator, spent 48 hours living and working at a depth of 432 feet in an underwater habitat called the SPID. Link designed the submersible *Sea Link* to carry divers into very deep water. It has operated at two thousand feet. The *Sea Link* has two separate chambers, one kept at atmospheric pressure houses the pilot and a nondiving scientist or observer and the other, maintained at pressure equivalent to that of the surrounding water, carries two divers and has a lock-out exit to permit them to enter the water. Link died in 1981 while working on autonomous dwellings that can be installed on the sea floor near a deep-water wreck so that divers could sojourn on the bottom while working. The *Sea Link* would transport the divers between the dwelling and a surface support vessel.

As a result of experiments conducted by the U.S. Navy and a number of commercial companies involved in the search for offshore oil deposits, divers using mixed gases have already reached depths of two thousand feet.

Oceaneering International, Inc. first introduced the Atmospheric Diving Suit to the offshore petroleum industry in 1974, and currently they own 27 ADS suits that have collectively logged over 5,000 hours of working dives worldwide. This system enables a trained operator to work in depths up to 2,000 feet while remaining in a surface pressure atmosphere. In a conventional mixed-gas saturation diving system, a diver descending to 1,000 feet would need approximately 12 days to compress to bottom pressure, carry out the work assignment, and decompress to surface pressure. With the ADS system an entire 1,000-foot dive can be completed in a manner of hours, with far less risk to human safety. The ADS suit places the diver in a natural, comfortable upright position that allows him to make working dives of several hours duration with excessive fatigue. Plans are currently underway to make use of the ADS suit on several shipwrecks in deep waters in the Philippines and in the Mediterranean.

It is believed that the maximum depth man can safely hope to reach will be three thousand feet. In certain applications, such as working in waters in excess of 2,000 feet, remote operated vehicles (ROV), which are unmanned, are desirable to employ. Carrying closed-circuit television they can be used to inspect targets located by side-scan sonar or other means and their manipulator arms can be used to make recoveries from as deep as 20,000 feet. Many of

The Alcoa Seaprobe *shown in action. Here it is recovering a missile nose cone. Note old wooden shipwreck on bottom. (Credit: Alcoa Corp.)*

the manned oceanographic submersibles already in use can also be used for deep-water inspection and recovery, but they are far more costly than the ROV systems.

In 1962, spurred by a lifelong interest in naval history and ancient ships, Bascom, who thinks important, and thus far unknown, archaeological data could be obtained by locating and raising deep-water wrecks, designed a vessel to do just that. Following his design, the Aluminum Company of America together with Ocean Science and Engineering, Inc., built the ALCOA *Seaprobe.* An all-aluminum, diesel-electric-powered ship, she is 243 feet long, with a beam of 50 feet and a draft of about 13 feet. The *Seaprobe* is propelled by vertical-axis cycloidal propellers fore and aft so she can hold a fixed position on deep water without anchors and can search along prescribed pathways. At the center of the *Seaprobe* is a derrick 125 feet high, like those on oil-drilling ships; beneath the derrick is a center well through which drill pipe is lowered.

This revolutionary vessel presently carries eight thousand feet of pipe, but can carry even more for work in extremely deep water. Using pipe rather than cable has several advantages. It is semirigid, can transmit torque and is easily weighted at the bottom with very heavy pipe which acts like the sinker on a fishing line. The pipe can also conduct seawater under high pressure to the bottom to operate hydraulic actuators, jets and other equipment for raising a shipwreck.

Attached to the bottom of the pipe is a search pod, not unlike the *Poodle* or other unmanned submersibles, equipped with sonar, television, lights, still and motion picture cameras, lights and strobe photo equipment. Signals to and from the pod are transmitted through a cable attached to the outside of the pipe. Two sonar units are used simultaneously. One scans directly ahead, covering an area four hundred feet wide; its chief purpose is to prevent the pod from running into obstructions. The other is a side-scanning unit which covers an area one thousand five hundred feet off each side of the pod. The resolution of this unit is such that at six hundred feet it can distinguish between two objects just three feet apart.

During the search the ship operates as follows: First, a precise local navigation system is set up. Far from land this consists of a pair of taut-moored buoys about ten miles apart, each supporting a radar transponder. The ship's radar triggers the transponders, which show up on the scope as brilliant points of light and can be accurately plotted to give the ship's position, moment by moment. An area of about fifty square miles can be carefully navigated with this system.

Next, the ship makes a general bottom survey to determine the depth of the search area so that a search plan (generally along contour lines) can be developed. The pipe with the pod is then lowered to within 180 feet of the bottom and the *Seaprobe* begins to move along the planned course at about a half knot, searching an area of approximately forty thousand square yards per minute, or a square nautical mile every two hours.

After the ship completes this gross search of the area, priorities for further study are given to targets found since the side-scan sonar only indicates that some object is sticking above the bottom. The pod is lowered to about sixty feet from the bottom and the most promising targets are reexamined with the sonar on a finer scale to get a better indication of their nature.

Then, the pod is lowered within twenty feet of the bottom so that selected targets can be visually examined via television and photography.

After a target has been selected for intensive study and possible recovery, the *Seaprobe* retrieves the pipe and pod, replacing the latter with examination-recovery equipment. This includes a set of tongs, or grab-bucket, mounted on an arm attached to the bottom of the pipe. The small exploratory tongs are guided by television cameras and can open to about eight feet by eight feet and lift more than five tons. The tips of the tines have water jets for propelling the tines into the bottom or for washing sediment from objects. Specific items can be recovered and brought to the surface through the ship's center well.

Bascom designed super-tongs that could lift an entire ship to the surface. They would weigh about fifty tons and be towed to a deep-water site supported on the surface by their own pontoons, which would have adjustable buoyancy. On the site, the super-tongs would be slung beneath the *Seaprobe*, secured to the tips of the pipe and lowered away. Controlled by television, the super-tongs would be capable of surrounding an object thirty feet in diameter and eighty feet long weighing up to two hundred tons, and could thus lift the majority of shipwrecks lost before 1000 A.D. The super-tongs could be used to lift even larger ships off the bottom by raising separately large pieces of a wreck which, while lying on the bottom, have been cut by a hydraulically driven band saw into manageable sections. The pieces could be reassembled later on.

After the super-tongs bring up an entire ship or a ship in sections, they would be retracted to a position just below the *Seaprobe*. The ship would then slowly carry her find into quiet shallow water and deposit it. There scuba divers could remove sediment and after recording everything, carefully remove ballast and cargo, lightening and strengthening the wreck for the final move. A special barge would be brought in and the wreck moved aboard it using a large-capacity marine derrick. The tongs would be removed and the ship carried away for preservation treatment and eventual display. This kind of underwater archaeological operation has not yet undergone trial, and there will certainly be modifications and changes. However, it looks promising and is attracting international scientific attention. The expense and effort of raising a ship from deep-water will be considerable, but chances are the results would justify them.

Recently, the exploration of the legendary *Titanic* captured the imagination of the world and is without a doubt the best example of placing shipwreck exploration in the modern "space age." Deep-water archaeology jumped from the bi-wing single-engine plane age to man setting foot on the moon. The saga started in 1980 when Texas oil baron Jack Grimm enlisted the assistance of various scientists and spent over $2,000,000 over the next three years in a vain quest to locate the *Titanic*. Then, during the summer of 1985, a joint American and French expedition led by Dr. Robert D. Ballard of the Woods Hole Institution of Oceanography decided to take a stab at locating the shipwreck. They narrowed the search down to an area of 150 square miles and began using high-resolution side-scan sonar and a towed sled containing cameras and lights named *Angus*. Finally, on September 1, 1985 at a depth of 12,500 feet the elusive *Titanic* was located and recorded on film to the great joy of the world.

The following summer Ballard returned to the site with the famous submersible *Alvin*, which was first launched in 1964 with an operational depth of 6,000 and carried a crew of three. Among the many remarkable accomplishments of *Alvin*, the most famous occurred in 1966 when she located and helped recover from a depth of 2,850 feet an H-bomb that was lost in the Mediterranean when two planes collided. Soon after she was reconstructed and now has a diving capability of 13,120 feet—just enough to reach the *Titanic*. After taking the tedious two-hour descent to the wreck site, the crew on the *Alvin* were able to obtain excellent photographs and also make many recoveries using the two manipulator arms. To get inside the shipwreck and also to obtain data in dangerous areas outside the hulk, a small tethered robot called Jason Jr. was used. Controlled by the pilot in *Alvin*, this 250-pound, 28-inch vehicle was worth its weight in gold. They were able to obtain 60 hours of video and 60,000 still photographs during a twelve-day period, compared with only two minutes of video and nine still photographs shot the previous summer with the more primitive tow sled *Angus*.

Ballard believed that the site should not be disturbed further and ended his explorations when bad weather set in around the end of the summer of 1986. In the summer of 1987 a well financed French expedition aided with a submersible similar to the *Alvin* and several sophisticated ROVs returned to the *Titanic* and obtained additional video and still photographs, and recovered an interesting collection of artifacts from the site. This last feat was considered to be plundering by many scholars and scientists around the world and met with great skepticism. However, they did prove the point that even shipwrecks in two and a half miles of water can be successfully located and salvaged.

Over the years *Alvin* has been joined under the sea by dozens of other manned submersibles, most being American and French. The deepest operational one at this time is the U.S. Navy's three-man *Sea Cliff*, which can carry a crew down to 20,000 feet and recovered objects weighing several tons. The big boon to the underwater archaeologists are the relatively new, compact ROVs such as the *Phantom* and *Mini-Rover*, which weigh less than 1,000 pounds complete with all cable and support equipment, and can reach depths of 5,000 feet to recover photographic data and small objects.

Although the future offers new vistas for deep-water archaeology, there are countless opportunities on shallow-water sites awaiting disciplined amateur underwater archaeologists who can work safely and productively, enjoying themselves and perhaps adding to the growing body of man's knowledge of his past.

Selected Bibliography

The Ships and Their History

Archibald, E. H. H., *The Wooden Fighting Ships*. 1968, London.

Artinano y de Galdacano, Gervasio de, *La arquitectura naval española*. 1920, Madrid. *Historia del comercio de las Indias*. 1917, Barcelona.

Baker, William A., *Colonial Vessels*. 1962, Barre, Massachusetts. *Sloops and Shallops*. 1966, Barre, Massachusetts.

Bass, George, *A History of Seafaring*. 1972, London.

Boxer, Charles R., *The Dutch Seaborne Empire: 1600–1800*. 1965, New York. *The Portuguese Seaborne Empire: 1415–1825*. 1969, New York.

Casson, Lionel, *The Ancient Mariners*. 1959, New York. *Ships and Seamanship in the Ancient World*. 1971, Princeton.

Chaunu, Huguette and Pierre, *Seville et l'Atlantique* (1504-1650). Nine vols., 1955, Paris.

Clowes, William L., *The Royal Navy*. Three vols., 1898, Boston.

Cowburn, Philip, *The Warship in History*. 1965, New York.

Duhamel du Monceau, Henri L., *Elemens de l'Architecture Navale*. 1758, Paris.

Duro, Fernandez Cesares de, *La Armada Española*. Nine vols., 1895–1903, Madrid; *Disquisiciones nauticas*. Six vols., 1876–1881, Madrid.

Fincham, John, *A History of Naval Architecture.* 1851, London.

Greenhill, Basil, *Archaeology of the Boat,* 1976, Middletown, Connecticut.

Hamilton, Earl J., *American Treasure and the Price Revolution in Spain 1501–1650.* 1934, Cambridge, Massachusetts.

Haring, Clarence H., *Trade and Navigation between Spain and the Indies in the Time of the Hapsburgs.* 1918, Cambridge, Massachusetts. *The Buccaneers in the West Indies.* 1910, Cambridge, Massachusetts.

Johnstone, Paul, *The Archaeology of Ships,* 1974, New York.

Landström, Björn, *The Ship.* 1961, New York. *Sailing Ships.* 1969, London.

Martinez-Hidalgo, Jose Maria, *Columbus Ships.* 1966, Barre, Massachusetts.

Marx, Robert F., *The Treasure Fleets of the Spanish Main.* 1968, Cleveland. *The Battle of the Spanish Armada: 1588.* 1965, Cleveland. *The Battle of Lepanto: 1571.* 1966, Cleveland.

Morison, Samuel Eliot, *Admiral of the Ocean Sea.* 1942, Boston.

Morrison, J. S. and Williams, R. T., *Greek Oared Ships: 900–322 B.C.* 1968, Cambridge, England.

Pares, Richard, *War and Trade in the West Indies.* 1936, New York.

Parry, J. H., *The Age of Reconnaissance.* 1963, London. *The Spanish Seaborne Empire.* 1966, New York. *Trade and Dominion.* 1971, London.

Schurz, William L., *The Manila Galleon.* 1939, New York.

Torr, Cecil, *Ancient Ships.* 1964, Chicago.

Veita Linage, Joseph de, *Norte de la Contratacion de las Indias Occidentales.* 1672, Sevilla.

Early Diving and Salvage

Davis, Robert H., *Deep Diving and Submarine Operations.* 1951, London.

Diolé, Phillippe, *4,000 Years Under the Sea.* 1954, New York.

Dugan, James, *Man Under the Sea.* 1956, New York. *Men Under Water.* 1965, New York.

Karraker, Cyrus H., *The Hispaniola Treasure.* 1934, Philadelphia.

Latil, Pierre de and Rivoire, Jean, *Man and the Underwater World.* 1954, London.

Marx, Robert F., *They Dared the Deep*. 1967, New York and Cleveland.

Diving and Modern Salvage

Carrier, Rick and Barbara, *Dive: The Complete Book of Skin Diving*. 1955, New York.

Ciampi, Elgin, *Skin Diver*. 1960, New York.

Cousteau, Capt. Jacques Yves, *The Silent World*. 1953, New York. *The Living Sea*. 1963, New York. *Diving for Sunken Treasure*. 1971, New York.

Ellsberg, Edward, *On the Bottom*. 1929, New York. *Men Under the Sea*. 1939, New York.

Falcon-Barker, Capt. Ted, *Roman Galley Beneath the Sea*. 1964, New York and London.

Gores, Joseph N., *Marine Salvage*. 1971, New York.

Hass, Hans, *Diving to Adventure*. 1951, New York.

Jefferis, Roger and McDonald, Kendall, *The Wreck Hunters*. 1966, London.

LePrieur, Yves, *Premier de Plongee*. 1956, Paris.

Link, Marion C., *Sea Diver, a Quest for History Under the Sea*. 1959, New York.

Lyon, Eugene, *The Search for the Atocha*. 1985, Port Salerno, Florida.

Marx, Robert F., *Always Another Adventure*. 1967, Cleveland.

Masters, David, *The Wonders of Salvage*. 1924, New York. *Epics of Salvage*. 1952, Boston.

Mathewson III, R. Duncan, *Treasure of the Atocha*. 1986, New York.

Morris, Roland, *Island Treasure*. 1969, London.

Nesmith, Robert I., *Dig for Pirate Treasure*. 1958, New York.

Owen, David M., *A Manual for Free Divers*. 1955, New York.

Rebikoff, Dimitri, *Free Diving*. 1956, New York.

Rule, Margaret, *The Mary Rose*. 1982, London.

Slack, Jack, *Finders Losers*. 1967, New York.

Stenuit, Robert, *The Deepest Days*. 1966, New York.

Stenuit, Robert, *Treasures of the Armada*. 1973, New York.

Tucker, Teddy, *Treasure Diving with Teddy Tucker*. 1966, Bermuda.

Wagner, Kip (as told to Taylor, L. B., Jr.), *Pieces of Eight.* 1967, New York.

Underwater Photography

Frey, Hank and Tzimoulis, Paul, *Camera Below.* 1968, New York.

Starck, W. A. and Brundza, P., *Art of Underwater Photography.* 1966, Philadelphia.

Rebikoff, Dimitri and Cherney, Paul, *Underwater Photography.* 1965, Philadelphia.

Shipwreck Locations

Anonymous, *Shipwrecks and Disasters at Sea.* 1851, London.

Barrington, George W., *Remarkable Voyages and Shipwrecks.* 1883, London.

Berman, Bruce D., *Encyclopedia of American Shipwrecks.* 1972, Boston.

Bowen, Dana Thomas, *Shipwrecks of the Lakes.* 1952, Daytona Beach, Florida.

Desperthes, Jean L., *Histoire des Naufrages.* Three vols., 1828, Paris.

Duffy, James, *Shipwreck and Empire.* 1955, Cambridge, Massachusetts.

Duro, Fernández Cesareo de, *La Armada Española.* 1878, Madrid.

Gibbs, James A., Jr., *Shipwrecks of the Pacific Coast.* 1957, Portland, Oregon.

Layton, J. F., *Memorable Shipwrecks and Seafaring Adventures.* No date, Glasgow and Sydney.

Lonsdale, Adrian L., and Kaplan, H. R., *A Guide to Sunken Treasure in American Waters.* 1964, Arlington, Virginia.

Marx, Robert F., *Shipwrecks in Florida Waters.* 1969, Eau Gallie, Florida. *Naufragios en Aguas Mexicanas.* 1971, Mexico City. *Shipwrecks of the Western Hemisphere 1492–1825.* 1971, New York.

Neider, Charles, *Great Shipwrecks and Castaways.* 1952, New York.

Nesmith, Robert I., and Potter, John S., Jr., *Treasure: How and Where to Find It.* 1968, New York.

Paine, Ralph D., *Lost Ships and Lonely Seas.* 1942, Garden City, New York.

Potter, John S., Jr., *The Treasure Diver's Guide.* 1960, New York.

Shepard, Birse, *Lore of the Wreckers.* 1961, Boston.

Snow, Edward R., *Great Storms and Famous Shipwrecks of the New England Coast.* 1943, Boston. *The Vengeful Sea.* 1956, New York.

Stick, David, *Graveyard of the Atlantic.* 1952, Chapel Hill, North Carolina.

Stirling, Nord B., *Treasure Under the Sea.* 1957, Garden City, New York.

Villiers, Alan J., *Wild Ocean: the Story of the North Atlantic and the Men Who Sailed It.* 1957, New York, Toronto and London.

Wilkins, Harold T., *Hunting Hidden Treasures.* 1929, New York.

Underwater Archaeology

Bass, George F., *Archaeology Under Water.* 1966, New York.

Blackman, D. J. (ed.), *Marine Archaeology.* 1973, London.

Blair, Clay, Jr., *Diving for Pleasure and Treasure.* 1960, Cleveland.

Borhegyi, Suzanne de, *Ships, Shoals and Amphoras.* 1961, New York.

Bush Romero, Pablo, *Under the Waters of Mexico.* 1964, Mexico City.

Cleator, P. E., *Underwater Archaeology.* 1973, New York.

Dumas, Frédéric, *Deep-Water Archaeology.* 1962, London.

Flemming, Nicholas C., *Cities in the Sea.* 1971, New York.

Franzen, Anders, *The Warship* Vasa. 1960, New York.

Frost, Honor, *Under the Mediterranean.* 1963, London.

Marx, Robert F., *Pirate Port: the Story of the Sunken City of Port Royal.* 1967, New York and Cleveland. *Port Royal Rediscovered.* 1973, New York. *The Lure of Sunken Treasure.* 1973, New York.

McKee, Alexander, *History Under the Sea.* 1968, London.

Muckelroy, Keith (ed.), *Archaeology Under Water.* 1980, New York and London.

Peterson, Mendel, *History Under the Sea.* 1969, London.

Poidebard, A., *Tyre.* 1939, Paris.

Rackl, Hanns-Wolf, *Diving Into the Past.* 1968, New York.

Sténuit, Robert, *Treasures of the Armada.* 1971, New York.

Taylor, Joan du Platt, editor, *Marine Archaeology.* 1965, London.

Throckmorton, Peter, *The Lost Ships.* 1964, Boston. *Shipwrecks and Archaeology.* 1969, Boston.

UNESCO Publication—"Underwater Archaeology." 1972, New York.

Wilkes, Bill St. John, *Nautical Archaeology.* 1971, London.

Preservation

Albright, Alan, "The Preservation of small water-logged wood specimens with polyethylene glycol." *Curator,* 1966, vol IX, no. 3, pp. 228-34.

Barkman, Lars, *The Preservation of the* Vasa. No date, Stockholm.

Caley, Earle R., "Coatings and incrustations on lead objects from the Agora and the method used for their removal." *Studies in Conservation,* 1955, vol. 2, no. 2, pp. 49-54.

Erickson, Egon and Tregel, Svend, *Conservation of Iron Recovered from the Sea.* 1966, Copenhagen, Denmark.

Graham, John Meredith, *American Pewter.* 1949, Brooklyn.

Katsev, Michael and Doornick, Frederick van, "Replicas of iron tools from a Byzantine shipwreck." *Studies in Conservation,* August 1966, vol. 11, no. 3, pp. 133-42.

Organ, R. N., "The conservation of fragile metallic objects." *Studies in Conservation,* November, 1961, vol. 6, no. 4, pp. 135-36.

Pittsburgh Plate Glass Company, "Embedding objects in selectron 5000 resins." 1946, Pittsburgh.

Plenderleith, H. J., *The Conservation of Antiquities and Works of Art.* (The most comprehensive work on the subject.) 1956, London.

Smith, James B., Jr. and Ellis, John P., "The preservation of under-water archaeological specimens in plastic." *Curator,* 1963, vol. VI, no. 1, pp. 32-36.

Thomas, M. W. and Dunton, John V. N., "Treatment for cleaning and preserving excavated iron objects." 1954, Williamsburg, Virginia.

Townsend, Samuel P., "Heat methods of preserving cast iron artifacts recovered from salt water." Report presented at the Third Conference on Underwater Archaeology, Miami, Florida, March 23-25, 1967.

Werner, A. E., "Consolidation of fragile objects." *Studies in Conservation,* November 1961, vol. 6, no. 4, pp. 133-35.

Dating Techniques

Aitkens, M. J., *Physics and Archaeology.* 1961, New York.

Brothwell, Don and Higgs, Eric, *Science in Archaeology.* 1963, London.

Michels, Joseph W., *Dating Methods in Archaeology.* 1973, New York.

Identification of Artifacts

Artillery

Foulkes, Charles, *The Gun Founders of England.* 1937, Cambridge, England.

Gibbon, John, *The Artillerists Manual.* 1863, New York.

Grant, Michael, *Armada Guns.* 1961, London.

Hime, Henry W. L., *The Origin of Artillery.* 1915, London.

Hogg, Oliver F. G., *English Artillery 1326–1716.* 1963, London.

Manucy, Albert, *Artillery Through the Ages.* 1949, Washington, D.C.

Mountaine, William, *The Practical Sea-Gunners' Companion or An Introduction to the Art Of Gunnery.* 1747, 3rd edition, London.

Muller, John, *A Treatise of Artillery.* 1780, 3rd edition, London.

Museo del Ejército, *Catálogo del Museo del Ejército.* Four vols., 1956, Madrid.

Robins, Benjamin, *New Principles of Gunnery.* 1742, London.

Saint-Remy, Pierre Surrey de, *Memoires d' Artillerie.* Two vols., 1741, The Hague, Holland.

Smith, George, *An Universal Military Dictionary.* 1779, London.

Streete, Thomas, *The Use and Effects of the Gunne.* 1674, London.

Thomas, Capt., *A Treatise on Gunpowder.* 1789, London.

Vigon, Jorge, *Historia de la Artilleria Española.* Three vols., 1947. Madrid.

Weapons

Greener, W. W., *The Gun and Its Development.* Ninth Edition, 1967, New York.

Jackson, H. J., and Whitelaw, Charles, *European Hand Firearms of the 16th, 17th and 18th Centuries.* West Orange, New Jersey.

Peterson, Harold L., *The Treasury of the Gun.* 1962, New York. *Arms and Armour in Colonial America, 1526–1783.* 1956, Harrisburg, Pennsylvania. *Daggers and Fighting Knives of the Western World.* 1968, New York.

Stone, George Cameron, *A Glossary of the Construction, Decoration and Use of Arms and Armor in All Countries and in All Times.* (The most comprehensive work on the subject.) 1934, New York.

Tunis, Edwin, *Weapons: a Pictorial History.* 1954, Cleveland and New York.

Wilkinson, Frederick, *Swords and Daggers.* 1968, New York.

Navigation Instruments

Brewington, M. V., *Navigating Instruments.* 1963, Salem, Massachusetts.

Garcia France, Salvador, *Instrumentos Nauticos en el Museo Naval.* 1959, Madrid.

Mountaine, William and Wakely, Andrew, *The Mariner's Compass Rectified.* 1754, London.

Waters, David W., *The Art of Navigation in England in Elizabethan and Early Stuart Times.* 1958, London.

Zinner, Ernst, *Astronomische Instrumente.* 1967, Munich.

Clay Smoking Pipes

Brongars, G. A., *Nicotiana Tabacum.* 1964, Amsterdam.

Dunhill, Alfred, *The Pipe Book.* 1924, New York.

Harrington, J. C., "Dating stem fragments of 17th and 18th century tobacco pipes." *Bull. Archaeological Society,* 1954, vol. 4.

Marx, Robert F., "Clay smoking pipes recovered from the sunken city of Port Royal: May 1, 1966–September 30, 1967." Jamaica National Trust Commission, Kingston, March 1968. "Clay smoking pipes recovered from the sunken city of Port Royal: October 1, 1967–March 31, 1968." Jamaica National Trust Commission, Kingston, August 1968.

Oswald, Adrian, *English Clay Tobacco Pipes.* 1967, London.

Glassware and Bottles

Buckley, Francis, *The Glass Trade in England in the 17th Century.* 1914, London.

Corning Glass Museum, *Glass from the Corning Glass Museum.* 1965, Corning, New York.

Frothingham, Alice Wilson, *Hispanic Glass.* 1941, New York.

Harrington, J. C., *Glassmaking at Jamestown.* 1953, Richmond, Virginia.

Hayes, E. Barrington, *Glass Through the Ages.* 1966, Baltimore, Maryland.

Honey, W. B., *Glass.* 1946, London.

Hume, Ivor Noel, "Dating English glass wine bottles." *Wine and Spirit Trade Record,* February 1955. *Here Lies Virginia.* 1963, New York.

Lee, Ruth Webb, *Victorian Glass.* 1939, Framingham, Massachusetts.

Marx, Robert F., "Wine glasses recovered from the sunken city of Port Royal: May 1, 1966–March 31, 1968." Jamaica National Trust Commission, Kingston, May 1968. "Glass bottles recovered from the sunken city of Port Royal, Jamaica: May 1, 1966–March 31, 1968." Caribbean Research Institute, St. Thomas, Virgin Islands, January 1969.

McKearin, Helen and George, *Two Hundred Years of American Blown Glass.* 1956, New York.

Rider, Dennis, *A History of Glass Bottles.* 1956, London.

Ruggles-Brise, Sheelah, *Sealed Bottles.* 1949, London.

Gold Plate

Castro, J. P. de, *The Law and Practice of Marking Gold and Silver Ware.* 1935, London.

Heal, A., *The London Goldsmiths, 1200–1800.* 1935, Cambridge, England.

Hill, H. D., *Antique Gold Boxes, Their Lore and Their Lure.* 1953, New York.

Jackson, C. J., *English Goldsmiths and Their Marks.* 1949, London.

Jones, E. A., *Old Silver of Europe and America.* 1928, London and New York.

Wyler, S. B., *The Book of Old Silver: English, American and Foreign.* 1947, New York.

Pewterware

Bell, Malcolm, *Old Pewter.* 1905, New York.

Cotterell, Howard H., *Old Pewter: Its Makers and Marks.* (The most comprehensive work on the subject.) 1929, London.

Markham, C. A., *Pewter Marks and Old Pewter Ware.* 1909,London.

Marx, Robert F., "Silver and pewter recovered from the sunken city of Port Royal." Caribbean Research Institute, St. Thomas, Virgin Islands, 1971.

Welch, C., *History of the Worshipful Company of Pewterers of London.* 1902, London.

Pottery and Porcelain

Chaffers, William, *The New Collectors Handbook of Marks and Monograms on Pottery and Porcelain*. 1914, London.

Cushion, J. P. and Honey, W. B., *Handbook of Pottery and Porcelain Marks*. 1956, London.

Frothingham, Alice Wilson, *Talavera Pottery.* 1944, New York. *Lustreware of Spain*. 1951, New York.

Garner, Frederic H., *English Delftware*. 1948, New York.

Godden, Geoffrey A., *British Pottery and Porcelain*. 1966, New York.

Goggin, John M., "The Spanish olive jar, an introductory study." Yale University Publications in Anthropology. no. 62, 1960, New Haven. "Spanish majolica in the New World: types of the sixteenth to eighteenth centuries." 1968, New Haven.

Savage, George, *Porcelain Through the Ages*. 1963, Baltimore.

Shepard, Anna O., *Ceramics for the Archaeologist*. 1965, Washington, D.C.

Thorn, C. Jordan, *Handbook of Old Pottery and Porcelain Marks*. 1965, New York.

Towner, Donald C., *English Cream-Coloured Earthenware*. 1957, London.

Watkins, Laura W., *Early New England Potters and Their Wares*. 1950, Cambridge, Massachusetts.

Wills, Geoffrey, *The Book of English China*. 1964, New York.

Spanish Coinage

Beals, Gary, *Numismatic Terms of Spain and Spanish America*. 1966, San Diego.

Dasi, Tomas, *Estudio de los Reales de a Ocho*. Five vols., 1950, Valencia, Spain.

Harris, Robert P., *Pillars and Portraits*. 1968, San Jose, California.

Lopez-Chaves y Sanchez, Leopoldo *Catalogo de la Onza Española*. 1961, Madrid. *Catalogo de la Media Onza o Doblon de a Cuatro*. 1961, Madrid. *Catalogo de las Onzas de la America Independiente*. 1961, Madrid.

Nesmith, Robert I., *The Coinage of the First Mint of the Americas at Mexico City.* 1955, New York.

Pradeau, Alberto F., *Numismatic History of Mexico from the Pre-Columbian Epoch to 1823*. 1938, Los Angeles.

Yriarte, Jose de, *Catalogo de los Reales de a Ocho Españoles*.1955, Madrid.

Coinage of Other Nations

Brooke, George C., *English Coins From the Seventh Century to the Present Day*. 1932, London.

Ciani, Louis, *Catalogue de Monnaies Françaises*. Three vols., 1926–1931, Paris.

Dieudonne, A., *Monnaies Royales Françaises*. 1916, Paris.

Lindheim, Leon, *Facts and Fiction About Coins*. 1967, Cleveland and New York.

Peck, C. Wilson, *English Copper, Tin and Bronze Coins: 1558-1958*. 1960, London.

Wood, Howland, *The Coinage of the West Indies, and the sou marque*. 1915, New York.

Yeoman, R. S., *A Catalog of Modern World Coins*. 1965, Chicago. *A Guide Book of United States Coins*. 1965, Chicago.

Brass and Copper Objects

Marx, Robert F., "Brass and copper items recovered from the sunken city of Port Royal: May 1, 1966–March 31, 1968." Jamaica National Trust Commission, Kingston, May 1968.

Wills, G., *Collecting Copper and Brass*.

Miscellaneous Reference Books

Bradford, Ernie, *Four Centuries of European Jewelry*. 1953, Geltham, England.

Bruton, E., *Clocks and Watches*. 1965, London.

Hume, Ivor Noel, *A Guide to Artifacts of Colonial America*. (This comprehensive book is useful in the identification of hundreds of types of artifacts.) 1970, New York.

Mercer, Henry C., *Ancient Carpenters' Tools*. 1960, Doylestown, Pennsylvania.

Index

253